MANAGING

HISTORICAL

RECORDS

PROGRAMS

About the Series
The American Association for State and Local History Book Series publishes technical and professional information for those who practice and support history, and addresses issues critical to the field of state and local history. To submit a proposal or manuscript to the series, please request proposal guidelines from AASLH headquarters: AASLH Book Series, 1717 Church St., Nashville, Tennessee 37203-2991. Telephone: (615) 320-3203. Fax: (615) 327-9013. Web site: *www.aaslh.org*.

About the Organization
The American Association for State and Local History (AASLH) is a nonprofit educational organization dedicated to advancing knowledge, understanding, and appreciation of local history in the United States and Canada. In addition to sponsorship of this book series, the Association publishes the periodical *History News*, a newsletter, technical leaflets and reports, and other materials; confers prizes and awards in recognition of outstanding achievement in the field; and supports a broad educational program and other activities designed to help members work more effectively. To join the organization, contact: Membership Director, AASLH, 1717 Church St., Nashville, Tennessee 37203-2991.

MANAGING
HISTORICAL
RECORDS
PROGRAMS

A Guide for Historical Agencies

Bruce W. Dearstyne

A Division of Rowman & Littlefield Publishers, Inc.

Walnut Creek • Boulder • New York • Oxford

ALTAMIRA PRESS
A Division of Rowman & Littlefield Publishers, Inc.
1630 North Main Street, 367
Walnut Creek, CA 94596
www.altamirapress.com

Rowman & Littlefield Publishers, Inc.
4720 Boston Way
Lanham, MD 20706

12 Hid's Copse Road
Cumnor Hill, Oxford OX2 9JJ, England

British Library Cataloguing in Publication Information Available

Library of Congress Cataloging-in-Publication Data

Dearstyne, Bruce W. (Bruce William), 1944–
    Managing historical records programs : a guide for historical agencies / Bruce W. Dearstyne.
        p. cm.
    Includes bibliographical references and index.
    ISBN 0-7425-0282-1 (cloth : alk. paper) — ISBN 0-7425-0283-X (pbk. : alk. paper)
    1. Archives—United States—Administration—Handbooks, manuals, etc. 2.
    Records—United States—Management—Handbooks, manuals, etc. 3. United
    States—History—Societies, etc.—Handbooks, manuals, etc. I. Title.
    CD3050.D43 2000
    025.17'14—dc21   00-035590

Printed in the United States of America

∞™ The paper used in this publication meets the minimum requirements of American
National Standard for Information Sciences—Permanence of Paper for Printed Library
Materials, ANSI/NISO Z39.48-1992.

To my family

Susan Dearstyne
Emily Dearstyne
Annmarie and Bryan Gregory

with gratitude for their patience and support during the many months that this book was under preparation.

CONTENTS

ACKNOWLEDGMENTS

Many people should be acknowledged for their assistance in the development of this book. David Hoober, State Archivist of Arizona, and Sandra Clark, Director, Michigan Historical Center, recognized the need for a book on historical records by AASLH and helped shape the original proposal. Terry Davis, Executive Director and CEO of AASLH, facilitated the review process that led to the final proposal. Erik Hanson and Mitch Allen at AltaMira Press were very helpful in getting the work under way and Pam Winding, my editor at AltaMira, has my enduring gratitude for working with me in the final stages of the manuscript, including review of the draft and final revisions.

My wife, Susan V. Dearstyne, read the entire manuscript and made many suggestions for improvements. Susan has been reading my drafts for a quarter of a century and never seems to tire of it or to run out of good ideas!

Many of the ideas in this book were derived from years of working with historical records repositories in New York State through the Documentary Heritage Program and working with the New York State Historical Records Advisory Board. I am grateful to the custodians of historical records at those repositories, and to my former colleagues at the New York State Archives and Records Administration, for the insights that I derived through many years of collaboration with them.

The Society of American Archivists, the nation's premier professional archival association, permitted the use of several of their publications, which are included in the book as appendices. Teresa Brinati, Director of Publications at SAA, was very helpful in facilitating the process. The Georgia Historical Records Advisory Board very generously permitted the use of their excellent self-assessment guide in the book. My special thanks go to Ed Weldon, Director of the Department of Archives and History, and to Anne P. Smith, Project Coordinator for the Board, for their assistance. I would also like to thank Susan Potts McDonald for permission to use the form for developing an arrangement and description work plan found in chapter 6.

Finally, I want to acknowledge gratitude to my students at the College of Library and Information Services, University of Maryland. Quite a few of the ideas in the book were first tried out in my courses there, and, through student reactions, questions, and constructive criticism, the ideas were improved and sharpened. The students—archivists and directors of historical records programs of the future—are a great source of inspiration.

While I appreciate all the assistance I've received, I alone am responsible for the contents and interpretations expressed in the book.

INTRODUCTION

THE STATE OF HISTORICAL RECORDS PROGRAMS

Historical records are a natural focus and collecting area for historical societies, history museums, and other historical agencies. They are rich, reliable, and revealing sources of history. They embody and reflect the history of people and institutions, are natural companions of theme-related collections of historical artifacts, and are right at home in historic houses and other historic sites. They are excellent sources for exhibits, seminars, and other public programs designed to reach people with engaging historical information and to allow the past to "speak" to the present. People in charge of historical agencies, who care about the preservation and perpetuation of history, readily appreciate the value and importance of historical records. It should come as no surprise, then, that the majority of historical records programs in the United States are situated in historical agencies.

It would be heartening to continue with the reassuring observation that most historical records programs in historical agencies are well administered, adequately resourced, and customer oriented, and that they plan and carry out their work systematically. However, that is not the case, according to recent studies, which include statewide surveys conducted in most of the states by their State Historical Records Advisory Boards.[1] The studies provide a detailed portrait of the historical records program mosaic. Historical societies are the most numerous custodians of nongovernment historical records, according to a recent national summary of state surveys, with college and university libraries, public libraries, museums, and records creators (e.g., religious organizations, nonprofit corporations, etc.) accounting for the rest. Most of the programs are small; nearly half of the programs in the survey were begun after 1970, and a sizeable percentage came into existence less than a decade ago. Fewer than 40 percent of the programs have written acquisition policies identifying the kinds of materials they collect and the conditions or terms that affect these acquisitions. Fewer than 20 percent have written disaster plans.

Nearly half of the surveyed programs reported lack of finding aids and processing backlogs as major impediments to the use of collections. Asked about their organization's annual spending for historical records programs, including salaries and building maintenance, over 40 percent responded that the amount is $1,000 or less. Over 80 percent have budgets below $10,000. Less than a third of the respondents have one or more professionals on staff and an amazing 28 percent reported operating with all volunteer labor. The survey showed a long list of critical, unmet needs—but also concern about those needs and a strong determination to address them.[2]

These statistics, and similar ones from other recent studies, can be interpreted in two ways. In one sense, they are a tribute to the broad, grassroots interest in and support for history and historic preservation of all types in this country. Americans are looking to the past for education and recreation, they are becoming more interested in genealogy and family history, and people who live out their lives in the towns where they are born join newcomers seeking to put down roots in enthusiastically organizing historical preservation. New museums and historic sites open with public fanfare and attract impressive crowds. Historical novels abound. The History Channel brings history and its dramatic, fictional counterparts into our homes. Movies about history make very impressive showings at the box office. Patriotic celebrations on the Fourth of July and on centennials and bicentennials of our states and local governments provide impressive evidence that our sense of history is alive and well.

Michael Kammen, who has studied the public's perception of history for many years, notes an ambiguous pattern: genuine grassroots historical interest alongside public ignorance about important historical events and evidence that students in schools lack a fundamental understanding of their nation's past. He asserts that an underlying *heritage*—a sense of a proud, inspirational history that "tends to be upbeat and affirmative in an unqualified way about the American past"—helps hold our country together and define what it means to be an American.[3] History is the glue that holds us together and gives us coherence and purpose as a people. Archival records are the grist for sound, well presented historical accounts; the interest in their collection is a natural reflection of broad-based enthusiasm for history. Historical records programs are springing up all over. Thousands of conscientious, dedicated archivists, volunteers, and others do an excellent job every day of preserving the records, serving their institutions, meeting the needs of researchers, and furthering the cause of history.

The recent archival reports and studies bear a second type of reading, however, that is unsettling. There is plenty of evidence of sincerity, dedication, and good intentions. There are many soundly administered historical records programs that are flourishing in their historical agency settings. But the reports provide evidence of how easy, and common, it is to underestimate what it takes to manage historical records in a responsible manner on a sustained basis. Many historical societies and other programs that collect historical records lack the resources, sense of purpose, sustained dedication, and support they need from their parent institution to carry out their archival work in a minimally acceptable way. The archival component of the historical agency's program is a permanent second-class citizen, underappreciated, and not well supported. The trustees of these programs are not fully carrying out their responsibilities for the adequate preservation of important cultural resources in the custody of the program. They operate at a resource level so low that they cannot discharge their archival responsibilities in an accountable, responsible fashion. Volunteers are immensely dedicated and helpful but their numbers cannot make up for the lack of paid, professional staff who have archival training. Lack of secure, climate-controlled storage space and preservation work may accelerate the demise of the very records dedicated people have worked so hard to save. Unprocessed backlogs without finding aids rest in a sort of archival abeyance—in the custody of a repository but unknown to researchers, and therefore, effectively unreachable and unused. Overworked staff members, no matter how energetic and conscientious, eventually tire. Research use trails off because researchers are not well served. The program may reflect conscientious dedication and exhibit limited or modest accomplishments, but it is not truly effective in caring for historical records. "Historical records repositories in Massachusetts are under-staffed, under-funded, and overlooked," concludes that state's Historical Records Advisory Board. "Most historical records repositories have multiple roles and care for records is only one of their many missions. Most rely on volunteers to ensure the preservation and accessibility of historical records. Most need more opportunities for collaboration, professional development, and funding."[4]

THE PURPOSE AND AUDIENCE FOR THIS BOOK

Managing Historical Records Programs: A Guide for Historical Agencies is intended for historical agency personnel who are considering starting a historical records program or who already have one and want to strengthen it. It has as a general goal the fostering of stronger, more vibrant historical records programs in historical agency settings. The book describes strategies, approaches, principles, and practices of strong historical records programs in these settings. It introduces archival theory but its main intention is to provide practical, applicable advice that its main audience, small- to medium-sized historical agencies, can readily use. It places *historical records* work within the context of *historical agency* work and includes many examples, checklists, and appendices that are intended to help these agencies find solutions and approaches that best fit their needs. It asserts that archival work needs to be carried out in accordance with professionally sanctioned practices, but that these are quite readily understandable and attainable. The book proceeds on the following assumptions:

- Historical records programs can be organized and thrive in historical agency settings—there is a natural, mutually reinforcing compatibility between archival work and the work of historical societies, historical museums, and comparable institutions. This requires sound judgement and planning and a recognition of how historical records work is similar to, but where it is distinct from, other things that the agency may do, such as maintaining historic sites and artifacts.
- Many historical records programs in historical agency settings are underdeveloped, underfunded, and in general need a clearer sense of mission and purpose. As presently constituted, they are not adequately serving their parent institution or the cause of history. They can and should do better.
- The archival field has developed only a few prescriptive standards but has established many canons of good practice, model approaches, and settled ways of proceeding to ensure the optimal management of historical records. That body of literature and practice is reflected in this book by way of expectations for how viable programs should proceed.
- Historical records work is engaging and exciting. It combines elements of investigation, historical analysis, service to historians and other researchers, and, ultimately, to the transmission of culture and understanding from one generation to the next. Archivists enjoy their work and they are dedicated and enthusiastic about what they are doing.

- There are two underlying themes in this work—challenge and change. Each can be good or bad, depending on how they are regarded and met by the people in charge of programs.

ORGANIZATION OF THE BOOK

The book is organized to systematically describe historical records program work:

Chapter 1, "Historical Records: Definitions, Concepts, and Importance," introduces the topic of the book, explains terms, makes the case for the fundamental importance of historical records work, and indicates its contribution to the work of historical agencies.

Chapter 2, "Prerequisites for Program Success," discusses the essential elements of successful historical records programs in the context of historical agencies.

Chapter 3, "Building a Historical Records Program: Sources of Assistance," describes the network of support, advice, and assistance that exists to help individual historical records programs with their work.

Chapter 4, "Leadership and Management of Historical Records Programs," provides advice on administration of successful programs.

Chapter 5, "Selection of Historical Records," describes approaches to what is arguably the most important archival function, the identification of records of enduring value.

Chapter 6, "Arrangement and Description," analyzes organization of, and access to, historical records.

Chapter 7, "Services to Users," has recommendations on how to provide services to researchers, including long-distance access through the Internet.

Chapter 8, "Preservation of Historical Records," discusses how to meet the fundamental obligation to ensure the survival and longevity of historical records in a repository.

Chapter 9, "Electronic Archives," explores the frontier of historical records work and offers some suggestions for coping with the challenge of digital archives.

Chapter 10, "Historical Records Programs in the Third Millennium," switches from analysis and recommendations to prognostication and offers some suggestions for how programs can prepare for what is ahead.

Each chapter has a "Checklist" summary at the end for a quick overview of the main points in the chapter and a means of gauging how well a particular historical records program measures up to what is recommended in the text. Several chapters have boxes or figures that elaborate key points.

The book includes several appendices:

Appendix 1, "Code of Ethics for Archivists," presents ethical guidelines and also has insights on archival principles.

Appendix 2, "Basic Elements of Historical Records Programs," summarizes the key elements of viable programs.

Appendix 3, "Self-Assessment Guide for Historical Records Programs," presents an extensive set of self-analysis questions.

Appendix 4, "Cooperative Approaches to Historical Records Programs," gives a boost to one of the book's conclusions—that programs should cooperate—by suggesting study questions that explore prospects for cooperation.

Appendix 5, "Historical Records Program Plan," presents a sample plan for a hypothetical historical agency.

Appendix 6, "Guide to Donating Personal or Family Papers to a Repository," provides advice on the issues surrounding the decision to donate records to a program.

Appendix 7, "Guide to Deeds of Gift," provides guidance on legal transfer of records to historical records programs.

Appendix 8, "Examples of Historical Records Descriptions," reprints some descriptions as examples of descriptive practices.

Appendix 9, "Checklist for Access and Reference Services," is intended to assist in the evaluation of those services.

Appendix 10, "Repository Security Checklist," provides an extensive list of questions for evaluating the adequacy of security for the records.

Appendix 11, "Selected List of Vendors for Archival Supplies and Services," is a listing of companies and products that are likely to be helpful in historical records work.

Appendix 12, "Suggested Readings," is for people who want additional information on various historical records topics.

I

HISTORICAL RECORDS: DEFINITIONS, CONCEPTS, AND IMPORTANCE

HISTORICAL RECORDS: TERMINOLOGY, CONCEPTS

This is a book about *historical records* in historical agency settings. Broadly defined, the topic is closely related to other work that such agencies carry out, including preservation and exhibits of historic houses and artifacts and education. But the work has its own terminology, which both shows its relationship to historical agency work and also its distinctiveness. Archival terms do not have prescriptive definitions that everyone in the field uses in an entirely consistent way. The Society of American Archivists' (SAA) glossary explains the most common, accepted usage and is a valuable reference tool.[1]

The use of terms in this book is more flexible than what SAA recommends and, hopefully, is suited to a historical agency audience.[2] *Record* means any type of recorded information, regardless of physical form or characteristics, created, received, or maintained by a person, institution, or organization. The definition is relatively easy to apply in the traditional, tangible information world where most records are on paper, microfilm, or another tangible medium and are recognizable by their file location, setting, format, or other characteristics, such as dates and signatures on letters. The definition is much more difficult to apply in an electronic information setting where records may exist alongside non-record electronic information. A record is unique, one of a kind. Records may be copied (leading to the use of the terms *original record* and *record copy* to distinguish the first from subsequent versions). If they are reproduced en masse, e.g., printed and published, they cease to be *records* the way the term is used here and in most archival literature.

Records generated by an organization or institution such as a government are often called *official records* or *institutional records*. Records created or received by individuals in the conduct of their personal work, family activities, or professional careers are often called *personal papers* or *personal records*. The broad definition of records encompasses correspondence, reports, diaries, journals, ledgers, minutes, photographs, maps, drawings, blueprints, agreements, memoranda, deeds, case files, and other material. Records come in many physical formats—parchment, paper, photographs, microfilm, cassette tape, film videotape, and computer tapes, disks, and hard drives. Often, they are referred to as if the *physical format* is actually the record. In reality, it is the *information* and not the physical format that is the essence of record. This is a particularly crucial distinction in the case of electronic records, where the content, context, and function are what counts and physical format is secondary.

Records management refers to administrative procedures for oversight of the creation, use, maintenance, and disposition of records. A more formal definition:

> Records management means the leadership, administration, coordination, and other work required to ensure that adequate records are created to document institutional functions and meet administrative, legal, and other operational needs; that record-keeping requirements are analyzed and included when information systems are developed; that professionally sanctioned management techniques are applied throughout the records' life-cycle; that records are retained and disposed of based on analysis of their function and value; and that records of continuing value are preserved and accessible.[3]

Records management is usually applied in an organizational or institutional setting though individuals should also practice sound records management. In institutional settings, archival work and records management are actually two parts of a single, comprehensive approach to record control. Most records are not needed for long; their significance diminishes after the purpose of their creation has been satisfied. Most records may, therefore, be responsibly discarded at some point after their creation when it has been determined they are no longer needed. In fact, they *should* be discarded because their value is gone but their bulk remains; having too many records simply makes it difficult to keep track of and access the ones that have continuing value. Archivists use the term *life cycle* to describe the evolutionary process that records go through: they are created; are actively used for their intended purpose; become less frequently used (a phase sometimes called *semi-active* or *noncurrent*), and eventually are either destroyed or, for a small, elite subpart of the whole, identified for continuing preservation because of their enduring value. The small percentage of all records that have this enduring value are called *archives, archival records,* or *historical records.* The term *historical records* is used here rather than *archival records* because it is used more commonly in the historical agencies belonging to AASLH—the primary audience for this book. Such records contain significant information about the past and are therefore worthy of long-term preservation and systematic management for historical and other research. A deliberate, organized, sustained effort to collect, manage, and make available historical records is called a *historical records program.* The contrast between a *program* and a casual, disorganized collecting effort is important, as discussed in chapter 2. Such programs exist in many settings; in this book, the primary concern is historical societies, museums, and other historical programs. The physical location for the historical records is referred to as a *historical records repository.*

What about the term *archives?* Its use is not totally consistent, even among archivists. The historical records of an organization or institution may be called its *archives, archival records,* or, sometimes, *archival materials.* The term *archives* or *archival program* may also mean the agency responsible for selecting, preserving, managing, and making available archival records. There are at least three types of archival programs: (1) Institutional archives, i.e., those programs that acquire the records of enduring value of their parent institution. For example, a corporate archives would be a program that acquires, preserves, and makes available the archival records of the corporation. (2) Collecting programs, i.e., programs that actively collect historical records that are not created by their parent institution. A historical society that actively collects in a particular geographical or subject area would be a good example. These programs, sometimes called historical records programs or historical records collecting programs, are the main audience for this book. (3) Hybrid or combined programs that both acquire their parent institution's archives and also collect from the outside. *Archives* may also mean the repository or place where such materials are kept, e.g., the building called the State Archives. This book uses the term *archivist* to describe people who, through training and experience, are qualified and competent to identify, acquire, manage, make available, and encourage and guide the use of historical records. *Archival* is an adjective that refers broadly to historical records issues and the work and concerns of archivists. The term *document* means approximately the same thing as *record* and *historical document* therefore means roughly the same thing as *historical record.* The term *manuscript* literally means a handwritten or typed record, but the term *historical manuscripts* is often used to refer broadly to historical records.

The term *collection* means all the historical records acquired and held by a repository—its total holdings. The term *holdings* is used nearly interchangeably with *collection*. But collection also means a grouping of records created by a private individual, group, or organization, and acquired and held by a repository. Thus the records created by Annmarie Gregory over the course of her career and later acquired by a repository might be called the Annmarie Gregory Collection. The term *record group* in an institutional archives means roughly the same thing as *collection* in a collecting program. Thus all the records of the Department of Transportation in a state archives might be called the Transportation Record Group. Within collections or record groups, records are likely to fall into several *series*. The series concept is important; series are like archival workhorses, the best entities for both appraisal and description purposes. A series is defined as:

> File units arranged in accordance with a filing system or maintained as a unit because they result from the same accumulation or filing process, the same function, or the same activity; have a particular form; or because of some other relationship arising out of their creation, receipt, and use.[4]

Having attempted to state what historical records *are*, it is helpful to add what they *are not*—at least as discussed here. They are not:

- *Published materials.* As noted above, records are essentially one-of-a-kind items, produced for particular purposes. If they are published and disseminated, they take on a different character and nature and need to be managed differently. For instance, the original letters of a particular individual might be called her records, but an edited, printed, published version of those materials is not a record as used here. A newspaper may be an invaluable primary source, but it is not a record according to our definition.
- *Necessarily old.* A common misconception is that historical records are old records—materials from the distant past. Actually, records created today and tomorrow may well be as valuable as a record from two decades or two centuries ago. Age does not equal value. What counts is informational content and research use potential.
- *Always produced by well-known, great people.* Historical records may be the products of important, talented, influential people who had great influence in their communities, business, or society as a whole. This is not, however, necessarily the case. The diary of a farmer, for instance, may have substantial information about farming conditions and community affairs even though the creator of the diary was himself an ordinary person. Archival records of institutions such as governments may be the result of routine

business carried out every day by someone with limited influence or impact on history. But the record itself is valuable because of its information.

Many historical agency programs collect and blend true records with other primary sources that might be called quasi-records in a way that serves researchers and simply does not address the fine points of record versus non-record. Sometimes, these collections are called "special collections" and are more likely to be found in library settings where they are included in the same set of finding aids or databases as historical records. These quasi-records may include such things as:

1. Maps, which may exist in a limited number of copies and so go beyond the strict definition of a record, but which constitute invaluable research resources and supplement records holdings.
2. Newspaper clippings, sometimes pasted into ledgers or scrapbooks. Newspapers *per se* are not records, but clippings related to a particular topic, or collected by an individual and maintained along with their records, can be interpreted as being a record.
3. Oral histories, deliberately created to elicit and record information that is not prominent, or that is sketchy, in the records themselves.

These and other similar materials may rest comfortably alongside records or even in their midst. The historical records tent is a big one. Many of the principles set forth in this book for the management of historical records also pertain to these closely related materials.

HISTORICAL RECORDS: DOCUMENTATION AND TRANSMISSION OF HISTORY

Records are extensions of human and institutional memory, purposefully created to record information, document transactions, communicate thoughts, substantiate claims, advance explanations, offer justifications, and provide lasting evidence of events. Their creation results from a fundamental human and institutional need to create, store, transmit, and retrieve important information. Records are essential to personal and institutional business. Historical records are those selected from among the totality of all records that have enduring value because of the information they contain or the important research purpose they are likely to serve. They have broad societal value. In a sense, they are the elite among records because of their transcending importance. These records have special significance: they are particularly revealing about the institutions and people who created them, provide especially helpful insights about important topics and events, or are adjudged to have great potential for documenting the institution or providing the basis for historical study and analysis. "There is a fascination about handwritten papers from other days, a feeling of genuineness, a personal touch about them that brings one close to the people who produced them," wrote archivist Philip Brooks.

> This sense of reality is more than a superficial impression. On it rests the faith that historians have in "original" source materials, and it is basic to a great part of the serious research involving the past . . . no other type of material tells us as much about the past as the documents in which the actors of an earlier era recorded their doings, their thoughts, their actions, and their reactions.[5]

Using historical records leads to excitement and discovery. Historian David McCullough described his excitement through "direct personal contact" with materials at the National Archives:

> [Handling an actual document] can be an experience you never forget. [The National Archives holds] an incredible documentary record of everyday affairs and of people who never ever imagined themselves as Historical. . . . Each new fragment of information leads to something more, almost always, and the personal satisfaction, the education, that comes with the search only increases the farther you go. What may have seemed at first a lot of mountainous dusty old paper—deadly stuff from the dead past—becomes vital evidence. You are caught up, carried forward by all the elements of surprise and fascination in detective work. You find things you were not looking for and these trigger new ideas that never would have occurred to you otherwise.[6]

Historical records have broad and enduring usefulness. "Society at large uses archives and the information they contain in a variety of ways. Anyone who looks on the care of archival records as esoteric, isolated, and irrelevant to any but a small group of specialists misses an important part of the story. Especially in recent years, archivists have come to recognize that their clientele is diverse and extensive."[7] Historical records are important to society as a whole for understanding the past and providing guidance for the future. In a broader sense, historical records constitute an important part of the collective memory of our society and of our cultural heritage.

Historical records have multiple values.[8] For instance, institutional and organizational archives constitute an institutional memory that can be invaluable to administrators. They may use the archival records to study the origins of programs and policies, analyze program development and performance, ensure administrative continuity, and probe past successes and failures. The new bank president who is interested in his company's historical relationships with its community, the clergyman who wants an extended view of the church's income and expenditures, the trustee of a fraternal group who wants to know how his predecessors came to a key decision—all may find answers in their institutions' archives. Archives are thus an important, practical tool for retrospective analysis and sound administration.

Government archives may have information on development of legislation and on legislative intent that make them important for understanding and interpreting laws. Some archival records document agreements and obligations, substantiate legal claims, protect individuals' rights, and show both the government's responsibilities and the limits on its power. Vital statistics records (births, deaths, marriages), official maps, incorporation documents, and wills and deeds filed in local government offices are essential legal documents. The citizen who visits City Hall to verify his property boundary, the worker who needs proof of birth and age to obtain Social Security or other benefits, the attorney who checks a will in the County Court House to advance her client's claim to an inheritance—all, whether they realize it or not, are drawing on archives.

Government archival records may be scrutinized by the press and citizens concerned with open, responsive government because they constitute evidence of the care and faithfulness of government administrators. In recent years, Indian tribes have used archival records to establish legal rights to lands and claims to privileges from the state and federal governments. Texas attorneys used three-century-old Spanish boundary maps to establish state ownership of submerged oil-laden lands in the Gulf of Mexico. Barbara Tuchman's discovery in the National Archives of the original copy of the Zimmermann telegram contributed to our understanding of the origins of World War I. Research at the Archives called into question the claims of "military necessity" for relocation of Japanese-Americans during World War II and helped lead to reparation legislation. Studies based on Freedman's Bureau records have changed our interpretation of Reconstruction after the Civil War.

Records are often newsworthy. For example, records from the Holocaust and World War II eras have been used to document the transfer of gold looted from Holocaust victims, the role of bankers in stolen assets, and the role of companies in using slave or forced labor during the war. Multibillion-dollar tobacco litigation has been decided in part on the basis of tobacco company records, including some that apparently show that the companies deliberately misled the public about the risks of smoking. The federal government's antitrust litigation against the Microsoft Corporation turned in part on records, including e-mail records created by Chairman Bill Gates. Historical records have been featured in articles in the *New York Times* and the *Washington Post*. In 1998, *U.S. News and World Report* identified archives as one of the ten "hottest" careers for the coming century, in large part because of the rising recognition of the value of archival records, particularly those in modern digital formats.

Of course, not all uses have such broad-scale or far-reaching results but every day people make use of historical records for practical purposes and with notable beneficial results. Engineers have used land use permits, maps, photographs, and other archival records to document the location of toxic dump sites and prepare environmental studies. Engineers and public works specialists study old maps, plans, reports, and other records for information on the age and physical characteristics of bridges, buildings, and other elements of the infrastructure, an important use in areas where the infrastructure is in need of repair. Building owners and other people use building files, original blueprints, engineering drawings, and old photographs for historical restoration projects designed to restore aging structures to their original appearance. Medical historians study patient records to trace genetic and familial diseases that are transmitted from generation to generation, and to study the spread of contagious diseases and epidemics.

Historical records can help educate by presenting firsthand information to students. Records are created by *people* and tell about the experiences of *people*; they therefore have an inherent interest about them that makes them appealing to young people who may otherwise find history remote or unexciting. They help people connect directly with the past. Their use livens up, enriches, and extends the classroom experience. Historical materials, when used in this way to supplement social studies and history courses, stimulate development of analytical skills and challenge students to reach conclusions about historical evidence that may be inconclusive and even contradictory. College and university students carry out research in historical records to derive firsthand evidence about topics in history and other courses.

Historical records can stimulate the historical imagination, illustrate historical accounts, and even entertain. Businesses use them in advertising and promotional efforts. Newspaper writers draw on them for background to provide perspectives on current news stories. Historical photographs are particularly useful because they provide striking visual images of the past and permit people to actually "see" images from the past that contemporaries of the photographs saw.

In short, historical records reflect and transmit our societal past in all its glory, with all its shortfalls, with all its diversity, complexity, and exuberance. Records reinforce the mission of many museums and historical agencies to collect and make available "local stories"—information about the community and its people that would otherwise be lost.[9] In the words of a recent State Historical Records Advisory Board report,

> Diaries of a farm woman, account books from a hardware store, minutes of a local zoning board, an oral interview with a traditional Mohawk basket maker, photos of a Puerto Rican baseball team, and the membership rolls of a Black Baptist church—these are some of the ways New Yorkers preserve their history, their culture, and their collective memory. Together, they are an incomparable resource for students and teachers, for the business community, for journalists, for folklorists, for documentary film makers, for genealogists, for government officials, and for all New Yorkers.[10]

THE ARCHIVAL MISSION

Archivists identify, select, manage, preserve, and make available records with enduring value. Their work is essential to a variety of users, as indicated above, but also to the cause of history. "History is not what happened in the past. It is, as the word itself suggests, a story, written by subsequent generations. The veracity and accuracy of the account, however, is totally dependent upon the surviving record at hand—documents, manuscripts, letters, publications, photos, and memorabilia—from which the story must often be pieced together and reconstructed, item by item, clue by clue." Archivists identify the best of the documentation for use in the future.

> Archivists have accepted the challenge, and the responsibility, to collect, preserve, and protect this fragile, constantly changing record of who we are and what we do. From the smallest shoe box stored in a hall closet to the voluminous National Archives, documents and memorabilia require special handling and an awareness of the material's particular value and possible use. Archivists are trained and experienced to deal with the various questions and problems which arise in the preservation of such material. They are able to bring a specialized perspective and an informed interpretation to decisions concerning the material's worth and usefulness. . . . [T]he archivist must first identify and appraise the value of the material, deciding what to keep and what to dispose of. The criteria used in this regard is a combination of the material's uniqueness, usability, and importance. . . . The next step is organizing the collected material(s) in a coherent and systematic way. This, in turn, insures its accessibility to researchers, compilers, analysts, information services, and other potential users. Finally, the archivist must provide for outreach opportunities that give the material an ongoing life outside of its safe storage—publications, exhibits, and other visible displays and applications.[11]

The archival mission is central to the well-being and future course of an open society. The obligation is a profound one:

Appraisal [the selection of archival records] imposes a heavy social responsibility on archivists. In the stirring words of Pam Wernich, a South African archivist writing in 1988, archivists are doing nothing less than "moulding the future of our documentary heritage." Archivists determine "which elements of social life are imparted to future generations. . . ." As a profession, we archivists need to realize continually the gravity of this task. We are literally creating archives. We are deciding what is remembered and what is forgotten, who is visible and who remains invisible, who has a voice and who does not. In this act of creation, we must remain extraordinarily sensitive to the political, social, and philosophical nature of documents individually, of archives collectively, of archival functions, of archivists' personal bias, and most especially of archival appraisal, for that process defines the creators, functions, and activities to be reflected in archives. . . .[12]

Archivists carry out at least eight functions, sometimes simultaneously:

1. *Acting as agents of the present and the past for the future.* Archivists are important participants in the process of passing on information of enduring value from one generation to the next. While they are practical in how they go about the work, they keep in mind that posterity is, in effect, their most important customer. Their role helps determine what gets identified, saved, preserved, and passed on, thereby contributing to what individuals and societies know about their own past, and the past histories of others.

2. *Partnering in the information field.* Archival work is seldom carried out in total isolation from other professional information work. Depending on the program setting, archivists need to work in partnership with allied information professionals such as librarians and records managers. Increasingly, they need to be involved in the creation of electronic information systems to help ensure that electronic records with archival value are identified, and that provision is made for their management and preservation, throughout their life cycle. The information field, broadly defined, is changing rapidly and archivists need to continually refine, and redefine, their roles.

3. *Organizing and managing coherent, comprehensive programs.* Archivists are not only custodians of important materials; they are also program managers. Even in a small or modestly sized program, the archivist must set priorities, determine goals, allocate resources, make and measure progress, and carry out other managerial functions. This is true in programs of one person, who is sometimes humorously referred to as a "lone arranger," where a single individual's time, talents, and energy are the

main "resources" to be managed. Management involves the allocation and wise use of resources—even if those resources are limited to the time and talent of one or two people and a physical facility that is not very large.

4. *Deciding which records have enduring value and therefore warrant continuing retention.* The systematic identification of records of enduring value and maintenance of a program for their collection may well constitute the most important roles that archivists play. The identification and selection process is far from perfect: the total universe of relevant documentation may not be known or available; insights into research trends and likely research use need to be balanced with practical considerations such as the amount of storage space available; the selection process may be rushed; the results, measured in terms of actual research use, won't be known for many years after the decision is made. The appraisal process is also the most intellectually demanding aspect of archival work.

5. *Asserting control and order.* Archivists value orderliness. They try to maintain orderliness when it exists in the records they acquire; to impose it in some sensible fashion where it does not exist; and to describe it, in finding aids and other access tools. Records are likely to have been more or less systematically created to suit the purposes and needs of their creators but they may not have been filed or maintained in an orderly fashion over the years, or the order may have been lost through transfers or neglect. Order is important as the size of collections grows and as more and more researchers attempt to use historical records.

6. *Preserving and protecting.* Archival work has at its heart an important curatorial and custodial responsibility. Archivists who take charge of records of enduring value also take on a substantial, continuing responsibility to ensure the continuing security and physical survival of the materials in their custody. This responsibility includes providing clean, temperature- and humidity-controlled storage conditions, keeping the records safe from theft or misplacement, and regulating their use to promote maximum life expectancy.

7. *Fostering access and use.* At the same time the archivist preserves records, he or she must also encourage people to access and use them. Balancing the two responsibilities involves good judgment and experience but *use* is the paramount purpose for all archival work. It is difficult to argue that a record in an archival repository is serving any useful function if it is never used by anyone for any purpose. Access includes making the existence of records known; promoting their research potential; keeping them in order; and administering a search room that is open reasonable hours so people can do research.

8. *Broadening awareness and support.* Historical records in general tend to be underutilized: people are unaware of their existence, underappreciate their value, or don't know how to access and use them. Therefore, an important archival function is *promotional*—calling attention to the records themselves, explaining the program and what it does (and, incidentally, why it needs a fair amount of resources), and educating people about the archival function in general.

ARCHIVAL PROFESSIONALISM

The field of archives has defined itself as, and grown into the status of, a profession. A profession is marked by sound judgment based on learning and knowledge; a coherent body of theoretical and practical knowledge, high skill levels, and relative independence and autonomy in work; a code of ethics; adherence to high service standards; high education requirements; and control over entry into the field through certification, licensure, or some other device. The archival code of ethics is a particularly impressive indication of high dedication and archival professionalism; it is reproduced in appendix 1. Archivists meet all of the expectations for a profession except possibly the last two, education and certification, and these are becoming more prevalent. Increasingly, the minimal educational attainment for entering the field is a master's degree, in library/information science, history, or occasionally other disciplines. There are no hard and fast standards for archival education, but the Society of American Archivists issued guidelines some years ago and publishes a directory of archival education programs.[13] There is no formal control over entry into the field, but the Academy for Certified Archivists, an organization that is separate from the SAA but works with it, gives examinations and provides the designation of Certified Archivist (CA) to those who qualify. Increasingly, CA is becoming the mark of a qualified, experienced, archivist. The basic requirements to qualify for the exam are a master's degree plus at least one year of experience in the field. (Provisional certification is possible for students and others who lack the experience.)[14]

Availability of certification brings up the important and sensitive issue of whether historical records programs need professional archivists on their staffs. Ideally, every historical records program should have an archivist to direct it. Not every historical records program may be able to afford a professionally qualified archivist on its staff, but that should be the eventual goal for any program that aims to be substantial and successful. Historical records work, like other types of historical work, is more than an avocation or a calling; well-developed expertise is required. This book is meant to provide helpful advice on program development and management but the success depends on the energy and ability of the person in charge and the people doing the work. As a minimum, historical records work requires someone in charge who is qualified through education and experience to competently carry out the work at hand.

ARCHIVAL EXCITEMENT

People carrying out archival work are likely to be enthusiastic about what they do. Archival work is enjoyable and exciting. It's more than just a job—it's an inspired calling of sorts! In this way, archival work is much like allied historical agency work—the sense of preserving history and perpetuating social memory is a powerful motivator. John Fleckner, longtime director of the Smithsonian Institution's archival collecting program, when asked how he became an archivist and what he valued about it, responded in part:

> I loved the combination of handicraft and analytical work and I loved the intense, intimate contact with the "stuff" of history. . . . My job [was] to be imaginative in listening to these records. My judgments would be critical to building paths to them for generations of researchers, across the entire spectrum of topics, and into unknown future time. . . . Part science, part art, and—when done properly—part showmanship, our ability to quickly understand and evaluate the record—especially when it is old, large, or complex—is a unique facet of our craft. . . . What we archivists do is essential to the well-being of an enlightened and democratic society. . . . The archival record . . . is the bastion of a just society. . . . Our allies are all those who struggle to understand and protect the past for the benefit of the future. . . . This is my joy in doing archives.[15]

Archivists are sometimes stereotyped as people who have withdrawn into the solitude of the stacks to care for old records and occasionally let someone use them. They are seen as curatorial and custodial to a flaw. Like most stereotypes, this one is hollow and false. Archival work, properly practiced, is rewarding and downright exciting! Archivists take great pride in their work; dedication, conscientious service, and a feeling that the work is worthwhile and socially significant are hallmarks of the best people in the field. Ask archivists what they like best about their job and their profession and you will hear responses like the following:

Experiencing variety. The work is seldom boring or repetitive. Like any job, archival work follows certain routines and procedures, but the inherent nature of the work itself is interesting. In the course of a day's work, an archivist may make a decision about a cache of records that will determine whether they survive or vanish; guide a thoughtful researcher to a particularly rich lode of material with information that is later reflected in an important study; answer a reporter's questions about the historical background of a current controversy that is documented in the records; and prepare materials for an exhibit that will travel to local schools.

Providing service. Many archivists are intensely service oriented. They take pride in carrying out responsibilities to serve the parent institution (the setting for the program and its main financial supporter); to serve potential donors of historical records; and to serve researchers who come to use the materials for a wide variety of purposes.

Working with people. Much historical records work doesn't involve working with *records* so much as it does working with *people.* Working with people is a central source of satisfaction and pleasure to most archivists. Helping someone find a particular record, satisfy an information need, shed new light on a family's past, or just satisfy personal curiosity—all bring a satisfying sense of a job well done.

Serving posterity. Archivists derive a deep feeling of satisfaction from the profound cultural transmission aspect of their work. They're concerned with documenting the past and the present for the future and often call to mind the fact that most of their "customers"—the ultimate users of the materials that archivists collect and preserve—probably haven't been born yet.

Analyzing records. Historical records are fascinating glimpses into the past. Sometimes, they constitute the only surviving evidence of a given event, accomplishment, or tragedy; other times, they are intensely personal, having been created without any expectation that they would ever be considered "archival," collected, and used for research; in still other cases, they present dramatic, eyewitness descriptions. Records are of great interest just because of what they are and what they present. The processes of appraising, arranging, describing, and providing researcher services on them are of great interest.

Being part of a dynamic profession. Archival work is constantly changing. That may be no surprise, given the fact that the nature of records is changing (particularly with the shift to electronic records); the nature and expectations of parent institutions are changing; and the range and expectations of users are changing. Archivists value the experience of building on the best of their traditions while keeping their profession dynamic and responsive to changing needs.

DEFINITIONS, CONCEPTS, IMPORTANCE: CHECKLIST

1. Are historical records–related terms clearly understood and used in a way that is consistent with professional archival practice and appropriate for the particular historical records program?
2. Is the working definition of "historical record" sufficiently clear, narrow enough to focus collecting and other work but also broad enough to include a wide range of potentially useful materials?
3. Are program managers aware of the multiple values and potential uses of historical records, including uses beyond traditional, narrowly defined historical research?
4. Are the archival mission and the archival function in society clearly understood, sources of pride and motivation, and actively interpreted and explained in promotional work beyond the program itself?
5. Is there an emphasis on the fun, excitement, and satisfaction of archival work—the joy of archives?
6. Does the program have a sense of destiny and mission, and of being about the work of intergenerational cultural transmission, documentation, and serving history?
7. Does the historical records program have a clear sense of where and how it fits into and contributes to the mission and work of its parent institution?

2

PREREQUISITES
FOR PROGRAM SUCCESS

HISTORICAL RECORDS AND HISTORICAL AGENCY MISSION

Historical agencies are natural, compatible settings for historical records programs. Fundamentally, archival work, like historical work in general, is about the business of *remembering*. "Remembering is the basis for knowledge and reason, because the capacity to learn depends upon memory—the accumulation of experience not only from our own lifetimes but from lifetimes across the ages," notes the president of the Missouri Historical Society. "We create ourselves from stories that cojoin us to places; bind us to each other; blend individual and community identities; and provide definition, context, continuity, perspective, and personality."[1] "A frequent question asked of me is just what it is, exactly, that the historical society does," notes another agency director. "[I] remind them of the personal agony and tragedy when a family member is struck down by memory loss [and] then . . . suggest that communities and states are in danger of losing their memories, too, with an equal amount of pain and disruption. What . . . the historical society really does is to ensure that the community does not lose its memory. In a sense, the society becomes the community memory." This director notes that, in general, historical agencies stress one or more of the following themes:

1. The transmission from one generation to another of a community's treasures, community-prized mementos, and evidence of everyday life.

2. The need to care for and preserve these things indefinitely.
3. The capability to interpret and present these items in intriguing and informative ways—showing every age of the community's past, for people of every age.
4. The significant and special qualities of history as a humanizing discipline, as a form of cultural literacy, and, conversely, the problems of illiteracy that result when history is neglected.[2]

Historical records have the potential to contribute to all of these themes and to the broader historical mission of maintaining a societal memory. They can enhance and enrich the work of a historical agency whose main business may be maintaining a historic house or maintaining exhibits of three-dimensional artifacts (as opposed to two-dimensional historical documents). "To those of us who do state and local history—local historians, historical agency personnel, historical exhibit designers, writers, teachers, and lecturers—the archives is our silent partner," Carol Kammen has noted.

> It is where projects begin, where they take on new and interesting twists and turns, and where they are grounded in particular information. . . . [The] records are varied and, while they are historical, they are not history. It takes an archivist to make the records of the past accessible, just as it takes the mind of the historian or the exhibit curator or researcher to make the information in an archives intelligible.[3]

Why should a historical society or other historical agency consider initiating a historical records program—one that may involve collecting or, as discussed later in this chapter, might take other approaches such as encouraging the establishment of institutional archives? There are at least three reasons:

1. Historical records work is often consistent with the agency's mission, which usually involves identifying, preserving, interpreting, and presenting history—serving as a bridge between past and future. Historic sites, historic houses, historic artifacts, and historical records have a commonality: they're all evidence of the past that is worthy of preservation and study in the future. Historical agencies that take a holistic view of historical sources often conclude that it is logical and consistent for them to become involved with historical records work.
2. Historical records can enhance and enrich an agency's collections and programs. Records are the embodiment of personal or institutional experience and knowledge. They were made to preserve information and their use for historical research and understanding in effect presses them into additional service, long after their creation, for the cause of history. To

take some relatively straightforward examples: understanding and interpreting the aged mansion that serves as a historical society's headquarters
are enhanced if the society also has the records of the families and people
who lived there; the exhibit of agricultural implements is made more
meaningful by an accompanying exhibit of farm diaries from people who
used the equipment; and the exhibit that features locally manufactured
home appliances is enriched by a display of advertising materials from the
manufacturing companies.

3. Historical records extend historical understanding. Archival work in general is closely tied to *research* of many types, as discussed in chapter 1.
   The research use of historical records helps illuminate the past, deepens
   historical understanding, identifies underlying patterns and trends, and
   aids understanding of what life was really like in times past. Often, this research has long-term and far-reaching ramifications because it results in
   articles, books, and other presentations that influence the way people understand the past.

BUILDING ON PROGRAM STRENGTHS

Historical records programs fit squarely within the traditions and missions of
historical agencies. They may well thrive there if the parent program is strong
and the historical records program's role is clear and compatible with the
agency's mission. Historical agencies need to develop strategies to find resources to handle the dynamic nature of their work: more accessions, more
visitors, more programs—all hallmarks of dynamic programs. There is a need
for strong, forward focused, energetic leadership. "All leaders of historical
programs and agencies face similar underlying issues of harnessing institutional direction, availability, and deployment of organizational resources,
maintenance of personal and institutional relationships, and development of
methods and values to achieve existing or new goals," in the words of an
AASLH *Technical Leaflet* on administration. "Leadership is much more than
technical competence. . . . A leader defines the cultural framework or core
values of the institution for staff and constituents; is the primary keeper of the
vision; establishes pathways for others to realize the vision; and establishes the
balance between continuity and change by building on institutional
strengths."[4] Historical agencies need to keep fresh and dynamic, to stay responsive to the needs of the community that is being served, and to change
with the times even when that means making difficult choices about new di-

rections. Programs must avoid "obsolete traditions of elitism [and] aloofness" and be open to new ideas:

> While we now define ourselves as educational institutions, we see ourselves as interpretive authorities, not facilitators; and as curators not community advocates committed to the search for common ground in the midst of diverse voices and multiple perspectives on the past, the present, and the future. . . . Change will not be forced upon us; we will merely be left behind.[5]

Historical records programs may flourish in well administered historical agencies and, in turn, contribute to their work. Planning and development of programs of the sort described in this book needs to take place within the context of the parent agency's program. *Compatibility* and *integration* are the keys to ensuring a good fit. They are particularly important in these areas:

- *Mission.* The fundamental purposes of the historical records program—its reasons for existing, its aspirations, what it aims to achieve—must be consistent with the mission of the parent agency.
- *Collecting policy.* The topical or geographical scope of collecting should be consistent with and reinforce the collecting strategies of the parent agency.
- *Budget.* The historical records work needs to draw resources from the same budget as the rest of the program's work. The historical records program needs to be adequately supported, but not at the expense of other agency programs.
- *Exhibits.* There is a natural partnership between the historical records program and other agency initiatives, such as displays of artifacts. The archival materials and the other collections materials reinforce each other, together carry a rich historical message, and enhance the experience of people who visit the facility and view the exhibits.
- *Outreach and public programming.* These efforts, broadly defined, aim to bring the resources of the agency—archival and other holdings—to the attention of researchers, students, and others who can benefit from their use.

PROBLEMS AND NEEDS OF HISTORICAL RECORDS PROGRAMS

Historical records programs may exemplify historical societies and other historical agencies at their best. In many cases, however, there is in fact plenty of room for program improvement and growth. Many historical records programs

face a series of interrelated challenges and needs, repeatedly documented over
several years:

- *Tendency to work in isolation.* Historical records programs tend to operate independently, in relative isolation or at least without closely cooperating with other programs in their regions or area of collecting interest. This
may lead to gaps, overlap, and occasional competition, and generally does
not contribute to a systematic, cost-effective preservation of our documentary heritage.
- *Inadequate resource levels.* In general, historical records programs need
more wherewithal—particularly program funding, staff, and space—to
meet current responsibilities and the growing, organic nature of archival
work in general: constant collecting, more holdings, more processing
work, and increasing researcher traffic. As responsibilities grow, so also resources should grow. Chronic overstretching of resources does not make
for a strong, dynamic program.
- *Underappreciation of the importance of historical records.* People who are
historical professionals, who genuinely love and respect history, who know
its power to inspire, entertain, and provide insights may assume that nearly
everyone naturally understands the importance of archival records. In reality, misunderstanding and lack of appreciation are actually very common.
Particularly important are four groups: records creators, who need to understand what an archival record is; researchers, who need to know their
value; agency directors, trustees, and other decision makers and resource
allocators whose actions may determine the fate of historical records programs; and the general public, which needs a better understanding of historical records and of the archival function in society.
- *Exponential growth in the volume of records.* Twentieth-century America
has been a records-producing dynamo. Records are generated at a dramatic rate by such information intensive institutions as schools and governments. Not all of it is archival, of course; only a small percentage actually warrants permanent preservation. Nonetheless, that volume
continues to grow simply because the rate of records generation continues to increase.
- *Inadequate storage facilities.* Custody of archival records is a long-term responsibility. It carries a responsibility for clean, secure, and controlled
storage surroundings. Many programs, particularly those housed in older
facilities, don't meet reasonable standards or are chronically short of storage space.

- *Physical preservation of records.* This problem is near or at the top in recent surveys. Paper records naturally deteriorate over time; newer, electronic (computer generated) records have their own set of preservation problems. Some of these problems can be addressed in a general way through sound storage and sensible handling restrictions. Others, however, require technical solutions and demand extensive resources.
- *Underdeveloped documentation, appraisal, and collecting policies.* The archival community in general needs a more systematic approach to documenting American history and life in all its variety and exuberance. Lack of a clear mission and collecting policy leads to drift and uncertainty about what to acquire. Many programs collect in an indiscriminate or unsystematic fashion, acquiring materials that relate only loosely to the parent agency's mission. The result is a collection that is uneven and unfocused.
- *Meeting researchers' expectations and needs.* Ironically, there is a pattern of *underutilization* of archival records—researchers don't know about them, don't appreciate their value, don't know how to access them, or don't have the patience or skills to make optimal use of them. Programs need to reach out to researchers and to tailor their reference services to meet their expectations and needs. The Internet and the World Wide Web provide the potential for reaching a broader range of users, but this promising approach requires strategies and resources.
- *Implications of digital technology.* Many governmental and institutional archives are dealing with the extremely complex issues associated with electronic records; most collecting programs have not met the issue yet and are concentrating on traditional tangible (mostly paper-based) records. The growth of electronic records has outdistanced our ability as a profession, and as a community of repositories, to respond and develop viable approaches to identifying and preserving archival electronic records. As a consequence, electronic archival records are being overlooked, neglected, and simply not collected.

ESSENTIAL PREREQUISITES FOR RESPONSIBLE HISTORICAL RECORDS COLLECTING

Historical societies that assume responsibility for historical records work are taking on a long-term commitment. Once the obligation is assumed, it is difficult to turn back. It is not wise to drift or leap into the administration of a historical records program without adequate planning, a clear notion of the resources required, and a commitment to sustain the work. Unless these elements are in place, or there are realistic plans for developing them in the short run, the responsible course may be to pursue options other than a collecting/curatorial role to reach the goal of identification, preservation, and availability of archival records; these options are outlined in the next section. The essential prerequisites to effective historical records collecting and maintenance work are:

1. *Legal authority and purpose.* The program must have something that defines its legal status and authority and a formal statement of purpose; usually this is part of, or at least closely related to, the charter of the parent historical agency.

2. *Clear and continuing commitment.* This must be a commitment by the institution's trustees and administrative officers to provide adequate staffing and storage space and to sustain the program at an appropriate resource level. This is a fundamental responsibility of the parent institution's trustees or governing body.

3. *Appropriate funding.* This must be dependably available on a sustained basis. It is the foundation on which sound historical records programs are built and prosper. Programs need regular budget lines in the parent institution's budget and the program director should have the opportunity to develop annual budget proposals for review and approval in the institution's regular budgetary process.

4. *Clear direction.* This includes a mission and vision statement and a planning document that articulates goals and objectives. Programs need to articulate a "sense of themselves"—the business they are in, the fundamental things they aim to accomplish, the groups they intend to serve, and what they expect to get done in the near and far term. Developing such documentation helps ratify the continuing importance of the program, shows the parent institution's commitment to it, and provides a point of departure for more detailed planning, establishing priorities, and developing budgets.

5. *Adequate staffing.* This is to ensure that there will be a sufficient number of people who are qualified through education and experience to carry out the work at hand and in prospect. Professional archival expertise and professionally approved archival techniques are of critical importance; in general, they are the approaches discussed later in this book and sanctioned by the associations and state archival programs described in chapter 3. Equally important is having enough people, at varying levels of expertise, to get the work done on a continuing basis.

6. *Adequate facilities.* This includes appropriate storage space, facilities for researchers to work comfortably, and the equipment and supplies need to house, preserve, reproduce, and otherwise care for the records, and provision for expansion of facilities as the program grows. Adequate facilities and responsible historical records curatorship go hand in hand. Records tend to be bulky, fragile, and in need of careful care; hence, facilities are a major concern.

7. *A dynamic approach.* This approach includes a commitment to grow as the volume of records and numbers of researchers increase, and to change with the times, including working in model archival practices and techniques as they evolve.

Appendix 2 presents a further elaboration of the basic elements of historical records programs. Appendix 3 is one of the most important items in this book. It presents a self-assessment guide for people who are considering starting a historical records program or people who are in charge of a program but need more information on how well they are doing and what steps they might take to improve the stance of their program.

ALTERNATIVES AND ACCOMPANIMENTS TO A CUSTODIAL ROLE

Historical societies, libraries, museums, and other historical agencies that wish to preserve historical records usually automatically assume that the most direct and expeditious strategy is to begin collecting themselves. Often, that *is* the right choice, provided they can reasonably expect to meet the prerequisites outlined earlier in this chapter and the expectations laid out later in this book. There are, however, at least three other roles that responsible agencies may play either as alternatives to collecting, or in accompaniment to a modest collecting program suited to their mission and resources. The three roles are by no means mutually exclusive.

Cooperation

The first option worth considering is cooperating with another institution, or perhaps more than one, rather than striking out alone. In this scenario, other programs, e.g., historical societies, libraries, and museums, are viewed as potential allies and partners in the fundamental business of historical preservation

FROM ASSESSMENT TO ACTION:
STRATEGIC PLANS AS INSTRUMENTS FOR CHANGE

"Seeing nothing less than a revolution in record-keeping, we have followed Churchill's dictum: 'Make no small plans,'" wrote George W. Scott, State Archivist and Coordinator of the Washington State Historical Records Advisory Board in the preface to that state's strategic plan. "Our goal is to make Washington's history more accessible, exciting, and understandable in the 21st Century." The Washington plan is an excellent example of clear, concise, convincing analysis and writing, and clear goals and action steps. It explains three fundamental assumptions: records are essential, records must be preserved, and records must be available. There needs to be a statewide perspective that is matched by local initiative.

The plan identifies several areas of need and sets forth strategies to deal with them, grouped around four issue areas:

1. Collaboration and leadership—a coordinated effort toward preserving and making accessible the state's historical records, including a leadership role for the Board and the State Archives and improved communication and networking within the records community.
2. Standards to serve preservation and access—technical standards for record-keeping, preparation for constant changes in technology, better planning for access, and improved management of current records, particularly electronic records.
3. Education, training, and technical services—including improved educational opportunities for all segments of the records community and expanded technical services from the State Archives.
4. Expanded access to historical records—particularly improved guides readily available via the Internet and broadened access to electronic records.

Source: Washington State Historical Records Advisory Board, *Preserving and Sharing Washington's Historical Records: A Strategic Plan for the 21st Century* (Olympia: State Historical Records Advisory Board, 1997).

rather than as isolated programs or potential rivals. Options worth considering include:

- *Sharing collecting responsibilities.* A local library and a local historical society, which serve essentially the same geographical region, might decide for strategic purposes to divide up the collecting responsibilities, e.g., by subject, by time period, or by some geographical division within the region.

- *Sharing storage.* Because storage space is at a premium in many agencies, it might make sense for two or more programs to jointly purchase, rent, or lease a secure facility to be jointly administered, which would house all of the partners' historical records.

- *Sharing staff and expertise.* Sharing staff and expertise in certain instances has many advantages. It permits pooling of what are likely to be limited financial resources for personnel. It permits both partners to draw on certain expertise that may be difficult or expensive to hire, e.g., preservation or electronic records specialists. It provides flexibility for allocating resources based on fluctuations in the work level of both programs. It provides the people involved with freshness and variety in their work. Of course, sharing staff goes well beyond the bounds of routine administrative practices and therefore requires careful management and supervision. It is, however, worth considering in the context of a search by programs for how they can work together.

Appendix 4 provides additional insight on cooperative approaches through a series of questions that explore the potential for cooperative work in various archival functions.

Coordination

A second potential noncustodial role, or one that fits with a modest collecting/custodial program, is to foster, encourage, and possibly coordinate the work of other collecting programs. In this option, for instance, a local library might take the lead in working with local historical societies, museums, colleges and universities, the state historical society, and others toward systematic collecting of historical records in the region, or at least toward communication and possibly coordination in collecting. The role is primarily *to facilitate*—precipitating, encouraging, leading—rather than assuming what may be an overwhelming unilateral collecting role and responsibility. It requires leadership, communication, advocacy, and honest brokering skills and leads to at least three products:

- A documentation or collecting plan that indicates which institution will concentrate on what records or topical or geographical areas. Such plans, sometimes called *documentation plans,* are not easy to develop and require good faith, an inclination to cooperate, and plenty of work. The concept is discussed in more detail later.

- A forum or meeting mechanism that convenes representatives of the involved programs on a regular basis to discuss collecting, issues and problems, future plans, etc.
- A means of measuring and reporting on the cooperative ventures.

Fostering Institutional Archival Programs

Historical agencies may consider encouraging the creation of government, business, church, educational, religious, and other institutional archival programs in their own communities. Many of the holdings in historical agencies today are, in effect, institutional archival records that did not stay at home because their institutions had no archival programs. Institutions that create records in the normal course of business often do not recognize any responsibility to identify and care for their archival records; indeed, the concept of archival records may be something they miss entirely. An institutional archival program, provided the institution itself has the resources to support it, can be interpreted as a normal part of doing business. In fact, it is a good "dollars and sense" business proposition for commercial firms because it ensures the preservation and availability of important documents that may be needed for legal or other corporate purposes, documents the development of policies and services, and provides documentation for retrospective policy analysis and study of past issues and program development by company staff.

Historical agencies can encourage systematic attention to institutional archival records by:

- Holding workshops, seminars, conferences, and other meetings where qualified archivists introduce the fundamentals of institutional archival programs, explain how to set them up, reiterate their advantages, and discuss resource and program development and support needs.
- Sparking archival conscientiousness on the part of executives, administrators, members of boards of directors, trustees, and others. The dual themes of documenting the institution's development and contribution and preserving important documents with legal or operational significance to the institution itself can be developed and applied to good effect here.
- Raising archival consciousness on the part of the public served by the historical agency. This can be done, for instance, by sponsoring conferences that showcase archives-based historical research, getting the news media interested in using historical records as background or illustrations for news stories, encouraging teachers and school students to use community historical records, and suggesting attention to these records for centenni-

als, bicentennials, and other historically oriented commemorative events.
- Serving as an informational resource, e.g., by maintaining a small library of archival literature, publicizing the availability of professional associations and conferences, maintaining a roster of archival experts, or maintaining a directory of local archival programs.

The accompanying box suggests some questions that might be used to initiate a discussion of the adequacy of historical records programs in a community.

MARKS OF EXCELLENCE
IN HISTORICAL RECORDS PROGRAMS

Historical records programs known for their excellence and achievement meet the suggested prerequisites explained above: adequate support, sufficient funding, clear direction, appropriate staffing, and secure facilities. Their dedication and competence, concern for both historical records and the people who need and use them, and responsible, planned growth, mark them as good models for others to emulate. They may be large or small, new or old, and located in a variety of settings. Exemplary historical records programs, whatever their size or setting, are usually characterized by:

- *Customer focus.* The best programs in this business have a clear fix on their customers—the individuals, groups, and institutions they aim to serve. Customers are not people who purchase products, as the term implies. Instead, they are the people who produce historical records, the institution of which the historical records program is a part, and the people who use records. These programs understand they have a daunting obligation to posterity—most of their customers are yet unborn.
- *Quality service.* Consistently quick, accurate, responsive service is a hallmark of the most successful programs. "Pleasing the customer" is an operating assumption that reinforces the customer focus.
- *Realistic planning.* Successful programs take planning seriously. A considerable amount of their collective time and energies are devoted to developing, sharpening, and keeping vital their mission and vision statements and developing and being guided by goals and objectives. At the same time, plans need to be dynamic, change with the times, and permit the programs to take advantage of opportunities and dodge or deal with problems.
- *Evolution and change.* Historical records may imply a steady, static state of affairs. Actually, the best programs are more likely to be characterized by

ASSESSING THE STATE OF HISTORICAL
RECORDS PROGRAMS: TWO STARTING POINTS

The strategic plans developed by State Historical Records Advisory Boards in the 1990s have provided insights into the condition of community historical records programs in each state. The starting point for development of many of these plans was a series of questions about issues and needs. The list below is a good example of open-ended questions designed to promote discussion and lead to further analysis about statewide needs. From New York State Historical Records Advisory Board, "Focus Group Questions," 1996.

1. What have you observed about the way the history of your community in New York is currently being collected and/or presented?
2. What do you like and dislike about the way history is being collected/presented? What do you see as the strengths/weaknesses of the current situation?
3. What kinds of information would best tell the story of your community in New York (events, topics, community life)?
4. Which specific individuals or organizations would you select to collect and store historical materials about your community?
5. If some organization started working to gather the history of your community, what things would they need to do to gain the interest, trust, and support of the community?
6. What potential problem areas and barriers might there be to collecting historical materials about the history of your community?
7. Other than yourself, who could be helpful in supporting efforts to collect historical materials about your community? What are some good ways to reach these people to interest them in participating in efforts to document your community?
8. What organizations do you know that are already collecting historical materials about your community? What kinds of things are they collecting?
9. What role do you think your local library currently plays in collecting historical materials about your community? What kinds of things are they collecting?
10. What role, if any, should the state play in assisting your community to collect historical materials?
11. What value would it have to your community if historical materials were collected?
12. Do you have additional suggestions, comments, or concerns that you can offer us to guide our efforts to be sure that there is better representation of your community in the history of the people of New York State?

Continued.

A similar set of questions might be developed and applied to assess the archive conditions in a specific community as opposed to the state as a whole. The following are from the New York State Archives and Records Administration, *Ensuring a Usable Past for* Your *Community* (Albany: NYS Archives and Records Administration, 1988):

1. Is significant documentation of the community's institutions, governments, and citizens identified, collected, preserved, and made available?
2. Do community groups and organizations, and individual citizens, take an active interest in, and provide support for, strong historical records programs?
3. Do historical records repositories, such as historical societies, libraries, museums, and archives, have written guidelines that guide what they collect?
4. Do religious, cultural, civic, business, and other community institutions have archival programs for the preservation of their records? If not, do they systematically transfer them to historical records repositories for preservation?
5. Is there coordination and cooperation among historical records programs, to ensure systematic documentation of the community's history?
6. Do historical records program staff have the training, experience, and expertise needed to care for historical records?
7. Do historical records programs have a secure facility and other resources needed to adequately care for historical records?
8. Do programs produce and make known finding aids for their records so that they are available to researchers?
9. Is adequate provision made for the preservation of historical records, to ensure their long-term survival for research use?

change; the makeup of the program one year differs from the previous, and the following year's makeup will probably continue the evolutionary pattern. The reason is that the home institutions are often caught up in change; the nature of records themselves is changing, particularly with the shift to digital technology; the makeup of the research community is changing; and the nature of research use itself is also dynamic.

- *Dynamic, balanced expansion.* Historical records programs by their nature are likely to be organic—they grow as their holdings increase and as research use expands. Growth is therefore a common underlying characteristic, but it is responsible and balanced. For instance, an increase in holdings is matched by new capacity for arrangement and description;

promotional marketing efforts are accompanied by more researcher services staff to deal with the resulting rise in research traffic.

- *High visibility.* The best programs are not quiet. They call attention to
  their holdings and services, and to the importance of archival records and
  the archival function in society generally, through such things as news releases, newsletters, exhibits, publications, speeches, Web sites, and other
  devices to catch the attention of current and potential customers and others with an interest or stake in what the program does.
- *Peer recognition.* The archival community gradually recognizes the best
  programs through such things as reading their written reports and products, interacting with their staff at professional meetings, participating in
  projects with them, observing how they cope with important problems,
  and getting positive feedback from researchers. More formal mechanisms,
  such as the Society of American Archivists' Distinguished Service Award,
  recognize the very best in the field.
- *Professional engagement.* Strong programs and active professional involvement have for many years tended to go hand in hand and to be mutually
  reinforcing. People from excellent programs contribute their time and talents to professional associations such as AASLH and the Society of American Archivists. They also learn from, and build on the insights of, their
  peers through professional meetings and other forums. Professional involvement lets them keep up with the best practices in the field. Finally, it
  is a way of coping collectively with some of the most intractable problems
  in the field, such as how to manage electronic records.

PREREQUISITES FOR SUCCESS: CHECKLIST

1. Is the program manager familiar with the State Historical Records Advisory
   Board's strategic plan, the issues it identifies, and the strategies it proposes?
2. Will the program actively participate in the solutions to those issues and
   problems?
3. Is the program's placement in, and relationship to, the mission of the parent historical agency clear?
4. Does the program have in place the essential elements needed for sound
   program administration and maintenance?
5. Has the program considered roles in addition to or as accompaniments to
   a collecting/curatorial/custodial role?
6. Does the program meet, or have sound plans and prospects to meet, the
   standards exemplified by programs that are recognized for their excellence?

3

BUILDING A HISTORICAL RECORDS PROGRAM: SOURCES OF ASSISTANCE

A NETWORK OF COLLEGIALITY AND ADVICE

Rugged individualism may be an admirable trait in people, but there is no need for historical records programs to "go it alone." In fact, trying to master historical records work through trial and error or through extrapolation from related fields (for instance, librarianship and artifacts curatorship) is unlikely to work, a disservice to historical records, and, moreover, just plain difficult. The archival community has built a tradition of openness and sharing approaches, solutions and advice, as well as tackling problems. Hundreds of historical records programs, dozens of professional associations, state archival programs, a good range of excellent literature, and other sources make up an effective network of support, advice, assistance, and informal discussion and consultation on archival issues. For agencies planning or beginning a program, this network can be a source for getting started on the right track; for new programs, a place to turn for advice on program development and administration; and for seasoned veterans, a source for advice on complex administrative, technical, or other issues. Sharing best practices and effective solutions to problems helps save resources, strengthens programs, avoids reinventing the wheel, and in general promotes consistency and good management.

STATE ARCHIVES/STATE HISTORICAL
RECORDS COORDINATOR'S OFFICE

In many states, the state archivist's office provides advice, assistance, and support for historical records programs. State archives, which may be located in state historical agencies, secretary of state's offices, state library agencies, or elsewhere, have responsibility for overseeing and determining retention and disposition procedures for municipal and county governments, including advice on their archival records. State archival offices issue retention and disposition schedules indicating how long various series of local government records must be retained, set standards for protection from fire, and issue guidelines for the application of information technologies such as optical disks used for the digital conversion of paper records. State archives are themselves good models of archival practice and their facilities in most cases reflect the standards that should be recognized for the preservation and security of historical records. They may also hold workshops, issue newsletters and other publications, sponsor conferences, and develop other vehicles for demonstrating sound archival practices for application in nongovernment settings. The Web site of the National Association of Government Archives and Records Administrators, *www.nagara.org*, includes links to each state archives Web site.

Moreover, most state archivists also function as State Historical Records Coordinators and chairs of State Historical Records Boards. The National Historical Publications and Records Commission, a federal historical records project funding agency located at the National Archives and Records Administration, requires the appointment (usually by the governor) of an advisory board and designation of a Coordinator as a condition for grant application by historical records programs within the state. The advisory boards review the applications from their state and the Commission takes their critiques into account when deciding on grant applications. Their role, however, is more pervasive than just reviewing federal grant proposals. State Coordinators and Boards may also actively encourage coordinated approaches to historical records collecting, carry out surveys and prepare reports, develop state legislative proposals, and sponsor grant-funded initiatives. The Coordinators and Boards carried out the surveys and issued the reports discussed in the introduction and summarized in chapter 2. These reports, available upon request from the Coordinator's office or the state archives Web site, analyze conditions and needs in the state, establish statewide directions and priorities, and often attempt to define responsibilities for progress toward established goals. Reading the state report can help establish a context for a particular historical records program, reveal common problems, and provide information on the state's archival community. The State

Coordinators have developed their own association (Council of State Historical Records Coordinators), and its Web site, *www.coshrc.org*, provides links to each State Coordinator's office and also to their publications.

PROFESSIONAL ASSOCIATIONS

Professional associations define the professional nature of the field, establish standards and guidelines, and provide a forum for exchange of information and discussion of common issues and problems. Joining, and becoming active in, a professional archival association is perhaps the best way to find colleagues dealing with historical records issues, become part of a professional network, and generally keep up with changes in the field. The cost of dues is almost always outweighed by the benefits of the educational opportunities, publications, and meetings.

The Society of American Archivists, the nation's oldest and largest professional archival association, is the place to turn for authoritative guidance on archival issues, best practices, and insights into difficult, emerging issues such as the management of electronic records. SAA publishes a quarterly journal, the *American Archivist*, a very informative newsletter, *Archival Outlook*, and other excellent publications (discussed below). It holds an annual meeting in a different part of the country each year and offers workshops in various locations. SAA can be reached at 527 S. Wells Street, 5th Floor, Chicago, IL 60607, or on the Web at *www.archivists.org*. There are also over fifty regional, local, and specialty archival associations, including, for instance, the New England Archivists (NEA), the Mid-Atlantic Regional Archives Conference (MARAC, covering New York to Virginia), and the Midwest Archives Conference (MAC), and about a dozen more in Canada, including the Association of Canadian Archivists. SAA's *Directory of Archival Associations in the United States and Canada*, issued periodically, usually as an insert in *Archival Outlook*, provides contact information for all of these organizations.

The National Association of Government Archives and Records Administrators (NAGARA) is an association of state archivists and records administrators and local and national records programs, including the National Archives and Records Administration. It issues a newsletter, holds an annual conference, and carries out other activities related to improved management of government archives and other records. NAGARA can be reached at 48 Howard Street, Albany, NY 12207, or on the Web at *www.nagara.org*. For programs whose interests or responsibilities include records management, the place to look is the Association of Records Managers and Administrators (ARMA International), which issues *Information Management Journal*, a news magazine, *Infopro*, and books and manuals. ARMA holds an annual conference and has regional chapters across the continent. ARMA can be reached at 4200 Somerset Drive, Suite 215, Prairie Village, KS 66208-5287, or on the Web, *www.arma.org*.

The place to look for guidance on micrographics, optical disk, and other advanced information technologies is the Association for Information and Image Management (AIIM), which provides guidance, helps set standards, and issues publications in the area of advanced technologies. AIIM is located at 1100 Wayne Avenue, Suite 1100, Silver Spring, MD 20910-5306; its Web site is *www.aiim.org*.

The American Association for State and Local History (AASLH), the sponsor of this book, is the recognized source for publications, a news magazine, *History News*, continuing education, a national conference, and other materials related to local history in all its manifestations. AASLH can be reached at 1717 Church Street, Nashville, TN 37203-2991 or at *www.aaslh.org*.

The American Association of Museums (AAM) promotes excellence in museum management and assists museum staff in adapting sound management techniques for their operations. They are located at 1575 Eye Street, NW, Suite 400, Washington, DC 20005, *www.aam-us.org*.

The professional association for librarians, American Library Association (ALA), provides leadership in the library community and advances the profession of librarianship; ALA can be contacted at 50 East Huron, Chicago, IL 60611, or *www.ala.org*.

For those who are interested in preservation, a good place to begin is the American Institute for Conservation of Historic and Artistic Works (AIC), a national membership association of conservation professionals, at 1717 K Street, NW, Suite 301, Washington, DC 20006, or via the Web at *sul2.stanford.edu/aic*.

Besides these organizations, there are dozens of others with varying specialties, including preservation, electronic records, information policy, and history. One approach to finding them is through the American Society of Association Executives (ASAE), which issues a periodic directory of associations. ASAE is located at 1575 I Street, NW, Washington, DC 20005-1168, or at *www.asaenet.org*.

Even associations with a paid executive director and paid staff operate mostly through *volunteer* labor; their members do most of the actual work. This fact means that there are plenty of opportunities to contribute, discuss, and learn. Professional associations are in fact the most widespread source of historical records education in the nation. Given the relatively limited number of formal educational offerings, professional engagement is a rewarding way to learn more about the field, advance archival skills, and gain insights into program management. Professional work also helps remind participants why the work is important and can help inspire and energize individuals. Accomplishment at home often goes hand in hand with professional dedication. Working with peers on association business also contributes to strengthening the profession overall. These activities are suggested:

- Follow the affairs of the association, attend the annual business meeting, determine how the association identifies key issues, sets priorities, and develops membership services.
- Propose topics for sessions at the association's conference, suggest presenters, and volunteer to serve as chair/commentator or to present a paper.
- Serve on committees, particularly those that are dealing with topics of direct interest to your program.
- Contribute to the newsletter or the electronic bulletin boards on the association's Web site as a means of sharing insights, asking questions, following issues, and obtaining information.
- Run for a seat on the board of directors as a means of shaping the association's agenda and, at the same time, enriching your learning experience through gaining additional perspectives and insights on issues.
- Read the professional journal and propose and write articles for the journal (publication may be easier than many people suppose; journal editors are often very eager to print good articles, particularly on topics of wide interest to the journal's readership.)

PUBLICATIONS

It is a mark of the diversity and dynamic nature of the field that there is no single book that is regarded as definitive. There is, however, a growing body of excellent professional archival literature. The Society of American Archivists (SAA) is the place to start for people who are entering the field or beginning a program. Two decades ago, SAA issued a *Basic Manual* series that covered the main points of archival work. Those volumes were superseded by a new *Archival Fundamentals* series, all of which are worth reading (and owning) by anyone aspiring to be a practitioner in the field. They are available from the SAA:

- James O'Toole's *Understanding Archives and Manuscripts* (1990) is an eloquent introduction to the archival field and the importance of archives.
- Thomas Wilsted and William Nolte, in *Managing Archival and Manuscript Repositories* (1991), cover the basics of management.

- Lewis Bellardo and Lynn Lady Bellardo's *A Glossary for Archivists, Manuscript Curators, and Records Managers* (1992) defines terms.
- F. Gerald Ham, in *Selecting and Appraising Archives and Manuscripts* (1992), explains how archivists select records of enduring value.
- Frederic M. Miller, in *Arranging and Describing Archives and Manuscripts* (1990), covers the physical arrangement of archival records and the development of finding aids.
- Mary Jo Pugh's *Providing Reference Service for Archives and Manuscripts* (1991) covers services to researchers.
- Mary Lynn Ritzenthaler, in Preserving Archives and Manuscripts (1993), covers the basics of preservation.

Faye Phillips, in *Local History Collections in Libraries* (Littleton, Colo.: Libraries Unlimited, 1995), explains how to administer local history collections in library settings. There are several other helpful basic manuals and books on archival programs, including Beth Yakel, *Starting an Archives* (Chicago: SAA, 1994); Gregory S. Hunter, *Developing and Maintaining Practical Archives* (New York: Neal-Schuman, 1997); Richard Cox, *Managing Institutional Archives: Foundational Principles and Practices* (Westport, Conn.: 1992); Judith Ellis, ed., *Keeping Archives*, 2d ed. (Port Melbourne: Australian Archives, 1993); and Bruce W. Dearstyne, *The Archival Enterprise: Modern Archival Principles, Practices, and Management Techniques* (Chicago: American Library Association, 1993). SAA and other publishers bring out new volumes periodically; watching Web sites, attending meetings, and reading notices and reviews are the best ways to keep track of new publications.

UNIVERSITY ARCHIVAL EDUCATIONAL PROGRAMS

Nearly three dozen universities in the United States offer archival training programs, ranging from single introductory courses through full-scale archival specialty programs with multiple course offerings. Practically all are at the master's level, usually in library/information science or history departments. Historical records program administrators and practitioners who need a grounding in archival methodology may find an introductory course helpful; specialists on the staff may be interested in courses in appraisal, reference, preservation, electronic records, or some other aspect of archival work. Some of the programs also offer courses in advanced archival administration, which help develop management and leadership skills. These programs sometimes sponsor seminars and institutes that cover selected topics intensively, often in one or two days, and are well suited to practicing professionals who want to update their expertise in a particular area. The educational programs may have students who seek practicums or internship opportunities in historical records settings. This kind of practical experience helps students learn the realities of archival work and also provides the programs with welcome and much-needed assistance in getting the work done. A partnership between the archival education program and the historical records program can be a winning proposition for both parties. The Society of American Archivists' *Directory of Archival Education in the United States and Canada*, updated periodically, describes all the programs and their course offerings.

MODEL HISTORICAL RECORDS PROGRAMS

Notably successful archival programs are themselves a source of inspiration and guidance to programs that are under development or experiencing problems. These dynamic programs, whose characteristics were outlined in chapter 2, carry out exemplary archival work every day, and have a storehouse of knowledge on problem-solving. Archivists tend to be friendly people who welcome a chance to share their experiences and insights with colleagues—and to display with pride the accomplishments of their programs. Peer-to-peer learning is an excellent way to gain insights, learn approaches, and avoid mistakes. Spending a day inside such a program, talking with staff, touring storage space, and generally finding out how things work can provide guidance and help avoid problems. Visiting more than one program provides multiple perspectives. An informal list of things to look into might include:

- *Relationship within the historical agency.* A visit can probe the role of the historical records program within the context of its parent agency, including mission, collecting policy, and cooperation with other parts of the agency on such things as preservation, exhibits, and public programs.
- *Foundation documents.* These include charters or other operating authority, mission and vision statements, long-range and annual plans.
- *Budget.* This may be a sensitive issue or the host institution may not want to make public its budget, but, if the information is available, the questions to ask might include: what are the budgetary sources; how does the program obtain funding from its parent agency; what lobbying is done and how effective is it; is the budget going up, down, or staying the same; and what role does outside funding (e.g., grants) play?

- *Administrative procedures.* These may be found in manuals and are guidelines on how things get done.
- *Collecting policies.* Are there written or unwritten guidelines that determine the topical or geographical areas and other parameters of the program's historical records collecting work?
- *Personnel policies.* How does the program recruit, hire, train, supervise, and provide for the continuing development of the people on its staff? How does it deal with such issues as work overload and burnout?
- *Facilities.* How secure is the building; what is done to protect records in the stacks; what is the level of fire and intrusion detection and alarm systems; what is the state of the heating/cooling system?
- *Researcher traffic.* Who uses the historical records, for what purposes, and how is use measured? What (if anything) is done to increase it?
- *School of hard knocks.* What lessons have the program managers learned through experience, what mistakes have they made, and what would they urge a new program manager to avoid?
- *Sources of advice and assistance.* Where does the program turn for advice, assistance, and counsel? Who are the most helpful resource people in the region? How helpful is assistance from the state? What are the most helpful associations?

ADVISORY COMMITTEES

The most successful historical records programs often have advisory committees made up of experts, advocates, and program supporters. In fact, the documents that authorize and set up the programs often permit, or even require, the appointment of such a committee, either by the head of the historical records program or by the director of the parent agency. Advisory committees serve two functions. First, they provide advice, insight, guidance, and recommendations on program development and on particular issues. For instance, a committee with expertise in the area of historical or other research might be particularly helpful in guiding the development of a collection policy and appraisal/selection decisions. Committees can be helpful in assisting planning processes, serving as the collective voice of various constituent groups. The committee's expertise becomes, in effect, an extension of the program staff's expertise and therefore a valuable and cost-free resource for the program.

Second, advisory committees serve as advocates for the program. They can point out budgetary needs, call attention to the need for more staff, sound the alarm about inadequate facilities or security, or quietly make the case for more space or a new building. Advisory committees can sometimes advocate for things that the program's own director cannot ask for because the request appears self-serving or because the program director's boss has turned down the request. This "political" role for the board is sensitive and must be approached with caution. An understanding must exist between the committee and the program's director that the board's role is helpful because it will further the aims of the program. Played adroitly, the role can be very useful.

Advisory boards and committees require the application of sound management practices, which means a commitment of time and resources. If management lags, the board will languish or else its role will become muddled; for instance, it may gradually shift from an *advisory* role to a *directing* role and then come into conflict with the program's administrators. Successful administration requires attention at least to the following:

- Make sure the committee's role is clearly delineated in a written document that lays out the "job description" of committee members and is periodically revisited to ensure its currency.
- Schedule meetings when most people can attend, designate a meeting chair (for example, the program administrator or the committee chair), set the agenda, develop and follow procedures for discussion and decision making, and circulate a summary of key decisions following the meeting.
- Carefully select committee members, including developing criteria, soliciting suggestions for members (e.g., from key customer groups), and recruiting. Choose members for the expertise and experience that the program needs, which may include political advocacy, fiscal management, fund-raising, public relations, or some particular aspect of archival work such as appraisal.
- Provide for orientation and training for new committee members, e.g., through use of a manual, orientation session, and having existing members mentor newcomers.
- Make sure it is clear who speaks for the program. Generally, advisory committees provide advice to the historical records program director, and the director and staff represent and speak for the program. If advisory committee members assume this role, questions can arise as to who is in charge.
- Listen to the committee with an open mind, carefully consider all advice, but make it clear that in the end the program administrator makes final decisions for the good of the program.
- The relationship between the program administrator and the chairperson of the advisory committee is critical for setting expectations, ensuring good

working relationships, keeping channels of communication open, ironing out misunderstandings, and generally keeping the advisory committee playing a positive role of advising, guiding, and supporting the program.

- When problems emerge, discuss them openly and frankly rather than hoping that problems will go away. Small problems, which are often the result of misunderstandings or lack of communication, can often be solved before they become large problems, and the board–program relationship is strengthened in the process.

CONSULTANTS

People establishing programs and program managers facing particularly difficult issues often turn to consultants for advice and assistance. For consultants to make a lasting, cost-effective contribution, several conditions must be present. First, the need and objective must be clearly defined. Otherwise, valuable time (and money) will be lost while defining the consultant's task. Second, the problem or issue must be one that a consultant can actually address. Typically, such issues include: (1) strategies for initial program planning and development; (2) advice on fund-raising, including competitive grants; (3) and advice and insight on particular issues, such as the management of electronic records.

Third, it must be clear that the consultant is advising for a limited time period on a particular issue or problem, and is not being hired to operate the program or put the proposed solution into effect over the long term. Consultants should not be treated as extra staff or temporary administrators; their appropriate role is to analyze, study, advise, report, assist—and leave. Fourth, the consultant must be well qualified through education and experience to provide the advice that is needed. The program manager should advertise the position, check with other programs in the area and with the state archives and appropriate professional associations, review résumés, and check references before making a selection. If the work required is sizeable and critical to the program, it may be advisable to interview finalists before making a choice.

Traits to look for in a historical records consultant include:

- *Educational preparation plus archival experience.* Consultants need a solid academic grounding in archival theory and practice and also actual hands-on experience working in a program. The insights and wisdom that flow from the right combination of sound education and rich experience are what sets a good consultant apart from a mediocre one.

- *Technical expertise coupled with broad program perspective.* The best consultants understand the technical issues thoroughly; they read the literature, attend conferences, contribute to the profession, and have experience in the particular issue at hand. But narrow technical expertise is not enough, because of the interrelationship of archival functions and the tendency of a development in one part of the program—for instance, appraisal and accessioning—to affect and have an impact on other elements of the program, such as researcher services. A recommendation that is advanced without regard to the rest of the program will be of limited value. Therefore, the consultant needs to have had experience in working in an archival program, an understanding of how things get done in such programs, and patience to learn about the make-up, priorities, and resources of the particular program.
- *Well developed analytical, listening, and communications skills.* These traits are essential to fully understand the dimensions of program issues and problems, to gain the best insights from program personnel, and to convey solutions in a way that is not only technically correct but also understandable and convincing to the staff who will actually carry out the solution.

As a fifth condition for a successful contribution, the consultant's work must be affordable, a reasonable expenditure of funds based on a fair rate, the nature and importance of the work, and the size of the program's operating budget. Consultant's fees, usually calculated on a per diem basis, often seem high; they are usually considerably higher than the average daily pay of professionals on the staff. That, however, is only one form of measurement of value, and usually not a very helpful one. A better approach is to gauge the overall importance of the issue or problem to be addressed and then judge whether the proposed fee is worth the cost to the program.

GRANT FUNDING

Grant funding can be a mixed blessing. It can give a new program a boost and help an established program get over hurdles. But grant funding should usually *not* be considered a substantial source of support. In general, there is only limited grant funding available for historical records projects. Grants are often awarded on a competitive basis, are usually a single award, and must be applied to particular types of records or problems that are of interest to the grant-making foundation or agency. Also, outside competitive grants should not take the place of ongoing, sustained, adequate funding from the parent agency—the agency's primary obligation to the historical records program. All-too-common stories in the annals of archives tell of programs that started with a grant, then crashed when the funding ran out; of partially processed collections; and of other work that was started but then sidelined when the outside funding dried up. The executive officer of the parent agency may feel that historical records work can be carried out exclusively with grants and volunteers, an assumption that is likely to severely limit or even kill the program. Grants should be sought as part of an overall fiscal planning effort and fund-raising campaign. This process would factor in the essential funding from the parent agency and then evaluate contributions available from local businesses, individuals interested in the work of the historical records program, and other sources. Grant funding may be particularly appropriate for:

- Planning and initial program development, including engaging a consultant to advise on the make-up of the program, facilities, and budget; paying for initial meetings of an advisory committee or board; producing a strategic report which will then provide the launch pad for program development; etc.
- Supporting a well thought out fund-raising effort; in effect, the grant becomes seed money or leveraging money.
- Arranging and describing particular collections that have been selected because of their topical information or high research value.
- Performing initial surveys and inventories of records that are needed to develop records retention and disposition schedules, lead to appraisal and selection decisions, and inform a new program about the volume and condition of records it is likely to have as it begins operations.
- Carrying out preservation work or microfilm priority collections.
- Engaging an expert consultant to advise on a particular issue or help the program address a technical problem.

A few states, including New York, provide grant funding for a variety of historical records program development projects. The National Historical Publications and Records Commission (NHPRC), a federal funding agency headquartered at the National Archives and Records Administration, offers competitive grants for historical records arrangement and description, program development, and selected initiatives, such as developing a capacity to preserve archival electronic records. Applications are reviewed by the State Historical Records Advisory Board, which may establish priorities for grant proposals from within the state and which reviews all applications. More information is available from the State Historical Records Coordinator's office or by writing the NHPRC, National Archives and Records Administration, Washington, DC 20408, or from their Web site, *www.nara.gov/nara/nhprc.* Their main publication, also available on the Web site, provides guidance on funding priorities and procedures: *Guidelines for Getting a Grant from the National Historical Publications and Records Commission.*

Federal and state government programs are only part of the grant funding picture, however. For small- and modest-sized programs, a more fertile source of funding may be local or regional foundations, community businesses, or even individuals. These sources may have an interest in a particular community, in the parent agency's program, or in a particular collection of records. The funding may be more limited than that from larger agencies, but it is also less competitive (or not competitive at all) and easier to obtain. The funding source may be particularly interested in the visibility and public relations advantages that result from funding the care of important historical records, and thereby supporting history and heritage. Finally, the "administrative" requirements—reports, forms, etc.—may be less burdensome for these types of grants than they are for programs administered by larger agencies.

There is yet another source of funding that is often overlooked by historical records programs: support from the donors of historical records. The simple donation of grandfather's papers after his death or the local company's records after going out of business is a mixed blessing for historical records program: it receives potentially valuable material but may lack the wherewithal to care for it. In some instances, potential donors can be asked to provide two types of support to accompany the transfer of the records. One is funding to process (arrange and describe) the materials. The rationale is that the materials need to be made available for research, so it is logical to seek support from the source of the materials to accomplish this. The second type of support is funding for long-term maintenance, including perhaps a staff position (or positions) to have primary responsibility for the collections. This is perhaps more difficult to justify because it requires continuing support and raises issues of the repository's long-term capacity and commitment to maintain the materials. But it may be worth a try, depending on circumstances.

In planning for grant-funded initiatives, large or small, several factors warrant consideration:

- Careful preparation is essential. This might include carefully reviewing the grants guidelines; reviewing other successful applications if they are available; asking the grants program officer to review a draft; and internal critiquing of the draft through reading and discussion by program staff before it is finalized. Evidence of hasty preparation is often enough to sink a proposal.

- To the degree possible, planning for grant funding should be integrated with the regular budget development process. This approach helps ensure that grants are an appropriate supplement to the main operating budget, which needs to come from the parent agency.
- It is essential to follow the funding program's guidelines. Funding agencies promulgate guidelines that reflect their interests and priorities and that lay out a rational process for grant applications and awards. Many grant applications fail simply because the applicants don't read the guidelines or don't take them seriously.
- The project or initiative to be supported by the grant should be defined as clearly as possible and should be clearly related to the program's overall work plan.
- If possible, ask funding agency staff to read a draft of the grant proposal. In most cases, they are more than willing to provide advice that will clarify and strengthen the proposal.
- The plan of work should be clear, concise, and complete. Specificity is a virtue; verbosity, a vice. The proposal should lay out the strengths of the institution, tell what will be done, describe the records, and explain the project and its importance. Including a time line is a good way to relate the work to the time available.
- The proposal should indicate how the project will conform to generally accepted archival principles and practices.
- The case for funding must be strong and must be skillfully presented. If an institution is well known and the records have apparent historical importance, programs may assume they need limited detail to present their case. That assumption is almost always wrong. Successful proposals need to describe the program, highlight the importance of the records, explain the plan of work clearly and in detail, set forth the budget including cost-sharing or matching funds from the applicant, and persuasively make the case funding needs.
- The results, outcomes, products, or impact should be spelled out. It's not enough to show that the work will be done well. The intended products need to be described as well as broader results, for instance, expected research in processed collections, numbers of people expected to see an exhibit, or dissemination of a report on a proposed symposium. The criteria for evaluating the success of the project also need to be included.
- The amount requested should be appropriate—enough to get the job done well, but not more than is actually needed. An approach that shows an intention to make optimal use of available grant resources will make a

good impression on the funding source, possibly opening the way for additional funding in the future.

- The application needs to demonstrate that the personnel involved are qualified through training and experience to carry out the work that is to be accomplished. Funding sources look particularly closely at the qualifications for the staff to be hired for the project through grant funding. They want to ensure that the grant dollars are used to support people who can clearly be expected to do excellent work.

Assuming the project is funded, it needs to be carefully and conscientiously administered. Administration of a grant-funded project needs to be handled as carefully as administration of the main program. A few principles to follow are:

- The funding should be spent according to the submitted and approved budget and plan of work. This advice may seem obvious, but in fact programs may be tempted to spend some of the money on related priorities rather than strictly on the work that is authorized.
- Sound, prudent financial management is critical; programs have a heightened fiscal obligation because they are using "someone else's money."
- The funding source should be credited in publicity and in the introduction to final products such as finding aids and guides.
- After the project concludes, a debriefing should be held with the staff involved to determine how well the project was carried out, what was learned in the process, and what, if any, insights the project provides about seeking additional grant funds.
- Every outside funded project should have a concluding narrative and financial report that describes the work that was done, the results, and how funds were spent.

SOURCES OF ASSISTANCE: CHECKLIST

1. Is the program aware of, and does it take advantage of, the publications, workshops, and other advisory services available from the State Archives/State Historical Records Coordinator's office?
2. Are program members active in professional associations, using them as an opportunity for learning, a forum for discussion, and a chance to contribute to the profession itself?
3. Is there a library of basic publications and provision for keeping up with the literature, including articles in journals?

4. Does the program take advantage of internships by students in regional graduate archival programs?
5. Has the program "plugged in" to the local and regional archival community and taken advantage of contacts to visit and learn from model programs?
6. Is there an advisory committee that advises, guides, and supports the program?
7. Is there a carefully thought out role for consultants?
8. Does the program seek and use grants for well defined projects and initiatives?

4

LEADERSHIP AND MANAGEMENT OF HISTORICAL RECORDS PROGRAMS

LEADERSHIP, MANAGEMENT, AND PROGRAM PROGRESS

Most thriving historical records programs, and most that are not doing well, can trace their condition to the same cause: the program's administration. Programs are not self-managing and self-perpetuating; attainment and success require sustained effort; challenges and change never seem to take days off. Even the smallest historical records programs require skilled, facile leadership and management, for several reasons. They are always part of a larger organization, whose mission is necessarily larger and broader than just historical records, so there is a need for clear program definition and assertion to get a place in the sun but also careful integration with the larger program. Resources are always an issue, so attention to budgeting and advocacy is needed and also to planning and prioritizing to ensure that funds, space, and people are not overstretched. The nature of the field and the make-up and expectations of the customer base are shifting, so strategic approaches are needed to advance the program. The most critical resource of all—the person or people doing the work—need care, nurturing, encouragement, and supervision.

Leadership and *management* are often referred to as if they were the same thing; actually, they are two distinct, but related, sets of talents. They may be found together in the same person, or they may be separate. Leaders are dynamic, visionary, future-oriented, and motivational. They are concerned about the direction of the program, its mission and vision, strategies for forward motion and dynamic change, and inspiring people and engaging their hearts as well as their minds and hands in the work. They think about *destination*. They work with others to develop the vision that defines the program's desired future course and destiny and then keep the program focused on it as a means of motivating, making tough decisions on priorities, and measuring progress. Archivists make good leaders, and they respond well to good leaders, because they tend to be highly motivated, dedicated, and committed anyway.

Managers are more practical and concerned more with the short term. They think about *getting the work done*. Managers work through other people to carry out tasks; they develop work plans to get the work done; oversee employees and provide them feedback and constructive criticism; and in general are concerned with systems, routines, reporting, and solid but incremental progress. Sound management is a good fit for historical records work because, as a practical matter, much of the challenge consists of hands-on work such as processing collections, writing finding aids, and providing services to researchers. It is practical, roll-up-your-sleeves work that requires dedication, energy, accuracy, and professional know-how. Leadership relates to vision, change, direction, perspective; management relates to getting the job done every day. Both are needed for a healthy program.[1]

FOUR PROGRAM FUNDAMENTALS: OPERATING AUTHORITY, PLAN, BUDGET, AND REPORTS

Operating Authority

Every program needs an operating authority in the form of a charter, incorporation document, or administrative directive. It is the point of departure, and later the fundamental point of reference, for a new program. The charter of the historical agency may indicate purposes and mission for the parent agency as a whole, but usually a longer document, derived from the charter but more detailed and focused only on historical records, will be needed. The authority-bestowing document should assert the program's right to exist and operate, indicate at least in general terms what it is supposed to accomplish, make it clear that the operation is a continuing one rather than intermittent or time-limited, and tie the historical records work to the work of the parent organization. The foundation document may also provide such information as geographical service area/collecting scope and indicate the priority groups or institutions for service. This information, in turn, is the launch point for more detailed delineation of collecting and service scope, as discussed in chapter 5. The point-of-departure document does several things: provides a solid legal basis for operation; ratifies the importance and permanence of the program; and provides insights about the aspirations of the program's originators for what it was expected to be and to accomplish.

Plans

Programs need to develop and follow plans in order to ensure steadiness of purpose, make optimal use of resources, signal to employees, executives, and customers alike what the program intends to do, focus the work, and take the program in new directions as needs, challenges, and opportunities change. Plans are blueprints for work and provide a standard for measuring progress and holding the program accountable for what it says it will accomplish. There is no prescriptive approach to planning. The process varies from one program to the next. It needs to involve the program's manager, who has primary responsibility for both developing the plan and overseeing its implementation; executives above the manager in the parent organization, whose support and provision of resources is critical; employees, who work with the materials and users every day and whose insights are therefore particularly pertinent; representatives of customer groups; and the program's advisory board, described in chapter 3. Plans have two characteristics. They indicate *what is to be done* in terms of expected outputs, products, and accomplishments. These are in effect the "deliverables" of the program—how many records it expects to accession, the rate and degree of processing, numbers and types of researchers anticipated to be served. They also indicate *how the work is to be done*, including strategies for approaching it and who is to actually do the work. Archivists and others in this field used to have relatively long planning horizons, e.g., five years. Recently, the professional literature has urged something much shorter, e.g., a year or two, because things change so fast. Plans tended to be long and detailed; more recently, they have tended to be shorter, state more general outcomes, and leave more room for managers and staff to determine the details of what to do and how to get it done.

Whatever their time frames or lengths, plans usually have five levels:

1. *Vision.* The vision statement sets forth in concise but bold, dramatic, and catchy terms the program's most fundamental aspirations and loftiest expectations. The vision presents everything the program would like to accomplish. But visions don't stay put. They are meant to be revisited and changed over time, to be compared to what is actually being done, and to be refined to represent the continuing hopes of the program.

2. *Mission.* Related closely to the vision statement, the mission indicates the business that the program is in, the work that it is doing, and the broad impact it hopes to have. Vision and mission should be based on, and need to be compatible with, the operating authority document.

3. *Goals.* Goals represent broad, general statements of expected accomplishment and products over the course of the plan. Goals are consistent with the mission and they clearly point the way toward the vision. For a long-term plan, accomplishing all the goals (seldom fully achieved in practice) would be tantamount to achieving the vision (which then, of course, would need to be changed).

4. *Objectives.* Objectives are concrete, measurable intermediate steps to each goal. Objectives are the workhorses of most plans: they're the things that require the most detailed attention, are the focus of day-to-day work, and are measured and reported on periodically.

5. *Activities.* Under each objective is a set of activities that need to be done to reach the outcome set in the objective. Activities are sufficiently discrete and detailed that they can be tied to individual workers' personal work plans, and can be used to measure workers' accomplishments and accountability.

Appendix 3 provides study questions that are helpful in plan formulation; appendix 5 provides a sample plan.

Budgets

Adequate budgetary resources that are dependably available to the program constitute the third fundamental. Providing an adequate level of resources on a continuing basis is primarily the responsibility of the parent program's trustees or overseers, but appealing for that budget and spending it well is the responsibility of the historical records program manager. Historical records programs are often underresourced, in part because of limited understanding of how demanding and resource-intensive the work can be, particularly if carried out in line with professional principles and practices. Therefore, an initial and continuing strategy is to make sure that the decision makers and resource allocators have a thorough understanding of what the program does and what it needs to do it. Some ways of getting the message across include: issuing reports; making presentations to the board of trustees; having trustees and top administrators visit the program, tour the stacks, and talk with employees about their work; giving people who operate the parent program professional literature to read; sharing with them the state strategic plan, issued by the State Historical Records Coordinator's office; taking them along to professional archival meetings; and bringing in an objective, outside consultant who can appeal to the executives and who brings an outsider's objectivity.

In appealing for annual budgets, some themes and strategies worth considering include:

- Historical records are a *growing* business. Stress that the program is organic and dynamic; it constantly grows as new accessions are received and as the number of researchers increase.

- Budgetary categories often include personnel, space, supplies and materials, technical services, travel, professional work and publications, and other areas. In developing and presenting the budget, it is helpful to itemize each of these, show the purpose and need, and stress how some naturally grow. To take a straightforward example, more historical records require more storage cartons. High-quality, highly productive employees require salary increases and, if the institution's policy permits, merit pay.

- Be ambitious—but realistic. Asking for far more than the parent agency's budgetary process can realistically be expected to support is usually not a good strategy and sacrifices credibility, particularly if it is done so often that everyone recognizes it as the program's repetitive strategy of choice. Making a businesslike case for resources that are needed, and backing up the case with a careful explanation of needs, documentation that shows conformance to generally accepted professional practices, and evidence of having identified the lowest cost supplier, are likely to be winning strategies.

- Make the budgetary case in terms that the decision makers can understand and appreciate. The historical society, library, or museum director who must allocate resources among several departments, including historical records, often must make hard choices, sometimes very quickly, on the basis of available information. It is advisable to avoid unfamiliar terms and concepts, unless they are clearly explained. Making the case directly and concisely in terms that are easy to understand is usually the best approach.

- Build the case gradually. Many times, the desired increase in the budget to hire a new person, install a new computer system, or microfilm a collection isn't awarded the first time around. The case may not be strong enough or the timing is off for any number of possible reasons. But persistence often pays off in archival work. Refining or revising the approach, repackaging the argument, building up points that seemed to inspire receptivity, and downplaying those that met with resistance or indifference, all increase the chances of eventual success.

- Dramatize the issue. It's too easy for budget analysts and hard-pressed program heads to assume that historical records issues can be deferred. After all, the argument (or unstated assumption) may hold that the records have survived for decades or even centuries, so what difference can a few more years make? Why not defer for now and address other, more pressing (not historical records) priorities? The person in charge of the historical records program has to find messages and strategies to break through that mind-set. A general set of arguments includes: We've waited too long already and need to act now or records (or opportunities) will be lost. Certain records will simply be discarded. Not acting means that we actually fall further and further behind. Deferring until the future will mean a higher cost (for instance, for preservation work); it's like waiting to fix the hole in the roof until the damage requires the entire roof to be replaced. Our customers (e.g., researchers) expect us to take action now, not wait. There is a high degree of public interest in these records.
- Get others to make the case. This is an excellent role for advisory committees, introduced in chapter 3. Advisory committees have an objectivity that the historical records program manager does not have since he or she is obviously directly interested in the program and would benefit from a higher budget. They have a different kind of credibility. An advisory committee can sometimes reach decision makers and resource allocators with appeals even after the program manager has worn out his or her welcome. Representing outside interests and customer groups, they have the potential for broadening the appeal for support.

One final budgetary point is worth making: historical records programs need to rely primarily on mainline, continuing budgets rather than on grants or other intermittent, unpredictable outside funding. Grants have a role to play in initiating programs, engaging consultants and subject area experts, and tackling specific problems, but they will not provide sustenance for the long run. Too much reliance on competitive grants can also take the pressure off the trustees and others to recognize that responsible historical records program work requires adequate resources.

Reports

The fourth fundamental program element is reporting. This may at first seem to be much less important than the three outlined above, but in fact it is tied to them. As stated earlier, many people beyond the professional field simply do not understand archival work, the archival function in society, or the need for wherewithal to sustain the work. Reports may include periodic updates and briefings, reports on special issues and problems, and an annual report that is printed and widely distributed and are an important vehicle for displacing ignorance. Reports highlight and document needs, helping to build the case for a higher budget. They can show exactly how funds were expended, underlining an inclination toward frugality and making every dollar do its duty. They can bring to life and dramatize the historical records, showing how important they are and how much interesting and valuable research information they hold. Perhaps best of all, reports can showcase *use* of historical records. With a researcher's approval, a report can take the mystery out of the research process by showing how the researcher located the records, why the researcher used them and how valuable they were, and provide insight about how the information from the records will further the research. Reports demystify, explain, advocate, and inform; they are, therefore, important tools for the historical records program.

MANAGEMENT PRACTICES OF PROFICIENT HISTORICAL RECORDS PROGRAMS

Successful programs are likely to follow several management practices that keep their program fresh, draw out the best in people, and reinforce the program's orientation toward service and excellence.[2] They relate to how people are recruited, managed, and generally regarded in the organization, on the assumption that in the final analysis it is the *people* that make the program.

1. *Careful, selective hiring of new personnel.* The strongest programs have a tradition of investing heavily in the new employee recruitment and hiring process. Getting the right person—with an appropriate educational background, the right mix of experience, and personality and other traits that are a good fit for the organizational climate—can take considerable time and effort. Through an extensive advertisement and recruitment process, including informal contacts in the archival community discussed in chapter 3, the job is publicized. A broad pool of applicants is worth the money spent on advertising. A multi-stage interview involving several staff members can reveal traits that do not show up in the résumé, including such subtle but essential characteristics as analytical skills, communication skills, customer service skills, initiative, ability to work as part of a team, and an inclination to grow, change, and take on new assignments and responsibilities. This is the time to pose tough questions: What are the per-

son's motivations for being in the field and aspirations for the future? How would the person handle a particular pressing problem? How would he or she balance conflicting priorities, a common situation in historical records work? How would an ethical issue be handled? How about dealing with a difficult colleague? The objective is to find out as much about the person's abilities and work style as possible before making a decision that is likely to be a lasting one.

2. *Extensive training and professional development opportunities.* Even the best employees need opportunities to grow as people and as professionals. Their high motivation and high productivity is often coupled with an inclination to constantly learn and "reinvent" themselves. Training opportunities and active participation in professional associations are sometimes regarded as frills or relegated to a secondary category because they require the outlay of funds and the commitment of the person's time. Actually, they should be high priorities, particularly in programs that rely on employee commitment, imagination, and initiative rather than close supervision and control as a standard operating procedure. Professional training should include enhancement of technical archival skills but also opportunities for growth through courses in leadership, institutional change, personnel management, and career enrichment. The best training programs are ones where the employees themselves suggest topical areas and approaches and/or actually design training courses that include hands-on, participatory activities. Professional association work, as noted in chapter 3, provides a chance to learn, to exchange ideas, and to grow outside the workplace. It also serves as a means of ratifying the importance and status of the work and an added reason to feel good about it, even if the work itself is not always exciting and conditions on the job are not as good as might be desired. Managers should set expectations that professional training and participation are a normal part of the job, and they should model their expectations by taking seminars and courses that advance their own skills.

3. *Relatively high compensation and job security.* Many people in this field are so dedicated that salary levels are not as critical an issue as is the case in some other fields. Nonetheless, pay is important, and it is hard for a program to hire the very best people and expect the very best from them if its pay is very low. Managers need to appeal to trustees and other resource allocators for salaries at appropriate levels. Sometimes, a special case has to be made to convince those who control the purse strings that archival work is truly a professional calling requiring the hiring of qualified professionals. Some programs are trying merit pay tied to individual

(or team/group) achievement and promotion based on ability and accomplishment as a means of retaining and rewarding productive staff. Job security is a related issue. This has taken on an added importance during the past two decades of downsizing, reorganization, and other developments that have cost many people their jobs and generally caused a chilling effect in many programs. Security is a worthy motivator, as well as a sign that the program really does care about and value the work of its employees. It encourages employees to take the long view of their program, to identify with it, to show concern for its welfare and fortune, and to make an extra effort to serve its customers well. On the other hand, constant worry about whether the job will last or whether a demotion or dismissal may come like a bolt out of the blue is sure to demoralize staff, distract their attention, and motivate them to look for other jobs. Points 2 and 3 are related: hire the best, pay them well, make them feel secure.

4. *Teams and decentralization of decision-making.* Management used to be more or less equated with supervision, which meant defining the work to be done, assigning it, closely overseeing the work while it was being done, checking it, and evaluating employee performance. That approach certainly did not motivate employees and it put a burden on the manager to somehow ensure that the employee carried out assignments. Enlightened management has changed in the past decade or so and now de-emphasizes such close supervision and constant checking and review. Empowerment of the individual is one new theme: let people know what has to be done, make sure they have the training and tools to do it, and turn them loose. Their own motivation and ability make it likely that the work will get done at a high quality level and in a timely fashion. Another relatively new approach is that of forming teams and pushing decision-making as far down into the hands of the teams and individuals as possible. The literature shows that self-managed teams almost always out-perform traditionally supervised groups; but it also shows that creating teams and making them operational can take a lot of time and energy, with occasional disappointments and setbacks along the way. Forming teams and making them work well requires management skills, time, patience, and an understanding of how challenging it can be to change traditional practices. But even if teams don't work for every area, the accompanying concept of decentralization of decision making seems to work in just about every case. The people who do the actual work have the knowledge and ability to take effective action, particularly when they must make an immediate decision and take action to make sure that a customer, for instance an archival researcher, is satisfied.[3]

5. *A climate that encourages initiative and innovation.* This trait is closely related to number 4. In striking a balance between "we have policies and procedures here that we all strictly follow all the time" and "we need consistency but we welcome innovation and new approaches," the program would do better to lean toward the latter. Rules are important, but they are secondary to good service and getting the job done, even if that may mean proceeding in some formerly untested way. Increased employee participation taps the knowledge, skills, commitments, and imaginations of employees. The program has about it a certain optimistic "can do" attitude, problem solving is a routine thing, innovation is welcome and in fact is built into performance plans, and mistakes and occasional setbacks are expected, tolerated, and used as teaching/learning experiences. Managers make sure that the program proceeds on a steady course and that reasonable expectations are met, but also that the program draws on the best ideas and energies of its most important resource—the people working there.

6. *Extensive information sharing.* Managers in the past have had a strong tendency to hoard information; in fact, information was equated with power. The top administrator had budgetary information, plans for getting grants, details on strategic approaches, and the latest policy discussions or decisions from the board of trustees. The administrator used the information for decision making. Other employees had only the information they needed to get their work done. In the newer approach to management, more decisions are made by employees and more initiative is expected from them, so it is only natural to give them more information. Broad sharing of financial, strategic, and operational information is now regarded as a hallmark of a high-performance organization. It has been made substantially easier in recent years through the use of computers, networks or intranets, and digital information. The policy of information sharing shows that the managers trust the people working for them, gives the staff the information they need to enhance performance, shows how the program is proceeding, and helps the staff see how their own program areas and their own accomplishments fit in.

7. *Valuing people and encouraging the heart.* What do people appreciate most from their bosses? "Appreciation, acknowledgment, praise, thank-you's, some simple gesture that says 'I care about you and what you do' . . . information that communicates 'You're on the right track. You're doing really well. Thanks.' . . . The heart of effective leadership is genuinely caring about people." This is the central message of the revealing and helpful study *Encouraging the Heart: A Leader's Guide to Rewarding and Recognizing Others.* Genuinely valuing people requires sincerity, dedication,

and genuine human empathy. The book provides several recommendations: set specific, high, but realistic work goals; make it clear that the very
best is expected from everyone; pay careful attention to what's happening
("Leaders are out and about all the time," say the book's authors. "They're
not in their offices much; the demands of the job keep them mobile.");
personalize recognition in a way that the person being recognized feels a
sense of understanding, caring, and appreciation; celebrate triumphs and
accomplishments together (going out to lunch, after-work activities, building a warm sense of community among caring people who enjoy working
together); and set a good example through absolute integrity as a caring,
concerned, leader.[4] Some programs go a step further by eliminating what
might be regarded as depersonalizing terms such as "staff" and "employees" and instead referring to everyone as an "associate" or some other
term which implies equality and respect. The particular approaches to encouraging the heart will depend on the program's traditions, culture, and
other characteristics. But keeping people at the center of the equation,
and constantly encouraging and recognizing their work, infuses energy
and potential for even more achievement in the program.

WORKING WITH VOLUNTEERS

Millions of Americans do some form of volunteer work; thousands of them
work in libraries, historical agencies, and historical records settings. The number of volunteers is growing for three reasons. One, many people are taking
early retirement, people are living longer, and they have more leisure time.
Two, volunteering is a way for people to infuse meaning and significance into
their lives, to "give something back," to experience satisfaction from having
contributed to a good cause. Three, national awareness of volunteerism has increased in the past decade because Presidents George Bush and Bill Clinton
have supported it (the latter through a presidential summit on volunteerism)
and the work of General Colin Powell and other civic-minded leaders who encourage it almost as a matter of patriotic duty. Many volunteers are retirees;
others are simply people with time to devote to volunteering, a desire to do so,
and useful experience or expertise to contribute.

Volunteers can be a particularly good fit for archival programs, for several
reasons:

- The programs tend to be underresourced or moderately resourced, so
  they need people.

- Historical records programs are mostly in urban and suburban areas, places that also have large numbers of potential volunteers.
- There are many things that volunteers, properly trained and supervised, can do well.
- Volunteers who like history, like serving people, enjoy working with conscientious and dedicated colleagues, and want to work in a pleasant, secure environment quite naturally are drawn to historical records programs.

Volunteers can help get the work done; they can take on certain tasks and free regular staff to do other things. For instance, volunteers who are properly prepared and supervised can help with processing, carry out indexing of genealogical research materials, provide orientation, give tours of the stacks, answer some reference questions, and carry out clerical duties. They can bring fresh insights and perspectives, often developed over many years of work and life experience. They may bring critical expertise; for instance, a retired history professor could help with appraisal and researcher service work in her area of expertise; a journalist could help with public relations; and a retired foreign language teacher could help with foreign language materials and researchers. They are often the program's most enthusiastic workers because they are dedicated, genuinely enjoy the work, and want to meet high expectations by doing a good job.

Volunteers can be valuable public relations agents for the program. Assuming their experience is positive, they will praise the program each time they talk about it with friends, family, and acquaintances. In some cases, volunteers have very willingly functioned as active advocates for the program, using their connections to help obtain resources and support. There are also other benefits. Volunteers may make a financial contribution to the program they have come to cherish. They may have historically significant records themselves that they are willing to donate. They may also be able to get friends, former colleagues, and others to consider offering their records to the repository.

Of course, there are disadvantages as well. Programs need to invest resources in their volunteer program, including time to identify, recruit, train, oversee, and provide feedback to volunteers. Some programs, after years of experience, conclude that the return is not worth the investment. Scheduling can be a problem if volunteers assume they may come in when they wish and leave when they wish. Volunteers can be independent-minded to the point of not accepting direction well, not taking criticism in a positive way, and in general being difficult to supervise. There is a constant challenge of ensuring that volunteers are given appropriate assignments and that their work is professionally acceptable. There have been instances where an influx of volunteers led to friction with regular, paid staff, who may resent having to orient and supervise the new-comers, may feel that the volunteers' work is not sufficiently professional, or may conclude that management relies too much on volunteers rather than pressing for more paid staff. In fact, managers need to guard against this very thing and avoid giving the impression to *their* bosses that volunteers are an adequate substitute for paid professional staff. Regular staff may even regard volunteers as threats to their own jobs. Finally, volunteers may be seen as security risks if they have unrestricted access to the storage stacks and records.

Volunteers have a place and role in historical records programs but, like other aspects of the work, good planning and management are the keys. An effective volunteer program has several dimensions:[5]

- *Designate a volunteer program administrator or coordinator.* This person should act as the advocate for the program, develop and oversee implementation of a volunteer plan, and where appropriate directly supervise the volunteers. The volunteer coordinator needs experience and expertise in program planning and organization, staffing and directing, team building and motivation, and an ability to work effectively with many different types of people.
- *Develop and plan for the role of volunteers in the program.* A volunteer program should not just grow on a hit-or-miss basis as people happen to come forward and volunteer. Instead, the role of volunteers should be clear in the program's planning document and there should be a formal volunteer job description, or more than one depending on needs, that describes such things as the work to be carried out, the knowledge, skills, and abilities desired or required, supervision, and evaluation.
- *Establish an organizational climate that is conducive to volunteers.* This includes provision for training, oversight, recognition, and strategies for retention. Careful, well-defined job assignments foster optimal use of the time of volunteers, provide a basis for measuring and evaluating progress, and make it clear to both the volunteers and regular, paid staff what the expectations are. There needs to be provision for soliciting, and where appropriate implementing, the insights and suggestions of volunteers. Managers need to establish and maintain a friendly, supportive, collaborative, and rewarding atmosphere; of course, such an atmosphere is helpful to all employees, not just volunteers!
- *Carefully match volunteer interest and experience to the work at hand.* Task design is an important predictive factor in both job satisfaction and in the quality of the final product. There must be realistic performance standards and expectations, matched by high levels of autonomy and responsibility.

- *Provide for orientation, training, and development opportunities.* These
  will not be nearly as extensive as the ones for regular staff, but they do
  need to include provision for orientation in the work the volunteer will do
  as well as some opportunities for personal enrichment and growth.
- *Establish a supervisory system.* This may include mentoring from regular
  staff. The supervision and mentoring should include such things as clear
  expectations for outcomes, delegation of decision-making responsibility,
  and regular evaluations and feedback.
- *Evaluate the program periodically.* This will determine its effectiveness,
  particularly in comparison with the time and resources that are being dedicated to it.

MANAGEMENT: PRACTICAL TOOLS

Historical records program managers often need a number of practical tools
and approaches in dealing with the day-to-day challenges of getting the job
done. These include:

- *Administrative manual.* A manual, which may be maintained in paper or
  more easily updatable electronic form, helps ensure that everyone is playing by the same general set of guidelines. The manual is the first thing that
  new employees or volunteers read, a point of departure when new initiatives begin, a point of reference and a source of know-how that reflects the
  program's preferred approaches. It needs to indicate expectations—but
  not be so detailed and prescriptive as to discourage individual initiative.
  The manual may include: program mission, vision, goals, and current
  workplan; code of ethics; procedures for appraisal, arrangement, and description; the preservation and disaster preparedness/response plan;
  guidelines for researcher services; and forms used for reports.
- *Individual work plans.* The program work plan presents the big picture,
  but individual work plans (usually prepared annually) guide people in their
  daily, weekly, and monthly work. The work plans, negotiated between employee and manager, should be tied to broader program work plans, should
  establish expected outputs and outcomes, should indicate performance
  measures, including qualitative as well as quantitative measures, but
  should also leave plenty of leeway for the employee to decide *how* to get
  things done, by exercising independent judgment.
- *Project-schedule-on-the-wall.* Some programs find it helpful to post in a
  common area a calendar with time lines and milestones for key initiatives

and projects. This has two effects: it reminds everyone of deadlines, and it reminds everyone that projects are accomplished on a team or program-wide basis rather than by individuals working solo.

- *Well organized staff meetings.* Ask many people in any organization what they dislike the most, and the answer is likely to be: *staff meetings.* That is because most meetings are poorly organized and nonproductive. Managers of historical records programs, cognizant of the time pressures everyone is likely to feel, should take care in organizing and conducting meetings. Some helpful hints: schedule meetings well in advance (a year-long schedule of regular meetings helps); seek employee input as to what needs discussion; prepare and distribute an agenda well in advance so that everyone can give thought to the topics at hand; begin and end the meetings on time; establish and follow ground rules about discussions and conclude discussions in a timely fashion by summing up major points and, where appropriate, action or follow-up items; and distribute a meeting summary with major topics, discussion points, and decisions right after the meeting.
- *Periodic one-on-one meetings.* Good management has good communication at its heart. Informal meetings with staff members every day and regularly scheduled periodic meetings to review work, discuss problems, and solicit input are a good way to keep the lines of two-way communication open. Some analysts call this "Management By Walking Around," a term originated by the management expert Tom Peters to denote a management style that stresses communication, awareness, and feedback. Frequent informal discussions and meetings are also a good way to underline the messages that management really does care about everyone on the staff, and that "we're all in this together."
- *Internal, informal communications devices.* There are other ways of staying in touch. Some programs use a bulletin board where announcements, notices, and other informational messages are posted. An informal internal newsletter can serve the same purpose. In this digital age, e-mail is a quick and easy (though impersonal) way to update everyone at once. In larger organizations, intranets serve the purpose of making certain information available to everyone all the time.

MANAGEMENT AND LEADERSHIP: CHECKLIST

1. Is the program well *led* in the sense that it has about it a sense of destiny, vision, mission, and a dynamic sense of change?

2. Is the program well *managed* in the sense that it proceeds in a systematic, businesslike way that makes optimal use of available resources, particularly people, maintains a service orientation, and gets the work done?

3. Are the fundamental operational elements—operating authority, work plan, budget, and reporting system—in place and active?

4. Does the program regularly employ strategies and practices that empower and motivate its people, draw on their best thoughts and energies, and help them to identify with the mission of the program?

5. If the historical records program uses volunteers, is there a systematic approach to recruitment, assignments, evaluation, and other aspects of their work?

6. Do managers make extra efforts to keep multiple channels of communications open and active?

5

SELECTION OF HISTORICAL RECORDS

SELECTION: A BLEND OF THEORY AND PRAGMATISM

The volume of records produced by people and institutions is overwhelming in quantity; however, only a small quantity of records merit continuing preservation because of their enduring value. How should a historical records program go about the business of identifying and selecting records to collect? The answer to this fundamental question determines the essential business of the program and the value of its services to history and to researchers in general. In too many programs, the question has not been fully addressed. There is no written collection policy and the holdings are an archival mosaic that reflects individual curators' interests over the years, the best intentions of people who donated what they regarded as important records, and other circumstances where records became available and were acquired even though they were not a particularly good fit for the program. In retrospect, the holdings seem to have accumulated informally, without a common theme, almost serendipitously. Many historical records programs thus have an uneven, inconsistent, set of holdings. Some are valuable; some are marginal, likely to be of occasional use; and some lack historical usefulness. Some are obviously related to the program's mission and setting, but others, though valuable, would be more compatible with another repository because of their nature.

A better approach is needed, one that takes into account the universe of recorded documentation, the setting of the program and its parent agency's mission, the value of the records, likely research traffic, and the practical matter of resources that can be obtained to care for historical records. The collection, by design, is built up in a systematic, orderly fashion. The repository gradually gathers a rich mass of related information, researchers develop an awareness of its dynamic nature and growing research potential, and the trustees of the parent agency sense a businesslike collecting approach that merits support and funding. The New York Documentary Heritage Program, which advises historical records programs on development and management, asserted that a systematic approach has six advantages:[1]

1. Affects the value placed on the repository by users, who will come to realize that the program has a substantive body of information to meet their research needs.
2. Helps determine the value placed on the repository by administrators, governing bodies, and others. If they believe the records are useful and have a high level of use by researchers, they are more likely to provide funding.
3. Affects the program's ability to raise funds, particularly from state and federal funding sources and private foundations. A well planned approach to appraisal and collection helps develop sound projects for which it is easy to justify funding.
4. Affects the kinds of programming that can be done beyond supporting research, e.g., teaching packets.
5. Determines all the rest of the work carried out by the program, since the program depends on—in a sense, is—what it collects and holds.
6. Most importantly, affects what ultimately constitutes the "historical record." For instance, for the nineteenth century, we know more about white males, politicians, those who were literate, and those who spoke English than others. These people were certainly important, but they were not the only people in this state, and for others the documentary record is limited and uneven.

Historical records programs, broadly defined, may have several potential sources of records. They may actively seek and solicit records, or records may be offered to them, sometimes for a price. Sources may include:

• *Their host or parent institutions.* As indicated earlier, this situation is typically the case for institutional archives, e.g., a business, university, or governmental archival program, and is not the main concern of this book.

- *Individuals.* People who are prominent in the geographical region of interest, or who have done outstanding work in the topical area of interest, may offer what they are likely to call their "papers" to the program. Or, as an alternative, their descendants may offer them. Such materials typically consist of letters, diaries, manuscript versions of publications, and miscellaneous items such as newspaper scrapbooks with information on the individual's career.
- *Groups and organizations.* Charitable, religious, fraternal, and other not-for-profit organizations produce some of the most interesting records anywhere because of the nature of their work, which often gets down to genuine individual human concerns. These records, which may include minutes, financial records, membership logs, and files on particular initiatives and activities, are often not sought or collected by historical records programs. Occasionally, the group itself creates an archival program; more often, the materials are simply eventually lost.
- *Institutions.* Governments and businesses are probably the most common examples of institutions that may wish to donate their archival records to a repository. In the case of government, in many states there are laws that actually discourage or prohibit this practice, on the assumption that government records belong to the public and are a governmental responsibility. In general, government archival records should stay with the government as part of an organized archival program. Businesses, particularly small, community-based companies with historical roots in the region, are more likely prospects. Institutional records may include such things as incorporation documents, minutes, plans, administrative files, and records showing the development of products, advertising, labor relations, advertising, etc. If the company is large enough, it should be encouraged to create its own archival program. If not, or if there is no interest in developing a program, the company may wish to turn over its archival records to an established historical records repository. But there is a catch here, too: if a business donates its records, it should be encouraged to also furnish financial or other resources to take care of them.

The picture is complicated by several factors. For one thing, some institutions in our society—government and education are probably the best examples—tend to produce abundant or overabundant records. Compared to other institutions, which are less influential and well resourced, these institutions tend to be *relatively* overdocumented. This does not mean that the nation's repositories have too many institutional archival records; it does mean that they tend to upstage and overshadow the rest. Some individuals and groups—typically, well educated, relatively affluent, and male—tend to produce more records than other groups and individuals, such as illiterate people, the poor, ethnic and racial minorities, and females. This last observation sometimes surprises people. Women make up the majority of the population but their records are a distinct minority of archival holdings. Archivists have also found that some groups, for instance certain immigrant populations, prefer to keep their records at home or in their communities rather than sending them to a historical records program that may be (or may just seem) remote, impersonal, and geared toward documenting traditional groups and history. Securing a representative, balanced, fulsome record of the past is one of the greatest challenges archivists face. It requires imagination, persistence in going after certain collections, and in some cases a proactive approach known as a documentation strategy, discussed below.

How does a program decide what to take, and what to pass up, from among the vast potential documentation that may be available? Selection requires wisdom, experience, good sense, and good judgment. It employs five concepts: (1) cooperative documentation; (2) collections policy; (3) program capacity; (4) appraisal; and (5) anticipating use.

COOPERATIVE DOCUMENTATION

Individual historical records programs have much in common: they are all in the same general business of identifying and saving historical documentation, exist to serve researchers, and with few exceptions have to make optimal use of limited resources. Their parent institutions—historical agencies, libraries, universities, etc.—share a common commitment to preservation and education. The challenge of saving all of the nation's historical records that warrant preservation over the long term is in reality beyond all programs' collective capacity. These facts ought to foster a natural inclination to cooperation, or at least coordination, in collecting. In fact, the opposite is usually true: programs develop collecting policies and strategies without consulting each other, communicate sporadically on collecting initiatives, compete with each other, and overlook important materials that should be collected and preserved. This is in part the result of the programs' parent agencies, e.g., libraries, historical societies, and museums, themselves lacking a tradition of cooperation. It is not uncommon for a public library and a historical society in a particular town to both seek and collect historical records from the town, with little regard to what the other institution is doing, and where neither is awash in resources to care for its holdings.

Historical records programs can do better through employing the concepts of *documentation* and *cooperative collecting*. The two concepts are often joined together in archival literature, but they are actually separate concepts. The concept of *documentation* holds that programs should back away from the traditional approach of passively collecting what comes their way, or appraising collections piecemeal without having a sense of the total universe of documentation that lies in their field of interest, e.g., a particular topic or a given geographical area. Instead, archivists need to work with major producers of records (particularly institutions), potential users, and other repositories to develop documentation strategies or plans. The plans look to improving future documentation as well as dealing with past records, and they should consider supplementing existing documentation when needed, e.g., oral histories for underdocumented groups of people. A documentation strategy is defined as:

> A plan formulated to ensure the documentation of an ongoing issue, activity, or geographic area (e.g., the operation of the government of the state of New York, labor unions in the United States, the impact of technology on the environment). The strategy is ordinarily designed, promoted, and in part implemented by an ongoing mechanism involving records creators, administrators (including archivists), and users. The documentation strategy is carried out through the mutual efforts of many institutions and individuals, influencing both the creation of the records and the archival retention of a portion of them. The strategy is refined in responses to changing conditions and viewpoints.[2]

Development of such a plan is a worthy role for a historical records program; in fact, it can substitute for, as well as accompany, actually collecting materials, as noted in chapter 1. The work requires an inclination to move beyond a unilateral approach toward a cooperative stance, for the common good of historical records and the people who will need to use them. It involves encouraging other institutions to take up the work, e.g., convincing a company to start a corporate archives. The work is demanding and time-consuming, which accounts for why it has only been attempted a few times, with mixed success, but the concept remains sound enough to warrant additional initiatives.

A successful approach involves two issues: (1) what should be documented and (2) how it should be done. The first question involves careful identification of a particular field of interest (most often for historical records programs this will be a geographical region such as a city or a county) and a thorough understanding of the history of the topic or area. The two key questions are:

1. What have been the most important historical developments and themes in this region? These may include such things as original settlement, growth and changes in the demographics of the population, the develop-

ment of the transportation network, business and commercial developments, and the impact of major events such as wars or depression.

2. What have been the most important and influential institutions in this region? Institutions include government, schools and other educational institutions, churches, and businesses.

The topics will vary from one area to another, but a good place to start is a general list of human activity developed some years ago as a framework for community documentation:[3]

- *Agriculture,* including the production, processing, and marketing of agricultural commodities ranging from small farms to large commercial operations.
- *Arts and architecture,* including the production, promotion, and sponsorship of music, painting, graphic and visual arts, performing arts, and other types of entertainment.
- *Business, industry, and manufacturing,* encompassing production of goods, processing of materials, buying and selling of goods, advertising and promotion, and other commercial activities.
- *Education,* which includes both public and private education, teaching, and learning, and includes all levels from elementary schools through universities.
- *Environmental affairs and natural resources,* encompassing activities related to energy, plants, animals, etc.
- *Labor,* broadly defined to include working groups and working conditions, as well as organized labor movements.
- *Medicine and health care,* including research, medical services, and health-related issues.
- *Military,* defined to include both wartime and peacetime military activity and affairs.
- *Politics, government, and law,* a broad category that includes both governmental services and the political life of the region.
- *Populations,* a term that is meant to include migration into and out of the region, ethnic groups, and groups such as children and women who are likely to be substantially underdocumented.
- *Recreation and leisure,* an area of growing importance in the twentieth century.
- *Science and technology,* a sprawling area that includes both research and applications.

- *Social organization and activity,* including not-for-profit institutions and voluntary groups.
- *Transportation and communications,* two areas with profound historical impact.

This list is meant only as a starting point and indication of potential topical areas. In the actual development of a documentation strategy, considerable study and historical analysis of a particular geographical area would be required to identify the most prominent historical activities or developments.

The second major issue—developing and implementing a documentation plan—involves six steps:

1. *Assemble a documentation coordination group or committee.* This needs to involve major repositories, representatives of government and major institutions, civic groups, academics, and members of the research community. The group needs to take responsibility for the development and implementation of the plan.
2. *Determine topical areas for priority documentation.* This step involves analysis of history and identification of a limited number of topical areas, drawing on the topical list developed for the particular area served by the historical records program.
3. *Survey existing collecting efforts.* The third step is to determine what existing repositories hold, and who is collecting in what areas. The gap between what is posited as desired in number 2 and the collecting work that is being done in number 3 is a measure of the magnitude of the work to be done.
4. *Develop a plan.* The plan should cover at least the following: (A) statement of the priority topical areas and details about them; (B) indication of the areas of specialization or priority for each participating program; (C) strategies for filling documentation gaps—areas of importance but where there is limited or inadequate collecting; and (D) mechanism for coordination, administration, and evaluation.
5. *Implement the plan on an ongoing basis.* This is the greatest challenge, involving oversight, coordination, and cooperation among a large and diverse group of players.
6. *Revisit and revise the plan as needed.*

A full-scale documentation plan is a major piece of work requiring sound leadership and an investment of considerable time and resources. For that reason,

DOCUMENTING THE PEOPLE: A POINT OF DEPARTURE

Documentation planning requires concerted analysis, discussion, development of a consensus on how to proceed, cooperation, and, perhaps more than anything else, a good deal of time. A project in New York City laid the basis for further work through first developing a four-point action agenda:

1. Documentation of 20th century New York City social history is inadequate, fragmentary, and scattered; records are often intellectually inaccessible for research and physically at risk.
2. Coordinated, cooperative measures are necessary to locate, preserve and make accessible records which document the experiences of the City's ordinary people—whether as immigrants, migrants or persistent residents, men or women, workers with collars of blue, white, or pink, as minorities who become the majority or vice versa, the politically "in" as well as the politically "out", those with homes and those without, as workers or as actors in other realms of their lives. . . .
3. Private and public funding should be allocated to upgrade and enhance the curatorial care and physical environment of historically significant records. . . .
4. The experiences of "ordinary people" as they themselves recorded them in words and images, should be presented through a variety of media for educational, research, and other purposes. Work for the interpretation and dissemination of New York City social history through publications, exhibits, film and video documentaries, landmark preservation efforts and tours should be encouraged and supported.

The project analyzed and reported on the state of documentation of successive ethnic groups, women's history, family life, politics, popular culture, labor and working class history, religious institutions, economic life, and activist and community groups. Recommendations for further action in each area pointed out ways to proceed in a cooperative fashion.

Source: Debra Bernhardt and Rachael Bernstein, eds., *Ordinary People, Extraordinary Lives: An Assessment of Archival Sources Documenting 20th Century New York City Social History* (New York: Robert F. Wagner Labor Archives, New York University, 1994).

in part, documentation strategies are rare. A more modest and feasible undertaking is *cooperative collecting*. This practical approach dispenses with the highly desirable, but also highly demanding, organization, surveying, and analysis work that a documentation plan requires. Instead, it proceeds on the assumption that a practical sharing of collecting interests and working agreements to divide up collecting responsibilities are to everyone's benefit. To take a simple example, a county historical society and all the town historical agencies and libraries within the county might agree on how best to divide up collecting historical records in the county. Cooperative collecting involves the following:

- A written understanding among the participating programs about overriding purposes and goals. The written document makes clear the purposes of the cooperation, spells out what each institution has agreed to do, prevents misunderstandings, and provides for continuity as individual program heads change and oral traditions of who agreed to what begin to fade. It also establishes expectations for all interested parties (including researchers, who are naturally interested in where they can expect to find particular materials).
- A steering committee or coordinating mechanism that keeps the cooperation on track, ensures communication, and if necessary makes decisions on particular issues such as disposition of a collection when there is contention among two or more programs.
- A communication mechanism, such as regular meetings, an informal newsletter, a common Web site, and an inclination to call or visit participating colleagues. Easy, informal communication is essential to keeping the cooperative approaches moving along smoothly.
- A common database or agreement to report regularly to a national database, or some other approach to make it clear which repositories have collected, and are prepared to make available, historical records.

COLLECTIONS POLICY

Every historical records program needs a written collections policy, whether it is part of a documentation plan or cooperative venture or not. The term *collection policy* is meant to refer to programs that seek and acquire materials from beyond their own parent agency; archivists sometimes use a broader term, *acquisitions policy*, to refer to the work of all repositories, including institutional archives that acquire archival records from their home program. Veteran archivist F. Gerald Ham notes:

> Whether or not archivists can significantly affect the larger ecology of the information universe—and have a professional mission to do so—they are not absolved from thoughtfully tending their own repository gardens, carefully developing program selection goals and methods. Their first task is to develop a repository acqui-

sition policy that defines the institution's role in contributing to a larger documentary heritage.[4]

Collection policies are signs of program maturity and accountability. In the absence of a policy, collecting is likely to be unfocused and haphazard; with the guidance of a policy, the program grows systematically, there is a basis for perusing or refusing particular collections, it is clear to trustees and executives that the program is proceeding responsibly, and researchers sense they can count on the program as a growing, reliable research resource. Collecting policies need to include several elements:

- *Mission and vision statement.* As discussed in chapter 4, every program needs a statement of vision and mission that is tied to the broader mandate of the parent historical agency. This statement establishes general expectations for collecting priorities.
- *Topical or geographical area of interest.* This part of the collecting statement is a natural product or derivative of the documentation planning work described above. But if that work has not taken place, the person in charge of the historical records work needs to state as clearly as possible the area of collecting interest, taking into account the mission statement, the repository's traditions and past work, the work of other collecting programs, and available resources. It should also indicate the chronological limits or preferences for collecting.
- *Types of activities supported.* The collection policy should provide some insight into the ultimate purposes of the collecting work.[5] It should indicate the types of research that the program is most interested in supporting and advancing. It should also describe other potential uses—for instance, exhibits, educational packets for schools, publications, videos—that are foreseen as potential beneficiaries of historical records collected. The statement should also indicate the intended audiences—groups most expected, and most encouraged, to use the records. As much specificity as possible is desired, without going to the opposite extreme and implying elitism or exclusivity. For instance, indicating "researchers" or "scholars" as high priority areas is not very insightful; describing particular types of research and outcomes (for instance, publication in a journal or a book) is more revealing.
- *Types of historical records collected.* The statement should give an indication of the physical types of records collected, e.g., letters, diaries, maps, account books, etc. If electronic records are sought and collected, the statement should so indicate, and provide some guidance on type, format, etc.

- *Broad criteria for decision making.* It is helpful, but not essential, for the statement to provide broad criteria for decision making on particular records. In effect, this is the launch pad for the appraisal process (discussed below). For instance, criteria might include:[6]
  - How well the records fit and support the program's mission statement.
  - The extent to which the function or subject is documented in existing holdings already in the repository.
  - The degree to which the function or subject is documented in alternative sources such as newspapers, periodicals, government publications, or books.
  - The holdings and collections programs of other programs in the same general collecting field.
  - Risk that the records will be lost if they are not accepted.
  - Clear expressions of interest, need, and intention to use, from groups of researchers.
- Low priorities and exclusions. The statement should include an indication of which records are regarded as low priorities and which ones are not sought or collected at all. This may seem out of place at first, but it actually reinforces the rest of the statement, which indicates what *will* be collected, and it provides a basis for politely refusing unwanted materials or directing them to some other, more appropriate institution.

PROGRAM CAPACITY

The level of resources that can reasonably be counted on, and the program's overall capacity, are important factors in selecting records. Every appraisal and selection decision has an impact on the program. It is all too common for programs to underestimate the amount of work required to take care of records, including arrangement, description, reference, and preservation requirements, and therefore to accept too much material. The quantity of materials simply outruns the capacity of the program to care for them. Among the "program capacity" factors to take into account when considering whether to solicit or accept a particular collection:[7]

- *Storage space.* Is there sufficient space to store the materials in secure, climate-controlled conditions? How near is the facility to being full? If these records are accepted and the program is near its storage capacity with no relief in sight, is it likely that other (perhaps more valuable) records will have to be refused later on? Storage space is a particularly critical issue with large volume collections, particularly if their research value is uncertain or is likely to be moderate.

- *Arrangement and description.* Does the program have the staff capacity to process (arrange and describe) the materials in a timely fashion so that they will be available for use? Processing needs vary with the size and state of arrangement of the collection. The issue is particularly critical with large scale collections that are likely to require extensive processing work before researchers can use them.

- *Researcher services.* The decision to accept any records worth having means that, eventually, someone will use them. That is the main purpose for all archival work; otherwise, there is little justification for taking in records. But this, in turn, means an increased demand on reference, or "researcher services," personnel who will serve the researchers. Are these increased service needs included in the repository's plans?

IDENTIFYING VALUES THROUGH APPRAISAL

The heart of selection is the process of *appraisal*, defined as:

> The process of determining the value and thus the disposition of records based on their current administrative, legal, and fiscal use; their evidential and informational value; their arrangement and condition; their intrinsic value; and their relationship to other records.[8]

The archival professional has developed two approaches to appraisal—*analysis to determine values*, the traditional approach, tested and used through years of experience, and *functional appraisal*, a newer approach that focuses on records-producing functions more than on the records themselves. The two are actually related and both have valuable insights for people who must make appraisals and decisions.

The traditional approach is tied closely to the notion of *values*. As a practical matter, archivists assume that records have two types of values, *primary* and *secondary*. Primary values include the administrative, legal, fiscal, and operational purposes for which the records were originally created, received, and used. These are the pragmatic purposes for records creation in the first place. The value diminishes or vanishes relatively soon after creation and use of the record. But a small percentage of records also have a secondary value, an enduring usefulness that transcends original creation purposes. In effect, records with a high secondary value are archival records and need to be preserved. But the process of identifying secondary value requires analysis and sound judgment. To help determine which records are valuable, archivists have developed the analytical insights of *evidential value* and *informational value*. Evidential value refers to the importance of the records in documenting the organization and operation of the institution or group that produced the records. Policy documents, operational directives, organizational charts, plans, etc., have high evidential value. The concept is more difficult to apply to individuals but refers to documentary material that shows how they organized their personal, political, economic, and social activities. The second category, informational value, is broader and deeper. It refers to how much revealing information the records present on people, things, and events. Records with extensive, rich information on important people and events are said to have high informational value and therefore are worthy of preservation. Those with low informational value—most records—are candidates for destruction after their primary usefulness passes.

Determining evidential and informational value requires an understanding of the producing person or entity, analysis of the records, awareness of research trends, and ability to compare the records to other sources. For good reason, appraisal is often called the most intellectually demanding aspect of archival work. Appraisal typically takes place at the *series* level, as defined in chapter 1. Appraising an entire *collection* or *record group* is possible, but usually this requires making a judgment at too broad a level. Appraising below the series level, e.g., file by file, takes too long and breaks up the natural organic coherence that series possess. In making an appraisal determination—deciding whether the records merit accessioning and preservation in the repository, it is useful to ask and answer the following questions:[9]

1. *Who created the records?* The answer to this question may seem apparent, but to some degree the importance of the records—and the likelihood that they will be regarded as authoritative, insightful research resources—depends in part on the role of the creator, his or her placement in and influence on a group, whether he or she was in a position to observe firsthand the events documented in the records, etc.
2. *What were the purposes and intentions of records creation?* This question essentially asks *why* the records were created. Purpose of creation sheds light on objectives, what functions the records were intended to accomplish, who was expected to use them, and why certain information was included in them.
3. *Is the information in the records unique?* As noted earlier, to meet the definition of a "record," an item needs to be unique, one of a kind. But a related question is whether the records contain information that can be found only in those particular records. If the same or similar information

is available elsewhere—for instance, printed sources or other records—then the records are of diminished significance and may not be worthy of preservation.

4. *What is the state of arrangement and description of the records?* The reason for asking this question is practical: records that were created in a disorderly fashion, are jumbled, and lack any kind of an index, finding aid, or other access tool may be a time-consuming challenge for the archivist to put in order. They also would be of limited value to the researcher who must try to determine order and relationships among individual scattered documents. If a choice must be made between records in good order and records in disorder, and the informational value is approximately the same, the scales tip toward the orderly records. Records that have accompanying filing system manuals or other indexes have an edge in the appraisal process because they come with the originator's finding aid.

5. *What is the degree of information intensity of the records?* Records with a good deal of well organized and well presented information in proportion to their volume and bulk are relatively good candidates for preservation; records with less information scattered over a larger volume of material are less promising candidates.

6. *What is the nature, quality, and importance of the information?* To what extent do the records provide rich, revealing information on people, topics, and events of importance, particularly in relationship to the mission of the program and the research interests of its priority research clientele? There should also be evidence that the records are accurate, that they were created in a timely fashion, and that the creator was an objective observer and recorder of events and facts as opposed to someone who may have had biases, preconceptions, or other traits that could have led to creation of a biased or inaccurate record.

7. *To what degree will the records be open for research?* Sometimes, people insist on restricting access to records or closing them for a given period of time because of the confidentiality of the information they contain, because they may reflect negatively on a family member, or for other reasons. Sometimes, reasonable restrictions are prudent and are a small price to pay for getting a particularly important collection. But in other cases, such as records with sketchy information about a topic that is tangential to the collecting policy, burdensome restrictions can tip the decision scale to the negative.

Appraising records requires skill, historical understanding, and experience. Often, it is benefited by consulting an expert in the topical field or a leading researcher, for added insight on the potential value of the records. Appendix 6 provides additional perspective by presenting guidelines aimed at potential *donors* who might be considering giving their records to a repository.

Some archivists, particularly those in government and other institutions who must appraise large volumes of records under intense time pressures, argue that the traditional process, summarized above, is too time-consuming and that the results, at best, may be uneven. They have advocated a varying approach, often called *functional appraisal.* Under this approach, the archivist, working with others in the institution, develops a list of the functions of the institution. For each function, a documentation plan is developed, taking into account existing records and also advocating the creation of additional records where necessary. The functional appraisal approach is conceptually similar to the "documentation strategy" approach. It is, however, much more focused and easier to achieve because it is applied on an institution-by-institution basis. Functional appraisal is still under development as a concept. It has been attempted mostly in university and governmental settings. Helen Samuels, longtime archivist at the Massachusetts Institute of Technology, in a pioneering work, identified seven generic functions of colleges and universities: confer credentials, convey knowledge, foster socialization, conduct research, sustain the institution, provide public service, and promote culture. She also developed a model for an institutional documentation plan.[10] Terry Cook, archival theorist and the program manager in charge of applying the concept at the National Archives of Canada (where it is known as "macroappraisal"), explains that archival analysis should focus on functions rather than records.

> By focusing archival research on analyzing . . . the importance of manageable numbers of these functions, programmes, and activities in the first instance rather than on appraising billions of records, or tens of thousands of systems, series, and collections, the archivist is able to see the whole forest, rather than just a few trees. . . . Using such knowledge gained by an institutional functional analysis, the main appraisal questions for the archivist are not what has been written down . . . where it is, and what research value does it have. Rather, based on this kind of functional-structural decomposition or analysis, [three] key questions are: What functions and activities of the creator should be documented (rather than what documentation should be kept)? Who, in articulating and implementing key functions, programmes, and transactions of the institutions would have cause to create a document, what type of document would it be, and with whom would that corporate person cooperate in either its creation or later use? . . . Which records creators (or "functions") (rather than which records) have the most importance?[11]

For most historical records programs that collect records from the outside, functional appraisal is an interesting, insightful concept but one they probably won't have the opportunity to apply directly. Traditional appraisal methods, in the context of carefully thought out collections policies, are probably easier and more practical to apply.

ANTICIPATING USE

Use of records by someone needing information is the ultimate purpose of all archival work. Therefore, to the degree possible, research use needs to be anticipated and taken into account in making selection decisions. To some degree, the concept of use is inherent in the four factors discussed above. The repository's mission statement or other document should indicate priority categories for use and users, which will provide guidance in the selection process. For in-

---

APPRAISING RECORDS: BACKGROUND INFORMATION

Establishing the background and context for records is a helpful basis for appraising them. The context reveals the setting, lets the archivist know where the person or institution that created the records fits in, and gives some predictive insights into their importance. The following questions help identify subparts of the needed information. From Anne-Marie Schwirtlich and Barbara Reed, "Managing the Acquisition Process," in *Keeping Archives*, 2d ed., ed. Judith Ellis (Port Melbourne, Victoria, Australia: Australian Society of Archivists, 1993), 150.

1. What relation does the person possessing the records have to the individual or organization whose records are being discussed?
2. What position did the creator of the records have in relation to the particular field being documented?
3. How long was the person or business active and when did they cease to be active?
4. Are these records unique or were copies distributed to a number of parties?
5. Who has legal title to these records? Were they inherited from a relative? Were they bought? Were they a gift? How is this ownership documented?
6. Are the records likely to contain much published material and is the published material readily available elsewhere?
7. Where are the records of other individuals or businesses relating to this collection held?
8. Are the records offered complete and representative evidence of the work of the creating organization or individual?

stance, if one of the program's priority user categories is researchers in demographics, that will predispose positive decisions on records that are rich with information on individuals, groups, immigration, emigration, and ethnic change. If historians of transportation are identified as an important researcher group, the program may tend to go after records relating to turnpikes, railroads, highways, airports, and such related topics as the growth of suburbs, commuters, and the growth of motels and roadside services. The time required to arrange, describe, and open the materials for use is another factor. Beyond that, programs need to plan for *promotional* activities—public notices, newsletters, presentations at professional meetings, calling attention to newly acquired holdings on Web sites, and generally proactively bringing them to the attention of researchers. The promotional activities need to be anticipated, at least in general terms, as decisions are being made.

TRANSFERRING ARCHIVAL RECORDS TO THE REPOSITORY

Once records are selected for the historical records program, there are still at least two more steps to be carried out to *accession* the records, or bring them under the legal and physical custody of the repository. The first is the *transfer of legal custody*. For most collecting programs, accepting a privately-owned collection involves transfer of legal title to the records. Occasionally, legal title may remain with the original owner of the record; the records are transferred physically to the repository but they are said to be "on deposit"—the repository has physical custody only. For records where both the physical and legal custody are transferred, the owner of the records and the receiving repository should negotiate a legal document usually referred to as a "deed of gift."[12] The deed of gift documents the understandings of both the transferring and the receiving party about terms and conditions of the transfer. It establishes clear legal title and its existence guards against misunderstandings later over rights and responsibilities. The deed of gift should include:[13]

- *The donor and the recipient.* The deed should indicate the name and address of the person donating the records, the name and address of the repository, and the name and title of the person accepting them for the repository. These people should sign the document.
- *Date of the transfer.*
- *Records to be conveyed.* The deed of gift should describe the records being transferred, including the title of the collection, a series-by-series description if possible, inclusive dates, and approximate volume. It may be

desirable to attach a box or folder level list if one is available. The objective is to describe the records with sufficient detail and specificity that there is no doubt later about what was transferred. The records description also serves as the starting point for the finding aid that needs to be produced for the records. In fact, it may itself serve as an interim finding aid because it provides essential information about the records and their content.

- *Physical form and condition.* The deed should indicate the physical types of the records and provide some indication of their physical condition.
- *Rights conveyed to the program.* The deed of gift should transfer not only physical custody but also copyright (assuming that the person transferring the records holds it), right to copy, and rights to discard material that has no research value in the process of arranging and describing the collection.
- *Restrictions on access.* Programs should strive to receive collections without access restrictions. Occasionally, donors impose access restrictions— that is, the collection or some parts of it are closed for a specified number of years—because of personal privacy concerns or out of a sense of caution because they do not know what information the records contain. For instance, there may be a provision that the entire collection, or certain series, are closed for ten years, or until a specified number of years after the death of the donor or some other event. Whenever possible, historical records program administrators should try to minimize restrictions, negotiate a time for their removal, or reach an understanding that sensitive documents will be identified during processing for further discussion. Whatever accommodation is reached, it should be spelled out in the deed of gift.
- *Financial considerations.* In some cases, repositories reach a decision to purchase material because of its outstanding research value and because the owner will not part with it otherwise. In other cases, the donor gives the material without charge but requires an estimate of value for income tax and other purposes. In still other cases, the program can negotiate for the donor to provide funding in addition to the material, to support its processing, preservation, and researcher services.

Deeds of gift are formal, legal documents. They are meant to be binding on both negotiating parties and to serve as a lasting record about the transaction. Therefore, deeds of gift must be drafted with care and with the advice and oversight of the repository's legal counsel to ensure that they are legally correct. The accompanying box about procedures to document acquisitions and appendix 7 provide additional information on deeds of gift.

PROCEDURES TO DOCUMENT ACQUISITIONS AND ESTABLISH OWNERSHIP

Every historical records program needs procedures to document its acquisitions, establish ownership, and document rights of use. The exact format will be different for each repository. The following checklist, in the form of yes/no questions, indicates what needs to be determined. From New York State Archives and Records Administration, *Strengthening New York's Historical Records Programs: A Self-Study Guide* (Albany: State Archives and Records Administration, 1989), 41–42.

1. Does the repository have clearly defined accession procedures for historical records deposits and donations and for documenting the selection process?
2. Do the accessioning procedures and forms used provide legal title to the repository's historical records holdings? Have all procedures and forms been reviewed by legal counsel?
3. Are the forms used adequate to capture the following information:
   a. Who is the owner?
   b. Who is the donor?
   c. Who is the recipient?
   d. What is the date of the transfer of title, if transferred?
   e. What is the material conveyed by the deed or agreement?
   f. Who holds copyright if any?
   g. What are the restrictions on use, if any? Is there a definable end date on the restrictions?
   h. Who can impose restrictions on use?
   i. To whom do the restrictions apply?
   j. Who can lift restrictions?
   k. Who has authority to dispose of records not wanted by the repository?
4. Does the repository fulfill its obligations to inform donors of their rights and responsibilities?
5. Has the historical records program informed donors of the rights and responsibilities of the repository?
6. Does the program avoid restrictions on access that appear inequitable or difficult or impossible to administer?
7. Has the program asked the donor to provide any financial support for the care of the historical records?
8. Will the program agree to accept further additions from the same records creators? If not, should the repository agree to take the first donation or deposit of historical records?

Continued.

> 9. If historical records offered to the repository do not fall within its acquisi-
> tion policy, will the repository direct the donors to other, more acceptable
> programs?
> 10. Will the historical records program provide records creators with any on-
> going records management advice and assistance?
> 11. Do disposition or retention schedules exist to serve as a continuing instru-
> ment for evaluation and deposit of institutional records?

The second action after making the decision on a collection of records and working out legal transfer is *transfer of physical custody*. This involves more than just going with a truck and loading the materials! It is the first indication of the level of care and concern that the program will show for its new acces-sion. As part of the transfer, it is important to develop documentation that de-scribes the records in as much detail as practical, depending on how much in-formation is included in the deed of gift. The transfer documentation should include information on the origin of the records; should describe them at the collection and series level; should note the informational content; and should include information about the *provenance* (origin) of the records. The transfer documentation, together with the deed of gift, make up the descriptive record of the material as it existed when acquired by the repository. It should include a box-by-box listing of the material. In fact, it may be considered the first step in arrangement and description of the records (covered in chapter 6).

SELECTION OF HISTORICAL RECORDS: CHECKLIST

1. Does the program participate in a documentation plan or engage in co-operative collecting with other programs that collect in the same or re-lated geographical or topical areas?
2. Is there a well developed, clear collections policy that indicates what the program collects, that is tied to the mission of its parent institution, and that indicates priority uses for the records that are collected and held?
3. In developing collecting policies and making appraisal decisions on par-ticular collections and series, are the realities of the program's storage ca-pacity, employees' capacities, and overall resource levels considered and taken into account?

4. Does the program have written appraisal guidelines and procedures that describe the appraisal process and indicate approaches to assessing records to determine which ones are truly valuable enough to warrant the program taking them?
5. Is the program "use and user oriented" and is likelihood of research use by priority research groups actively considered when appraisal and collecting decisions are made?
6. Does the program have and follow guidelines for accessioning of archival records?
7. Is there provision for reappraisal and for periodic revisiting of selection procedures?

6

ARRANGEMENT AND DESCRIPTION

ARRANGEMENT: THE KEY TO ORGANIZATION

This chapter and chapter 7 on researcher services are actually two parts of a common story: putting people together with records to satisfy an information need. Having people make productive use of the records is the ultimate goal of all archival work. *Arrangement* and *description* contribute substantially to that goal. Arrangement and description are so closely interrelated that they are often carried out together and sometimes described in archival writings as if they were a single procedure. In fact, the term *processing* is sometimes used to refer to accessioning (taking custody), arrangement (organizing records in accordance with archival principles to provide physical control), and description (assembling and presenting information to support access) as a collective entity of work.

Because arrangement involves physical handling and analysis of records, it tends to be one of the most time-consuming (and, therefore, resource intensive) aspects of archival work. It is also one of the most misunderstood archival functions and probably the one that is most often botched. The reason for this usually relates to the settings of historical records programs. Librarians may assume that historical records are actually enough like books that they can be cataloged in a fashion similar to that used for books. Historical curators may assume that they are actually enough like museum objects that they can be categorized the same way as artifacts. Researchers may add to the problem by pressuring repositories to organize materials so that they are easily accessible and quickly retrievable on a subject basis. What is actually needed is an approach that: (1) is true to, derives from and reflects the organization of, the records themselves; (2) responds to the realities of the repository's time and other resources; and (3) serves the best interests of the researcher. Arrangement is a vital part of archival work:

> The documentation processes involved in arrangement and based on provenance and original order are of great importance because archives, unlike books, draw much of their meaning from their context. Books, being discrete items, complete in themselves, can be catalogued and used individually. However, archives, being the organic products of continuing work or life activities, can only be fully understood through a knowledge of why and how they were created and used over time. As one's life or business changes, these new directions are reflected in the records and provide important evidence for the researcher. Each collection of records is different and the amount of arrangement that is necessary will vary. Some collections may still be in their original order, while others will need extensive reorganization either to restore the order in which they were created and used or to impose a new order if none previously existed.[1]

The Society of American Archivists' definition of arrangement is a good place to begin because it is comprehensive:

> The intellectual and physical processes and results of organizing documents in accordance with accepted archival principles, particularly provenance, at as many as necessary of the following levels: repository, collection, record group or fonds, subgroups, series, subseries, file unit, and item. The processes usually include packing, labeling, and shelving and are primarily intended to achieve physical control over archival holdings.[2]

Arrangement is based on five principles: (1) levels of arrangement and control; (2) provenance; (3) original order; (4) balanced approach; and (5) institutional resources.

FIRST PRINCIPLE: ARRANGEMENT TAKES PLACE AT SEVERAL HIERARCHICAL LEVELS

Many years ago, archivist Oliver Wendell Holmes asserted that arrangement is something that actually takes place at five separate levels.[3] Archivists have more or less followed his conceptual breakdown ever since that time. It works, sometimes with modifications, for most historical records in just about any historical records program setting—except possibly for electronic archival records, discussed in chapter 9. Records are grouped from the largest, most general down through a hierarchy to the most numerous and specific. Each level is related to, but different from, the other levels. Moreover, the approach is congruent with the principles of original order and provenance and also with descriptive practices. These five levels are:

1. *Repository.* A repository's holdings are sometimes divided into a few major and distinct categories. These categories are usually set early in the program's development and remain in effect unless and until there is a major change in its program. For instance, a museum archives might have two major categories: the museum's own archival records, and historical records that it collects from the outside. A major research library that collects business records and the records of individuals might maintain them as two separate major categories.

2. *Collection or record group.* These two terms mean approximately the same thing. Collection refers to all the records of a particular individual, institution, or organization. It is commonly used in programs that collect manuscript materials. A record group is a body of organizationally related records that are accessioned from a common source and are maintained together by the program on the basis of provenance. Record groups should clearly relate to the office or activity from which they came. For instance, the records of the state conservation department in a state archives are called the conservation record group; the records of the academic vice president's office in a university archives' would be maintained and referred to as the vice president's record group. Occasionally, the term and concept *subgroup* is used if there are clear and distinct subdivisions within a record group. The decision on whether to establish and maintain a subgroup depends on the volume and complexity of the records.

3. *Series.* A series is defined as file units or documents arranged in accordance with a filing system or maintained as a unit because they result from the same accumulation or filing process, the same function, or the same activity; have the same form; or because of some other relationship arising out of their creation, receipt, or use. Series are usually readily identifiable because they are records that were filed together in the same filing system; related to a particular subject or topic; or have the same physical format. Examples from the university vice president's office referred to above might include: correspondence (may be more than one series if clearly divided by topic and maintained that way), minutes of faculty meetings, minutes of meetings with the deans, and project case files. As previously noted, series tend to be the workhorses of the archival world. Series are often the appropriate level for appraisal; they are the

level at which the most important descriptive work will take place; and they represent an appropriate scope for researchers. If the archivist is lucky, the materials within the series were created, accumulated, and maintained in a logical order, which then requires very little arrangement work before it is offered for research.

4. *File units.* Within series, records tend to be maintained in discrete file units. Perhaps the best example is the common file folder. For the vice president of academic affairs, there might be alphabetical file folders for the correspondence series; each of those alphabetical folders is, in effect, a file unit.

5. *Item.* The fifth and final level is the item level. Items might include individual letters, memos, and reports. In the example above, each letter in the folder would constitute a discrete item. Items are, obviously, the most numerous of the arrangement levels. Because they are so numerous, as a practical matter they tend to get relatively little individual attention simply because the archivist does not have time to tend to them, i.e., appraise each item or describe each item.

SECOND PRINCIPLE: RECORDS OF A PARTICULAR RECORDS CREATOR MUST NOT BE INTERMINGLED WITH THOSE OF OTHER RECORDS CREATORS

This fundamental precept is usually called the "principle of provenance." As the term "provenance" implies, what counts here is the origin of the records. Records created by one person or institution should not be disassembled and intermingled or interfiled with the records of another, separate originator. The records of Juliette McAuliffe, a community leader and patron of music in the city of Chesapeake should not be interfiled with the records of the Chesapeake Symphony Orchestra even though they may relate, more or less, to the same topic of music in the community. Instead, they should be maintained separately, each collection according to its origin. This principle may seem so obvious and logical that it does not even need stating; but the thousands of collections in repositories all across the nation that have been broken up and reorganized by subject or in some other way bear testament to the need to assert and follow the principle. Violation of the principle has usually resulted from either (1) a misguided desire to group individual record items according to subject on the (false) assumption that they should be put together in the same fashion that books are cataloged by subject; or (2) a feeling that users are likely to seek materials on particular topics, so historical records should be organized to anticipate and meet their approach.

Provenance reveals important information about the creator, the conditions of creation, and the context in which the creation took place. Frederic Miller, author of the Society of American Archivists' manual on arrangement and description, has noted:

> Provenance is identified primarily with the creator. . . . A key practical argument [for provenance] is that a set of records must be put in place physically and/or administratively, and that the selection of a location strongly influences intellectual arrangement and description. Provenance permits archivists to avoid the librarian's need to select only one predefined subject for purposes of classification, by accepting the creator or source as the substitute for some defined system of classification. . . . In addition, provenance allows for an uncomplicated archival organization and a simple description of repository holdings. Collections and series are generally maintained as they were received. The holdings of archives and manuscripts repositories are described and organized on the general level according to inherited administrative structures or the names of individuals and families.[4]

As a practical matter, it is next to impossible to organize large collections of historical records on a topical basis for the simple reason that records, unlike books, are likely to relate to more than one topic. That is inherent in the nature of records; they may have a particular originator and a particular purpose, but each one is not necessarily confined to a single topical area. Therefore, provenance prevails on a practical as well as a theoretical basis. The principle is equally valid for small accessions (such as a three-volume diary from an individual) as for large ones (such as the archival records of a local company that went out of business).

THIRD PRINCIPLE: MAINTAIN RECORDS IN THEIR ORIGINAL ORDER

The concept of original order is the ally of the concepts of multilevel arrangement and provenance. Original order means that records should be maintained in the order in which they were created, filed, maintained, and preserved by the person or institution that created them. "The original order does not have to be neat, easily understood or obviously meaningful for it to be retained. If an order has been imposed on the papers by the original owner, this must be retained, for to do otherwise would destroy meaning in the material which may not be readily apparent or which needs special expertise to understand."[5] Like the principle of provenance, original order tells the researcher something about the origin of the records. It reveals something about how the person or organization that created them functioned, carried out business, and documented its activities.

Moreover, individual documents, while they may be interesting in and of themselves, take on added meaning when they can be considered along with other documents that were created at about the same time, and which document the same transaction, relate to the same topic, and were filed and maintained together. The whole picture becomes apparent by study of the documents in context, along with their original companions, in the original order in which they were created. Individual records take on added meaning when studied in context. This approach also keeps the records intact, buttressing their claims to be both authentic and complete. It also takes advantage of the originator's supposed self-interest in maintaining, and being able to retrieve, records that were needed to conduct business. Assuming there is a clear structure and organizational pattern to the records, then the presumption is that the archivist should simply preserve it. If the original order was good enough for the originator, the argument runs, it should be good enough for the researcher—and therefore acceptable to the archivist. Following this concept preserves the original order of documents within file folders, of folders within series, and of series within collections.

But the principle is not sacrosanct. For one thing, the original order may in fact reflect the eccentricities of the person who filed the records and the filing "system" may be incomprehensible to anyone else. Alternatively, the system may have changed over the course of years, even within a single series. For another thing, records often get out of order between the time they are filed and the time—often, many years later—they are appraised for archival preservation. They may have been transferred from their original files to some other storage containers, such as boxes, in a rough, slapdash fashion that disturbed the original order. They may have been moved, perhaps more than once, and disorganized and jumbled in the process. If the original order is too arcane to be comprehended, too complex to be practical, or simply has been lost over time, then archivists feel an obligation to put the records into some other, logical order that both reflects the originating activity (as far as it can be reconstructed) and also is likely to serve the needs of researchers.

The new order scheme may be by subject, alphabetical, chronological, by format, or another scheme suited to the material. For organizations, it is helpful to reconstruct the mission, goals, and functions if possible, to assume that records followed functions, and therefore that the records may logically be organized along functional lines. For individuals and groups, it may be possible to organize by functions, roles, or subjects. The finding aids produced need to indicate clearly that the original order was changed by the archivist during arrangement and description work, or that there was no original order, so the archivist created one. This information ensures that the researcher understands that the archivist as well as the records' originators had a hand in organizing the materials.

FOURTH PRINCIPLE: THE LEVEL AND INTENSITY OF ARRANGEMENT WORK SHOULD BE MORE OR LESS CONSISTENT FOR ALL THE REPOSITORY'S HOLDINGS

This principle is more difficult to name; perhaps *balance*, meaning keeping the work more or less even and consistent, is as good a term as any. What this means is that it is inadvisable to carry out detailed, exacting arrangement work (or, for that matter, description or preservation work) on one collection and, at the same time, do little or nothing on others. A good rule of thumb is to start at the top of the hierarchical breakdown noted earlier: perform work at the collection/record group level, then down to the series level, and only below that (to the file unit and individual document level) if time and resources permit. It is best to reach approximately the same level for all collections before going deeper (that is, more detailed work) on any particular collections. Because records are so voluminous, and because resources are so scarce in most programs, carrying out sound arrangement work to the series level is as far as the program may get—and probably good enough for most purposes. Of course, there will need to be exceptions to this principle of balance and evenness: a collection that has extraordinary research value, or that, after analysis, warrants processing to the item level because of its nature, the information it contains, and the anticipated research traffic.

FIFTH PRINCIPLE: INSTITUTIONAL RESOURCES ARE CRITICAL FACTORS IN ARRANGEMENT WORK

This principle is the corollary of number four and vice versa. Arrangement and description work, particularly of voluminous collections, is demanding in terms of personnel time, space, and other resources, including the folders and boxes used to rehouse the materials. It is easy to underestimate the amount of work that will be required to prepare the materials for use. Therefore, a practical factor comes quickly into play: the resources available for the work, in the form of staff, funds, space, and materials. Of course, this factor enters into the decision on appraisal and selection, as noted in chapter 5, and it needs to be taken into account in the program's overall administration and planning, particularly budgetary preparation. But the amount of work inherent in processing a given collection can only be anticipated, not fully known, until it is under the roof of the repository and undergoes a thorough analysis. Once that is done, and the extent of the arrangement and other processing work is estimated, practical decisions must be made which balance the needs against the time and energy available to do the work. For example, the decision may be reached that the collection can be arranged down to the series level but, at least for the time being, no work below that will be done because of lack of resources. Later on, perhaps, depending on resource levels and the work on other collections, it might be possible to return to the collection for work at the next level.

ARRANGING HISTORICAL RECORDS: PRACTICAL STEPS

There is no prescriptive way to arrange a collection of historical records; the best advice is to establish and follow certain principles, such as those outlined above. Some practical suggestions for proceeding:[6]

1. Develop a plan of arrangement on paper before the work begins. The plan should spell out, as precisely as possible, the existing state of arrangement; the proposed level of arrangement and descriptive, preservation, and other work that will be done during or along with the arrangement work; identify staff members to work on the project; and set forth an approximate timetable for performing the work. No plan will be exact, but it will provide a rough estimate of time required and will serve as a guide when decisions are required on how to proceed. (Figure 6.1 presents a suggested form for developing the plan.)
2. Assemble the supplies and materials that will be needed, including acid-free folders and cartons, labels, and materials for preliminary cleaning, before the work begins. This saves time and permits uninterrupted work on the materials.
3. Review the accession documentation for an overview of the records and use it, if possible, as the basis for arrangement and description work. The accessioning information is in effect a preliminary control device/finding aid and is the first building block in subsequent work.
4. Keep to the original order if there is one; it's worth spending time to determine whether one exists or not. Sometimes, collections that appear to have no order in fact reveal their order as the archivist goes through the steps below. It the archivist gets through steps 5 and 6 below and no order is apparent, then it's time to go to the next option, which is imposing an order on the collection.

ARRANGEMENT AND DESCRIPTION WORK PLAN

Call Number: Creator:

Title:

Date span: Volume:

Potential research value:
_____ High   _____ Medium   _____ Low

Arrangement analysis:

Current arrangement: Proposed arrangement:
_____ Alphabetical   _____ Alphabetical
_____ Chronological   _____ Chronological
_____ Numerical   _____ Numerical
_____ By record type   _____ By record type
_____ Other: _____ Other:
_____ No arrangement

Multiple series? _____ Yes _____ No

Records accessibility:

_____ Minimum rearrangement   _____ Medium rearrangement   _____ Maximum rearrangement

Proposed level of arrangement:

_____ Collection level   _____ Box level   _____ Folder level   _____ Item level

Proposed preservation during processing:

_____ Rebox
_____ Refolder
_____ Flattening
_____ Hardware removal
_____ Unbind postbinders/looseleaf notebooks
_____ Other:

Comments:

Estimated processing time:

Figure 6.1. Form for Developing an Arrangement/Description Work Plan. Form developed by Susan Potts McDonald and reproduced in Anne P. Smith and Jill Swiecichowski, Preferred Practices for Historical Repositories: A Resource Manual *(Atlanta: Georgia Department of Archives and History, 1999), Section 12, pp. 5, 6.*

5. Go quickly through the entire collection to get a feel for it as a whole, to verify the information in the accessioning documentation, to do a preliminary identification of series, and to identify any major problems. This preliminary overview gives a good sense of the collection and helps anticipate the amount of arrangement time that will be needed.

Description analysis:

Proposed level of description:

_____ Collection level   _____ Box level   _____ Folder level   _____ Item level

Comments:

Processing schedule:

Beginning date: Scheduled end date: Actual end date:

Staff assignment:

Submitted by: _____   Date: _____

Approved by: _____   Date: _____

Figure 6.1. Continued.

6. Separate the collection into series and put the series in the order in which they will be boxed and described. The collection should fall naturally into series; if it does not, the archivist may decide to create artificial series, based on function, document type, or some other criteria. If this step is taken, it should be noted in the finding aid.

7. Put series in a logical order, usually according to the value and importance of the information they contain. For instance, it makes sense to order series according to an administrative hierarchy of an organization (president or top administrator first, deputies second, etc.). The most information-

laden series should usually precede those with less information. For an individual, for instance, a series of rich, revealing personal correspondence would therefore precede a series of diaries with information of intermediate importance which, in turn, would come before a series of routine financial records (assuming these were important enough to accession in the first place).

8. Process each series to the file unit level if possible. This may involve some preliminary cleaning (brushing off loose dirt, for instance) and should also entail transferring the materials to standard, acid-free archival folders and cartons. This step requires perusing the material to get enough information so that the archivist is familiar with the order and contents of the material. The folders should also be labeled at this point.

9. Proceed to the item level only if there is time and if the plan accommodates it. As noted earlier, the repository may not have time—and there may not be an absolute need—to get to this level, examine every document, and make absolutely certain that everything is in order and in place. Archivists also need to avoid the temptation to read each and every item simply because the material is interesting! That is work for the researcher later on, not for the processing archivist.

10. Prepare a box-and-folder listing. List all the folders in each box in order. This will form part of the basis for the finding aid, to be prepared later on (and discussed below).

11. Don't set expectations too high or aim for perfection. Historical records work seldom reaches that level. For instance, it isn't absolutely essential to process to the item level and ensure that every document, e.g., individual letters in a file folder, is precisely where it belongs. Researchers expect, or should expect, that occasionally things will be slightly out of place, that the order will be less than totally clear, and that items that should be there will be missing. Part of the orientation for researchers needs to explain how the historical records program approaches arrangement and description, what its priorities and expectations are, and that researchers will need to do some searching for the exact materials and information that they need.

The work requires precision, dedication, and the ability to blend physical handling of records along with intellectual analysis of content and relationships. In many settings, the work is divided between professionals, on the one hand, and paraprofessionals, clerical staff, students, and volunteers, on the other. Professionals develop the processing plans, carry out the preliminary analysis and sorting down to the series level (steps 5 and 6 above), supervise the paraprofessionals and others, and prepare descriptions of the records. The other staff, with supervision, can easily handle such tasks as refoldering and reboxing, unfolding, cleaning and staple removal, and preparation of box and folder listings.

DESCRIPTION: THE KEY TO ACCESS

Description is the companion of arrangement; they are often carried out at the same time, share some of the same traits, and proceed in a hierarchical fashion, from the repository level at the top on down through series and file units and, occasionally, to individual documents. Description is:

> The process of analyzing, organizing, and recording information that serves to identify, manage, locate, and explain the holdings of archives and manuscript repositories and the contexts and records systems from which those holdings were selected.[7]

Description aims to bridge the gap between the records and the users; that is, to guide people to the records they need. Records are in most instances described to the level to which they are arranged; that is, if the arrangement work reached down to the file folder level, so too should the descriptive work. In that sense, arrangement and description are interlinked. Description takes the form of production of *finding aids*—tools that establish intellectual and physical control over the archival records. A repository should develop a descriptive program which has three goals:

1. *Physical and administrative control of the records.* Finding aids tell archivists and researchers where records are located physically in the facility, show their quantity, convey information about numbers of cartons or other containers, and show interrelationships within collections, such as numbers of series in a collection.
2. *Access to the records via provenance.* The natural access route into historical records is via their provenance or origin, which is how they are arranged. Finding aids naturally result from and follow provenance and original order. For instance, a collection from a given individual is likely to be described in an inventory for that collection.
3. *Access to the records via subject content.* Finding aids also permit access via the subjects or topics that are covered in the record. They do this in two ways: describing provenance and the business of the originator of the records in such a way that the researcher can tell that certain topics are

likely to be covered there; and subject-indexing, particularly via automated systems, which leads researchers more directly to desired material.

LEVEL OF DESCRIPTION

Finding aids may be created at any level of specificity and detail. At one extreme would be a short brochure that describes in summary the repository's holdings, perhaps mentioning a few outstanding collections and generalizing about subjects covered. At the other extreme, in theory at least, would be a system that describes each and every document. In reality, the first is helpful but of limited use; the second is virtually impossible to achieve because of time constraints and is possibly harmful because it may lose sight of provenance and relationships, e.g., series. In deciding what approaches to take, and how extensive and intensive the descriptive work should be, historical records repositories should attempt to take into account several factors:

- *Quantity of records.* As in arrangement and so much other archival work, quantity is an important determining factor in how to plan for description and the production of finding aids. There are at least two aspects to consider: numbers of collections and the total physical quantity in the repository. Obviously, a large number of relatively small collections is likely to require more descriptive time and work than a small number of relatively large collections.
- *State of arrangement.* Well arranged collections are relatively easy to describe; collections that are out of order much less so. That is why arrangement and description go hand in hand.
- *Rate of growth of holdings.* As noted earlier, a large number of repositories in the United States complain of having an "unprocessed backlog"— records that they have taken in but not yet arranged or described or records that they have arranged but still need descriptive work. In an optimal situation, the rate of new accessions should be approximately paralleled by the pace of arrangement and description work. If the new material is outdistancing the processing work, the rate of accessioning should be slowed down, or plans should be advanced for catch-up in the arrangement and description work.
- *Need for a balanced, more-or-less even approach.* This point is similar to the one above for arrangement. As a general rule, all collections in the repository should be described to about the same level. For instance, a repository that has a large quantity of undescribed records, many de-

scribed only superficially (for instance, the accession documentation is all that exists), and a few described to the item level probably needs to reexamine its approaches to description. Of course, there will be instances where substantially more or less descriptive work on a particular collection will be warranted, but that decision is one that should be deliberately made based on the nature of the records and researcher traffic.

- *Researcher traffic.* Finding aids are researcher service tools. Descriptive plans need to take into account existing researcher traffic, the repository's defined researcher priorities, and probable growth in researcher traffic. In addition, as a general rule more and better finding aids, particularly if coupled with publicity and promotional efforts, can be expected to increase researcher traffic.

- *Available staff, time, money.* This final, practical factor needs to be considered in just about all aspects of archival work. In small programs with large existing holdings and prospects for more coming in, it may be the most important factor. In effect, it relates to each of the five factors noted above. It also relates to the other aspects of the program in the sense that more resources for description may well mean fewer resources for other work, e.g., researcher services and preservation, and vice versa.

TYPES OF FINDING AIDS

Most finding aids are produced via computers, using special software purchased for the purpose or more common word processing and other software that is modified for the purpose. There is no taxonomy of finding aids but the following are commonly found in historical records programs:

- *Descriptive promotional brochure.* A short, snappy brochure is a useful item that introduces the program, outlines its mission and collecting scope, summarizes its holdings, points to topical areas of particular strength, and provides information on location and hours. It is a "finding aid" in the sense that it conveys at least a general sense of holdings and research potential. It has the advantage of being short, easy to produce, and relatively inexpensive and therefore a good item to mail out, hand out at conferences, etc.

- *Summary guide.* A summary guide provides access to all the holdings of an institution, in shorthand or summary fashion. It might, for instance, describe each collection in a page or two and list the series headings, but not provide any further detail.

- *Accession-level descriptions.* For programs with limited staff, production of a rudimentary finding aid based on accession information plus a quick overview of the materials may constitute a serviceable finding aid or a stopgap until additional work can be done. Such a description might consist of a main entry (the person or group that produced the records), title, dates, volume, brief indication of scope and contents, access restrictions (if any), and key indexing terms.[8]
- *Inventory.* The term inventory is a general one used to refer to a basic finding aid that contains and presents information about a collection or a record group. Inventories usually have most or all of the following features:[9]
- *Title of the collection.*
- *Preface.* This initial section explains the institution's collection policies, summarizes its holdings, and outlines its researcher service policies.
- *Introduction.* The introduction provides an overview of the collection, its provenance, and its research strengths, and how the contents relate to the history of the creating entity.
- *Biographical sketch or agency history.* This section sets forth concisely the history of the entity that produced the records or presents a biography of the person. This section is necessarily brief, presenting the highlights and suggesting the importance of the institution or person in history. It refers people to other sources, if there are any, for more details.
- *Scope and contents.* This is the heart of the finding aid. It includes inclusive dates, quantity, major types of material, an indication of the arrangement, and an outline of major subjects. The subject listing is particularly critical for several reasons: the subjects serve as indexing/retrieval points for automated systems, the listing is designed to attract the attention of researchers and to serve as a topic point of entry for the records, and the choice of terms also helps both archivists and researchers understand how various collections relate to each other.
- *Series descriptions.* Inventories should include series descriptions, which build on the scope and content note. For each series, the following information should be included: inclusive dates, quantity, types of material, arrangement, and major subjects.
- *Box or other container listing.* This is the part of the inventory that enables people to go directly to the material that seems relevant and helpful to their work. The box listing may in fact be the same one that accompanied the original accession and was part of the accessioning documentation; or, more likely, it will be a revision of the original listing, which reflects the actual contents discovered during arrangement work.

- *Access restrictions, if any.*
- *Other helpful information*, e.g., creator-supplied finding aids, or indexes to all or part of the collection.

CONSISTENCY OF FORMAT AND TERMINOLOGY

The archival community has, over the past two decades, gradually reached a consensus that it makes sense to follow a standard format in assembling and presenting information in finding aids and in access tools generally. A standard format provides for consistent placement of the same kinds of information in

---

GETTING THE DESCRIPTION INFORMATION OUT

In many states, there are statewide library bibliographic networks that offer to include summary descriptions from, or links to the Web sites of, individual historical records repositories. At least two national utilities are concentrating on dissemination of descriptive information about historical records collections.

National Union Catalog of Manuscript Collections (NUCMC), operated by the Library of Congress, has published descriptions of manuscript collections since 1959. NUCMC will create collection-level MARC bibliographic records in the RLIN (Research Libraries Information Network), where they will then be available to researchers and institutions who subscribe to RLIN's services. To submit to NUCMC, a repository must be regularly open for research and must submit data in a form NUCMC prescribes. This can be done on the Internet; no familiarity with computers or computer applications is needed. Submitting to NUCMC is an easy (and free of charge) way of spreading the word about significant collections. For more information: Library of Congress NUCMC Team, 101 Independence Ave., SE, Washington, DC 20540-4375, 202-707-7954, nucmc@loc.gov, or check their Web site, *lcweb.loc.gov/coll/nucmc/info.html*.

ArchivesUSA: Integrated Collection and Repository Information, published by Chadwyck-Healey, provides access to holdings of nearly 5,000 repositories and over 100,000 collections. *ArchivesUSA* includes all NUCMC entries as well as entries from two other major directories of historical records. It is available by annual subscription and is updated quarterly and on their Web site. It is available free of charge in a few states, which have provided statewide funding as part of a national campaign to eventually make *ArchivesUSA* free everywhere. For more information: *ArchivesUSA*, Chadwyck-Healey, Inc., 1101 King Street, Alexandria, VA 22314, 800-752-0515, service@chadwyck.com. or check their web site, *archives.chadwyck.com*.

the same location every time, makes it easier for researchers to use the finding aids, is consistent with automated systems (though automation is not required for using the format), and makes for more consistency from collection to collection and from repository to repository. The format that is the subject of the consensus is USMARC—U.S. Machine Readable Cataloging. The now-outdated term "Machine Readable" is a reminder that the format grew out of experimentation and research/development efforts in the 1970s and 1980s by the Society of American Archivists, the Research Libraries Information Network (RLIN), and others.[10] There are several key USMARC fields for archival description:

110	Personal name
245	Title and dates
300	Volume
351	Arrangement and organization
520	Scope and content

Appendix 8 presents some examples of entries from finding aids.

For many years, repositories made up and used their own collection and series titles and terminology for scope and content notes. This practice, like the one of each repository developing its own format, has gradually been superseded by a more consistent approach that is helpful to researchers and supports computer-based access. The approach has two parts to it. One, archivists are now using standard terminology as much as possible, particularly *Library of Congress Subject Headings* (updated periodically). Second, they are attempting to use approaches that are consistent with library cataloging, including standardized rules, subject classifications, and authority files. Archivists do not actually *catalog* their materials; that term is associated with library practice. But they are more likely than in the past to follow sensible, consistent procedures, many of which are set forth in *Anglo-American Cataloguing Rules* (usually referred to as AACR and updated periodically). The Society of American Archivists has published a manual that relates cataloging rules to archival practice, and a second publication that brings together and explains descriptive standards.[11]

DESCRIPTION ENCOUNTERS THE WORLD WIDE WEB

MARC represented a grand step forward for archival description but it did not provide for the kind of universal access and interchangeability that the Internet and the World Wide Web make possible. The rather dramatic advent of the Web in the 1990s is bringing in its wake many changes for archives, some of which are discussed in chapter 7. In order to take advantage of the Web's potential, archivists have developed Encoded Archival Description (EAD), a data structure standard that can be used for the encoding of finding aids. It follows the syntactic rules of Standard Generalized Markup Language (SGML) (used in programming data for posting on the Internet) and has been endorsed by the Society of American Archivists and the Library of Congress. EAD permits finding aids to be made available and disseminated over the Internet. This distribution permits finding aids to be accessed and searched effectively. EAD can be used for the conversion of existing finding aids and the creation of new ones. It permits the searching of finding aids at various levels; its inherently hierarchical approach to data structuring mirrors the information hierarchies that have long been the cornerstone of archival descriptive practices. EAD is not simple to apply; implementing it may require a new approach to finding aids, staff training, the purchase and mastery of new software, and administrative changes. It does seem worth the resources for repositories that intend to be active via the Web, and that is likely to be the majority. Repositories that have implemented it have found the results helpful. EAD is still in the early stages of implementation; the best approach to understanding it is to review some of the in-progress projects that are available through the EAD Web site at the Library of Congress.[12]

7

SERVICES TO USERS

DEALING WITH RESEARCHERS: OPPORTUNITIES, DILEMMAS

Researchers—people who use historical records to meet an information need—are the most important category of users of historical records. Archivists usually use the term *reference* to describe their interactions with researchers. That term is actually too narrow and reactive. A better term—and a more appropriate concept—is that of *researcher services*, which actually involves four aspects: (1) encouraging research use of holdings; (2) actively counseling and assisting researchers; (3) making records available; and (4) analyzing and measuring research use. Dealing with researchers is often considered the most rewarding part of archival work, the culmination of everything else, including appraisal, preservation, arrangement, and description. Getting researchers interested in the records, answering their questions, guiding them to the sources, watching them find historical nuggets, hearing their expressions of satisfaction (and, sometimes, gratitude) at the end of their work—these are heartening experiences that confirm the value of our work and help provide motivational fuel to do more!

However, experienced archivists will quickly admit that the work can also be frustrating and surrounded by dilemmas, including:

- *Historical records are underutilized.* As indicated in chapter 1, researchers as a group do not make as much use of historical records as their importance warrants and therefore there are gaps in reports, missing footnotes and citations in scholarly works, and other examples of information needs that are simply not fully satisfied because historical records were overlooked or ignored. In part, this is because academic training generally does not prepare researchers to use primary sources, including historical records. In part, it is the result of researchers being in a hurry, not knowing about the resources or not caring to use them. In part, it is the fault of archivists who do not actively seek out researchers or who exhibit too proprietary and custodial approaches to their work.

- *Researchers are often not well prepared to use historical records.* It is not uncommon for researchers to approach historical records before they have done preparatory work in secondary sources; to assume that historical records are in reality library materials and therefore organized as library materials are; to expect quick, easy and direct access to the exact materials they need; to anticipate that the historical records custodian has plenty of time to act as a research assistant; to assume that the repository must be open evenings and weekends, since those are the most convenient times for researchers; to be surprised by the presence of security requirements and restrictions such as not being allowed to use pens in the search room; and to proceed on the basis of unsound research strategies such as taking too many notes and spending too much time on particular records.

- *Researchers and archivists may initially talk past each other.* A good deal of archival researcher services work has to do with communication. Researchers, for instance, may find it difficult to articulate exactly what they are seeking, or may not want to disclose it for personal reasons. Archivists need to work hard at describing repository holdings and policies to compensate. Researchers come at things topically; archivists arrange things by provenance. Researchers ask about the index or the catalog; archivists respond with the inventory and the series description. Researchers expect and value concise containers of information; archivists are used to bulk. Researchers expect logically organized materials; archivists go by original order even if it is not neat. Researchers are often in a hurry because their research time is scarce and their travel money is limited; archivists, ever patient, understand that good research in historical records takes time.

The dilemmas and the opportunities come together in the search room—or wherever historical records custodians encounter researchers by phone, fax, e-mail, or, increasingly, over the Internet. For this reason, researcher services specialists—the archivists and/or other professionals who work with the re-searchers each day—need to play several roles:

- *Promotional marketer.* The initial role, to be played by the researcher serv-ices specialist or some other expert, is that of *marketing* holdings and serv-ices in the sense of making researchers aware of them and encouraging them to use the resources.
- *Negotiator.* Part of the work is communicating, informing, and negotiating with the researcher. This involves, for instance, zeroing in on the research topic and mediating among the researcher, the finding aids, and the records.
- *Research counselor.* Archivists should not actually carry out work for re-searchers; that crosses the line between professional archival work and re-search work. But the archivist should advise, assist, and counsel the re-searcher, pointing him or her toward appropriate finding aids, retrieving needed records, and advising on such things as provenance, original order, and appraisal/selection policies.
- *Records content expert.* Archivists get to know their records well—through appraisal, through processing, and through assisting researchers over the years and observing how they use the records, and through firsthand ex-amination of the records as time permits. This means they can go beyond the finding aids when appropriate in suggesting to researchers where to look for information.
- *Distance services expert.* Increasingly, services are sought and delivered on the Web via the repository's home page or its parent institution's Web site. The archivist must therefore become adept at dealing with researchers at a distance. This work is different from the traditional work of responding to mail and telephone inquiries, as discussed below.
- *Security enforcer.* Researcher services specialists must also be security specialists—they have a special obligation to protect the records in their charge as well as to make them available. This means stating and enforc-ing the rules and, at the same time, making researchers feel welcome and comfortable using the materials.
- *Copyright law and access restriction enforcer.* Archivists are sometimes likened to gatekeepers because they determine when to allow people into the historical records and when they have to restrict access and copying.
- *Reporter.* Reporting is often the forgotten or neglected part of researcher services because there seems to be insufficient time for it.

Historical records programs need to keep *use* at the top of their list of priori-ties. The table on page 105 contrasts *user oriented* programs with *custodial ori-*

ented programs that have not defined use as a priority but, instead, concentrate on custodial responsibilities. Neither approach is necessarily right or wrong, but the author urges programs to tilt toward the user oriented approach.

TYPES OF USERS

In general, the historical records repository should be open to anyone who wants to use it. There may be exceptions, such as a business archives that restricts its holdings to company employees, but in general openness should be the rule. Special treatment, unless sanctioned by the institution's policies, should be avoided. However, institutions can and should indicate preferences for certain types of research and researchers in their mission statements, should consider these in appraisal and selection processes, and should take them into account when setting priorities for outreach activities and researcher services priorities. An academic archives may well wish to encourage use by its faculty and students; a county historical society may decide that its priorities are in the area of use by local schools and community colleges. This does not mean that there is a discriminatory or exclusionary approach; it does mean that priorities have been set and resources allocated accordingly.

USER ORIENTED	CUSTODIAL ORIENTED
Researcher services is the common term.	*Reference* is the common term.
Use is the main rationale for archival work.	Use is one of several rationales.
Information on users is essential for program planning.	Information on users is interesting but of secondary importance for program planning.
Systematic gathering and analysis of user information.	Researchers are merely counted.
Marketing is a priority.	Marketing is secondary.
Promoting use, researcher services are regarded as program priorities.	Promoting use, researcher services are secondary to appraisal and other functions.
Subject indexing fosters retrieval.	Reliance on provenance as a means of retrieval.
Finding aids and services are geared to users' needs	Reference is mainly education users to appreciate records, contexts, how the repository works.

In setting priorities for researcher services, it is helpful to distinguish among five types of users:

1. *Administrators and other employees of the institution.* This category obviously has special meaning for institutional archives and probably automatically rises to the top of the list of priorities. But it is also relevant in any historical records program where, for instance, employees may use records for exhibits, document packets, and publications that the program is developing.

2. *Issue or topical researchers.* These include people who are searching for information on legal, environmental, health, economic, social, or other topics. Their research is "historical" in the sense that they are looking through records of the past, but their purpose is "current" in the sense that they have some current issue or problem that they are trying to solve or need that they are trying to address. They have a "need to know" which, hopefully, can be met in full or in part by the material in the archives.

3. *Historians.* Historical researchers are of various types, with a variety of historical topics that require historical analysis, better understanding and illumination of the past, new interpretations, etc. Their objective is dealing with the past and contributing to historical understanding rather than addressing current issues. They may include local historians whose interest is strictly community history, students doing historical research projects, and advanced historical researchers who are teaching and publishing.

4. *Genealogists and family history researchers.* These two groups, taken together, make up the largest number of users of archives overall. Typically, they are tracing their ancestry, the ancestry of someone else, or trying to gather facts on family history, often along with research in other sources.

5. *Casual researchers.* For lack of a better term, the final category is called "casual" to denote people who are studying historical records to satisfy their curiosity, because they are interested in a particular topic or collection, or simply because they enjoy going through historical records. Frequently, they are unsystematic, perusing individual items that have particular interest and skipping over the rest, not taking notes, but gaining satisfaction and edification as they work.

It is also useful to distinguish researchers by the *direct* and *indirect* uses of their research. Direct use refers to the quantity and quality of the information gleaned from the records. It is relatively easy to measure; it is part of the exit interview and the form that the researcher should be asked to fill out before leaving. Indirect use refers to the benefit that people may derive from the research. This refers to readers of books and viewers of TV shows and movies that are based in part on archival research; people affected by legal proceedings that draw on archival research; people whose health is affected by the study of diseases; and students and others whose education or understanding is advanced by studies based in part on archives. Indirect use is difficult to measure. For one thing, the results of research in archives are often blended in with the results of research in other materials; sometimes, it's difficult to discern which fact came from what source. The ramifications may be broad, cumulative, and distanced in both time and place from where the research took place and therefore difficult to trace.

WORKING WITH RESEARCHERS

Working with researchers who enter the facility's research room requires all of the skills noted above. The approach with any given researcher depends on at least five factors:

1. The researcher's interests, needs, state of preparation, and time constraints, as far as the archivist can determine these things through an initial interview.
2. The program's research priorities as spelled out in the mission statement or elsewhere.
3. The amount of resources available—as a practical matter, this is likely to mean how much time the researcher services expert has available to apply to this particular researcher. This, in turn, depends in part on how many other researchers must be served, other work that needs to be carried out, etc.
4. The records themselves, including their quantity, state of arrangement, number of series, age, variation in format, etc.
5. The state of the finding aids, including how detailed, whether there are indexes, whether all of the records are covered, etc.

Working with researchers usually consists of several steps:

- *Initial orientation.* The initial orientation may include an audiovisual production, asking the researcher to read written materials, an oral introduction, or some combination of the three. The orientation is designed to introduce the repository, including its administrative setting, mission and programs, collection policies, collection strengths, researcher service priorities, researcher services, and policies and restrictions.

- *Registration.* In this step, the researcher is asked to provide certain identifying information and to read, agree to, and sign the rules for the research room. (See Figure 7.1 for an example.)
- *Researcher interview.* Sometimes considered the most important part of researcher services, the interview consists of a structured dialog between the researcher and the archivist. The researcher attempts to convey the purpose and scope of the research, the topics covered, research already carried out, material that is needed (if known), time constraints or deadlines, and other requirements. The archivist listens carefully, responds to questions, offers suggestions, and explains the finding aids/access system. The process is interrogatory, analytical, and responsive at the same time.

  > In conducting a reference interview, the archivist is beginning the task of assessing the individual researcher's needs and matching them to the holdings and services offered by the archives. There is an important inferential process at work in the interview: the archivist is matching [his or her] knowledge of the records and the agencies which created them with the researcher's questions which are usually expressed in terms of subject/person/place. The archivist's questioning, listening, and negotiating skills are used to assist the researcher in the quest for information from the archives' holdings. During the reference interview, the archivist has to respond to the researcher's questions about specific records or about the likelihood of finding material on [his or her] topic.[1]

- *Retrieving records.* The archivist, or an assistant, retrieves records as needed and requested by the researcher, within the limits set by program policy for the amount of material (e.g., number of cartons) that a researcher may have at her table at one time, etc. The objective here is to be responsive to needs, keeping in mind that the amount of time needed to get through material varies greatly with the researcher, the topic, and the material.
- *Maintaining surveillance and security.* The archivist or someone else on the staff should double as the security officer, keeping an eye on researchers to ensure that search room policies are met, records are safeguarded and not damaged, and that theft is deterred through careful, obvious vigilance. (See box.)
- *Offering assistance during the research process.* From time to time, the archivist should engage the researcher in a brief conversation to continue helpful support. The inquiries should not be so frequent as to constitute annoying interruptions for the researcher and also absorb too much of the archivist's time. But neither should they be so infrequent that problems and opportunities are left unaddressed. Typical topics for discussion during the research process include: questions about the finding aids, the

I apply to use the Archives.

Name _____   Date: _____

Permanent Address (Street, City, State, Zip)   Permanent phone no.

_____   _____

Local Address (Street, City, State, Zip)   Local phone no.

_____   _____

Researcher Affiliation and Status (Choose one)

1. Parent Institution	2. University/College	3. General	4. Personal
a. Department	a. Name	a. Employer	a. Geneology

b. Tile	b. Position	b. Title	b. Other
	_____ Faculty		
	_____ Staff		
	_____ Graduate Student		
	_____ Undergraduate		
	c. Department		

Statement of Research Topic

Intended Use of Research (Check all that apply)

_____ Book	_____ Article	_____ Dissertation	_____ Thesis
_____ Term paper	_____ Speech	_____ Geneology	_____ Film
_____ Radio report	_____ TV report	_____ Government research	_____ Exhibit
_____ Videotape	_____ Personal interest	_____ Professional research	_____ Slide-tape

Other _____

Use of Information about You

May we tell others of the subject of your research? ___ yes ___ no

May we tell others which materials you used? ___ yes ___ no

May we contact you by mail or phone as part of future user studies? ___ yes ___ no

How did you learn about this repository? (Check most important)

_____ References or citations in published books   _____ Television, radio, newspaper

_____ Published guides to archives, bibliographies   _____ Brochure

_____ Guide to this repository _____NUCMC   _____ Presentation by archives staff

_____ Databases: _____ RLIN _____ OCLC _____ Local   _____ Visit to museum exhibition

_____ Teacher, professor, or colleague   _____ General knowledge, assumptions

_____ Archivist or librarian elsewhere

_____ Information from historical, professional, or geneological organizations

Other _____

Before your first visit on this project, did you write or telephone to get information about holdings or services?

___ yes ___ no ___ don't know

I have read the Rules for Use of Materials and agree to abide by them.

Signed _____

Identification _____   Archivist _____

Figure 7.1. Sample Researcher Registration Form. This sample form indicates the type of information that it is helpful to collect before a researcher begins his or her work. From Mary Jo Pugh, Providing Reference Services for Archives and Manuscripts *(Chicago: Society of American Archivists, 1992), 72.*

arrangement of the historical records, gaps in the records, etc.; inquiries about whether the research suggests additional lines of analysis into other records that the repository might hold; determination about whether there are additional ways that the archival staff can be helpful.

- *Exit interview and form.* At the end of the research process, it is helpful to discuss an exit interview to determine the degree to which the researcher's expectations and needs were met and how services might be refined or improved. The researcher and/or the archivist should also fill out a form that indicates what records were used and how much important information was gleaned from them.

Experienced archivists have an almost instinctive ability to assist researchers in a way that is helpful and supportive, but not intrusive or condescending. One of the best reference archivists, Mary Jo Pugh, offered this insight:[2]

The reference process in archives is often inferential, based on what is known about the records, their creators, and the circumstances of their creation. This process sometimes gives archivists an "illusion of omniscience" to users unfamiliar with archival research. For instance, a user inquired whether a noted Victorian author had ever visited Ann Arbor, Michigan. The archivist suspected that the author would have written to University of Michigan President James B. Angell and knew that Angell's correspondence was indexed by name. With this information, it was relatively simple to find a letter from the author discussing the date of his visit. Knowledge of the date gave access to local newspapers, university publications, and diaries for description of the visit.

By explaining their reasoning to users, archivists can help researchers build their own research skills. It is important to help users understand records creation, finding aids, and the process leading to a particular search strategy. Archivists strive to make users as independent as possible by helping them to think archivally—that is, functionally and hierarchically. As teachers, archivists help users to think, "Who would have been likely to record the information I am seeking, how would it have been recorded and filed, and where are the records now?"

Appendix 9 presents study questions that may be helpful in developing researcher services and access policies.

SECURITY IN THE RESEARCH ROOM: VISIBILITY, DETERRENCE

Damage and theft of historical records are all too common occurrences in programs across the nation. Policies and procedures are needed to discourage inappropriate practices, warn researchers against carelessness and inappropriate behavior, and actively deter the threat of outright theft. Two types of potential problem researchers warrant particular vigilance: the researcher who is overly demanding, impatient with the rules, and may try to bully the archivist; and the researcher who becomes overly friendly and intends to lull the archivist into a false sense of camaraderie and into letting his or her guard down. What is

RULES FOR THE RESEARCH ROOM

Every program needs carefully formulated rules to govern the use of materials in the research room. This approach sets expectations for both researchers and program personnel and is a hallmark of a well administered program. The following illustrates the areas that should be covered for a hypothetical historical society's program; the exact policies and wording will vary from program to program.

CHESAPEAKE COUNTY HISTORICAL SOCIETY
DEPARTMENT OF HISTORICAL RECORDS
RULES FOR THE RESEARCH ROOM

Researchers are asked to read and sign the following before their research work begins. This statement of rules and restrictions is meant to inform researchers about the Society's policies for serving them while at the same time protecting and preserving the historical heritage that is represented in its holdings.

1. The Search Room is open from 10:00 A.M. to 5:00 P.M. Monday, Wednesday, and Friday and 10:00 A.M. to 8:00 P.M. Tuesday and Thursday, except state holidays.
2. Researchers must provide name, address, institution if any, and phone number and provide a government-issued photo ID (e.g., a driver's license).
3. Researchers are requested, but not required, to fill out a form and provide additional information to the researcher services specialist about the nature of their research, records used, and the information from the records. This helps the Society analyze use of its holdings and improve its services to researchers.
4. Researchers are required to leave hats, coats, briefcases, and other containers in the lockers outside the search room.
5. Researchers are not allowed in the historical records stacks; program personnel will retrieve materials as needed.
6. To obtain material, researchers must fill out a request form provided by program personnel. No more than three cartons of material will be made available at any one time. Materials are retrieved from the stacks every hour, approximately on the hour; the last retrieval is one hour before closing.
7. Researchers must use care in handling historical records, turn pages gently, take care not to rip materials, and keep all materials in order.
8. No materials may be taken from the research room for any reason.

Continued.

9. Where appropriate, copies of records, e.g., photocopies or microfilm, will be made available in lieu of the originals.
10. Computers, typewriters, tape recorders, and other approved copying machines may be used for taking notes and making copies, with the approval of search room staff and in areas designated by them.
11. Historical Society personnel will make copies of records upon request for the posted fees. Copying is governed by the U.S. Copyright Law (Title 17, U.S. Code).

needed is a sense of visibility and deterrence that is consistent but does not go so far as to be stifling and make researchers feel uncomfortable. Some suggestions include:

• Develop clear policies in the area of security, including steps to be taken in the event that theft is suspected or observed. Ensure that these provisions are reviewed and approved by counsel. Include them in the program's administrative manual and in materials that are given to researchers (and/or posted on the program's Web site). Make sure everyone knows the policies.
• Include training in security for all staff, particularly those who have charge of surveillance and oversight in the search room. This needs to cover such things as the program's policies regarding theft, how to maintain careful surveillance without being intrusive, and what to do in the case of a suspected theft.
• Duplicate selected materials, particularly those considered especially susceptible to theft because of certain features such as signatures, and make the duplicates (e.g., photocopies, microfilm) available instead of the originals.
• Require researchers to provide identification, including a recognizable photo ID such as a driver's license.
• Require that researchers leave coats, briefcases, other enclosed containers and extra items outside of the search room. Many programs provide lockers for these materials as a means of both encouraging compliance and making things easy for the researcher.
• Do not allow pens near the records.
• Don't let researchers into the stack areas where records are stored.
• Limit the quantity of materials that a researcher may have at his or her desk at a given time.

- Make provision for easy, inexpensive copying either by the researcher (under the watchful eye of a staff member), by the program, or both.
- Maintain surveillance in the search room at all times. If staffing levels permit, this should mean a person in the room at all times whose sole job it is to watch researchers. If not, the oversight may be combined with other responsibilities such as processing or answering written or Internet inquiries. Security cameras help, but they are not a substitute for human eyes.
- Have an action plan for what to do in the event of a disruptive researcher or suspicion or detection of theft.

The box in this chapter on research room rules and appendix 10 have additional guidance on security in the search room.

ACCESS AND COPYING

Should records be open to everyone, and should copying be unrestricted? In answering these questions, historical records custodians must balance among at least three conflicting sets of expectations: records creators and donors, who may want to impose restrictions; researchers, who may want unrestricted access; and the law, which tries to mediate among conflicting interests and set conditions for access. In general, historical records programs seek to make as much information as broadly available as possible as a means of promoting scholarship and research. Openness and the archival mission seem compatible and mutually reinforcing. On the other hand, some records need to be restricted or closed (at least for a time), for several possible reasons. In the case of government records (not the primary topic of this book), Freedom of Information and privacy laws may prescribe closures or restrictions to prevent an unwarranted invasion of personal privacy, to safeguard police investigatory methods, to protect trade secrets included in required reports, or for other reasons. In the case of nongovernment records, considerations of privacy and confidentiality may apply. Privacy refers to the right of people to be left alone and to keep information about themselves out of the hands of others; confidentiality refers to the inherent characteristic of private communications (such as letters) to remain known only to sender and receiver. Both privacy and confidentiality may be issues, for instance, in a large collection that includes thousands of letters written among various individuals. They were written for a particular purpose, with no expectation of their being laid open for researchers later; in fact, that is one of their strengths as archival records. In such cases, the records may need to be closed for a number of years, or their use restricted, as a condition of the deed of gift. Usually, such restrictions should be kept to a minimum; but they may be necessary in order to get the person to turn over the records. It's a question of balance and judgment, as is the case in so much archival work. Archivists should recognize several responsibilities regarding access:[3]

- Understand laws and regulations relating to privacy, confidentiality, freedom of information, etc.
- Advise creators and donors about access issues.
- Negotiate clear, responsible agreements with donors and originating agencies.
- Be aware of where sensitive information is likely to be found in records that are acquired.
- Identify information that cannot be made accessible immediately.
- Develop appropriate restrictions for sensitive records and administer them consistently.
- Inform users about restricted materials.
- Strive to open as many materials as possible.
- Promote equality of access whenever possible.
- If necessary, advocate changes in law, regulations, or institutional policies.

The issue of copyright also requires balance and good judgment. The federal Copyright Law, Title 17 of the U.S. Code, Sections 102, 106, 107, and 108, substantially revised in 1976, provides that the creator of a work that embodies a unique expression—a sweeping concept that would include most historical records—has the right to benefit from the work and to control reproduction. The copyright holder owns the right to make and distribute copies. Copyright continues in effect until a certain time, currently the life of the author plus seventy years; the exact time period depends on whether the work was created before or after the effective date of the 1976 law, i.e., January 1, 1978. The situation is even more complicated when it is unknown whether the author has died or not. On the other side of the coin, another provision of the law, called "Fair Use," permits quoting or making copies for criticism, comment, teaching, or scholarship; the extent of the right to reproduce depends on context and purpose. Another section, 108, permits archives to make copies for preservation and for private use of their researchers, provided that the holdings of the repository are open to the public, the copies are not made for commercial purposes, and notice is provided that the material may be protected by copyright.[4] Section 108 has been interpreted broadly by archivists to justify copying by researchers, but several court cases and opinions by the Library of Congress Copyright Office have complicated the picture by seeming to interpret copyright broadly, narrowing the right to copy.[5] The Copyright Law thus attempts to balance the creator's right to control his or her own intellectual property against the social benefit of research, copying, and study of primary materials. The best advice is: study the Copyright Law, follow copyright developments, seek legal counsel when in doubt, and apply good sense and good judgment in balancing the conflicting interests of donors, users, and the law.

RESEARCHER SERVICES MOVE TO THE WEB

In the past, most interaction with researchers has been in person, over the phone, or by letter or fax. The Internet and the World Wide Web are dramatically changing the nature of archival work, particularly researcher services. Just about every major issue, including the one of access and copying noted in the section above, becomes more complex when services leap from the search room onto the Web. Some programs report that just putting up a Web site has a transformational effect—the number of inquiries increases dramatically, the mix of researcher traffic gets more complex and undifferentiated, and there is a pattern of rising expectations: the more that's available electronically, the more people seem to expect and want. Users of the Web generally have expectations for quick, easy, direct access not just to finding aids but to the information itself—in the case of archives, that means the archival records themselves. That expectation, in turn, puts pressure on the archives to make not only its finding aids and access tools available, but also to put up electronic records and to undertake digital conversion of paper records, a relatively expensive and technically demanding proposition. Even if the historical records program decides on the modest and sensible course of making only selected finding aids and a few records available via a Web site, there are immediate implications and changes in the archivist-researcher relationship:

- What has been called the "death of distance" comes into play—access can be had from anywhere a person can get to the WWW via a computer and online access.
- The program never closes; the opening and closing hours of the search room are irrelevant. Information and services are accessible any time.
- There is likely to be an upswing in user access, and the users are anonymous unless the archival program requires identifying information. Many programs have found that going onto the Net also increases their walk-in traffic because more people become aware of their holdings.

- The new users bring new expectations, as noted above, for instant access to relevant materials.
- The researcher archivist's traditional roles of gatekeeper, mediator, negotiator, and advisor, need to be revised.
- It is impossible to know which finding aids or records were used, or by whom.
- The use of the material, and the results of the research, are not likely to be known.

How does a program determine whether it should develop a Web site and go into business over the Web? The best advice is: *analyze, plan, test, and ease into this new business*. Of course, this is one of many areas where it is essential for the historical records program to integrate its work with that of the historical agency overall. The program's Web-based services need to be part of the parent agency's Web-based services. There are no guidelines yet for archival program services on the Web, so making use of the network of archival colleagues discussed in chapter 3 is a sound approach. Actually using some well-developed Web sites and evaluating their features is another good approach (see box). Several steps are recommended in developing services:[6]

- Assemble a program-wide team to plan the services. This is not just a job for technical experts or the parent institution's Web master; it requires multiple areas of expertise and perspectives to assure success.
- Carefully define purposes, goals, and audiences.
- Define criteria for selecting and identifying materials.
- Decide how to organize the work of providing services.
- Determine how to measure and report on use.
- Identify approaches to measuring how well the service meets customer needs.
- Assess resource implications and determine how to allocate resources to what will probably be an area that grows rapidly and unpredictably.
- Monitor and report periodically.

Successful historical records program Web sites have several critical characteristics:

- The site is well managed and monitored with minimal "down" time.
- The home page is clear and logical with menu elements organized the same way that users expect the information to be organized.

MODEL ARCHIVAL WEB SITES

Here is an informal list of archival program Web sites. They have been selected to illustrate clarity, organization, comprehensiveness, ease of use, and variety. While they are all good models, none embodies all the traits noted in the text for model Web sites.

- Duke University Archives. www.duke.edu/web/Archives
- Hartwick College Archives (Oneonta, NY). www.hartwick.edu/library/ archives
- Minnesota Historical Society Collections (St. Paul). www.mnhs.org/ library/collections
- Newberry Library (Chicago). www.newberry.org
- New York Public Library Archives and Manuscripts. www.nypl.org/ research/chss/rbk/mss.html
- New York State Archives and Records Administration. www.sara.nysed.gov
- North Carolina Collection, University of North Carolina, Chapel Hill. www.lib.unc.edu/ncc
- Rockefeller Archive Center (Pocantico Hills, NY). www.rockefeller.edu/ archive.ctr
- University of Wisconsin at Madison Archives. www.library.wisc.edu/ libraries/Archives

- Graphics are used to foster and facilitate use rather than for decoration.
- Key information is provided, including identifying title, source, date of production and update, mailing address, and phone number, etc., in order to establish authenticity and reliability.
- Site uses clear language that is likely to be familiar to users; it avoids jargon and technical terms unless they are necessary (and are explained).
- The material is current, outdated material is removed, and the date of the most recent update is shown.
- If e-mail inquiries are an option, there is provision for responding quickly and accurately to them.
- Researchers can determine quickly whether the information they seek is available and can access it easily.

Finally, here is a list of elements found on responsive, user-oriented archival sites. A site does not need all of these to be successful. In fact, it may be advisable to start with the basics and build up from there, testing interest and needs in the process:

- Logo, photo of building, or some other distinguishing illustration
- Technical information on viewing the site, e.g., web browser, need for telnet capacity
- Program name, address, phone, and fax numbers
- Map, directions to the facility
- Mission, goals, explanation of services
- News items: information on new accessions, exhibits, publications, etc.
- Order form for publications and/or posting of publications online
- Description of reference services—hours, retrieval policies, security, advice on calling before making a visit, etc.
- FAQ's (Frequently Asked Questions) and answers, derived through analysis of questions asked repeatedly through the site
- Short description of records related to particular subjects
- Summary guide
- More detailed finding aids, e.g., inventories
- Limited subject/topical search capacity
- Direct access to a limited number of digital records
- Provision for asking reference questions via e-mail
- Hyperlinks to other, related sites
- "Virtual exhibits"—digital versions of selected documents arranged as an exhibit
- Invitation to submit suggestions for improving the site and related services

MEASURING AND REPORTING IN RESEARCHER SERVICES

Historical records experts have made substantial strides in recent years in developing meaningful measures of researcher traffic, its significance, and its impact on the program as a whole. Most of the formal user studies have been carried out at large institutions such as the National Archives and Records Administration and, while insightful, have limited applicability to smaller operations.[7] The easiest approach is to simply count the number of researchers and to break them into a few simple categories, e.g., academic and nonacademic. That provides only limited enlightenment; something more extensive and revealing is needed. The measures discussed below are most applicable to onsite researchers; they are moderately applicable to researchers who are in contact by phone and letter; and much less so to the new Web customers, where new approaches are needed. The information should be gathered by a combination of questionnaire and the entrance and exit interviews carried out by the researcher services archivist. The approach needs to be consistent with whatever information gathering is used for the rest of the historical agency's programs, e.g., counting and measuring the degree of satisfaction of visitors to historical exhibits. Information and measures are needed in six areas:[8]

1. *Categories of users.* Who uses the records? Researchers should be grouped into categories that are developed by the repository, based on its mission, its holdings, and researcher traffic. For a local historical society, for instance, the categories might be: staff of the parent institution, local historians, genealogists, high school students, college students, professors of history, and people doing research on particular issues.

2. *Type of interaction.* How do researcher and archivist interact and communicate? Currently, the types of interaction include phone, fax/letter, in-person visits, and communication over the Internet via e-mail.

3. *Purposes of the research.* What are the various purposes, intents, and goals of research? This is similar to, but different from, the *types of researchers* category outlined under number 1 above. It is based on the assumption that researchers will willingly disclose their research purposes; if they don't, then this area can't be measured. These need to be established categories, based on analysis of researcher traffic. Purposes might include: legal research for a matter at law; historical research for publication; historical research for a film, TV show, or other nonpublication presentation; background material for a news media presentation; retrospective research to help develop new policies; genealogy; family history; and casual research for personal edification.

4. *Subjects of research.* What are the particular subjects or topics being researched? This, too, is based on the assumption that researchers do not mind disclosing what they are working on. This information, elicited initially through the questionnaire but refined and made precise through the reference interview, is likely to differ with each researcher.

5. *Records used.* Which records did the researcher use? This can be measured by keeping track of the records brought to the researcher, noted by collection, series, and carton.

6. *Intensity of use.* How long were the records used in relation to their volume and how much information was gleaned from them? This is in part a time measure—how long the researcher spent on various collections, series, and cartons—but it is mainly a subjective measure, based on the exit interview with the archivist. It might be measured by establishing numer-

ical scales (e.g., 1—Insignificant or trivial, through 5—Excellent, exceptionally helpful) and also asking for narrative responses to such questions as: How helpful were the records in providing entirely new information that you did not have before? In supplementing and extending what you already knew? In leading to new insights, perceptions, conclusions? In suggesting new lines of analysis and additional source material that warrants pursuing?

Historical records managers should urge researchers to share with the program copies of any eventual publications or other products based on their research. The information gathered through the process described in this section should be used for three types of reports. One, analysis and reporting that provides feedback to the program itself on how research use of the materials relates to appraisal and other work. Two, reports to the administrative directors of the parent agency to show the impact of the historical records program's work, relate it to the parent agency's mission, and justify the budget and buttress resource appeals. Three, public reports (for instance, via a program newsletter or in a special section on the Web site) that illustrate the variety of research being carried out as a way of reaching potential donors of additional records, getting the attention of additional potential researchers, and possibly enlightening potential outside funding sources about the value of investing in the program.

BEYOND RESEARCHERS: REACHING OUT TO OTHER USERS

People who actively carry out research in historical records constitute the largest and most important category of users but not the only one. Programs need to devote at least some energy and resources to outreach and marketing beyond the researcher community. The work involves a blend of public relations, advocacy, and public programming; it is similar to the publicity work that historical societies and museums are used to carrying out for their nonarchival collections. Outreach can take many forms.[9] Promotional and descriptive brochures introduce the program's services and holdings. A newsletter provides updates to potential donors, users, and others on program developments and particularly interesting records. Some programs have made promotional videos to highlight the human dimension of their program through featuring researchers as well as archivists at work. Exhibits are an excellent way of getting historical records (preferably, facsimiles) out into public spaces and of demonstrating how history can be conveyed through those records. An increasing number of programs are working with the schools through production of document packets that are tied to the curriculum and supplement textbook presentations. The educational use of historical records introduces young people to both archives and history, gives them experience in analyzing primary sources and reconstructing history, and develops writing and other presentation skills. It is a natural activity for a historical records program that is part of a historical agency that stresses education.[10] All of these promotional and outreach initiatives may be supplemented by, or actually moved to, program Web sites. For instance, a Web site may include a "News" section and documents and teaching plans that may be downloaded for classroom use.

SERVICES TO USERS: CHECKLIST

1. Does the program's planning document include a discussion of services to users, particularly researchers?
2. Does the program have a *user* orientation and philosophy that gives highest priority to encouraging, fostering, and facilitating the use of its holdings by researchers and others?
3. Has the program established priorities for categories of researchers and types of research?
4. Do program personnel effectively and consistently serve researchers, including serving an informational and mediation role through the researcher interview and assistance as the research is carried out?
5. Does the program have procedures for tracking and reporting on research use?
6. Are security provisions in place to ensure that the records in the program's custody are protected and secure?
7. Are there access and copying policies that take into account legal requirements, donors' restrictions, and researchers' needs?
8. Does the program have a Web site and if so is it being developed and managed according to carefully developed plans and with appropriate oversight and review?
9. Does the program use brochures, newsletters, videos, exhibits, and document packets to get the message out, including use of its Web site to supplement traditional formats?

8

PRESERVATION OF
HISTORICAL RECORDS

INTRODUCTION: PRINCIPLES OF PRESERVATION

"How should I preserve historical records?" is probably the question most often asked by historical agency personnel who have responsibility for documentary material. The question is often prompted by two concerns. One, records are "recorded" on an impermanent medium that will eventually deteriorate. The deterioration process is dramatically visible if a newspaper is left in the sun for just a few days; it turns yellow, then brown, a sign of a rapid aging process. Two, in most collections there are a few old and particularly tattered materials that have attracted attention, engendered concern, and seem to cry out for some sort of remedial, restorative effort. What is to be done? In formulating an answer, the first insight is simply that *there is no such thing as a permanent record*. Nothing lasts forever, not even the most important historical record. Even the nation's "Charters of Freedom"—the Declaration of Independence, the Constitution, and the Bill of Rights—have faded over time despite the best storage conditions that could be created for them. Even the most recent, sophisticated information technology cannot help very much; as noted in chapter 9, information that is "recorded" in electronic form may degrade, become unreadable, or simply vanish, even faster than records on paper.

The best that programs can do is to prolong the life of materials through the use of various *preservation* techniques. The Society of American Archivists defines preservation broadly:

> The totality of processes and operations involved in the stabilization and protection of documents against damage or deterioration and in the treatment of damaged or deteriorated documents. Preservation may also include the transfer of information to another medium such as microfilm.[1]

This book takes an even broader, and admittedly less focused, view: preservation includes everything that programs do to prolong historical records' usable life span. Preservation should not be confused with *conservation*, a subpart of preservation that deals with the physical or chemical treatment of documents.

Settling on broad *principles* is an important first step toward planning and action. Principles should include:

1. *Preservation is a broad, pervasive undertaking.* Preservation should be broadly conceived and should include, or at least be carried out with reference to, other program activities that foster longevity. It should shy away from the notion that preservation is mainly exacting work on a few old, choice documents.

2. *Setting priorities is essential.* Preservation, like other historical records work, requires analysis and planning. This, in turn, implies the necessity of setting and keeping to priorities. The program probably cannot afford optimal preservation provisions for everything. That needs to be considered along with the fact that not all records warrant the same level of preservation effort.

3. *Fundamental preservation and protection are obligations.* Programs have a certain bottom-line responsibility for the basic preservation of the materials they seek, accept, and make available for use. This responsibility includes secure storage in appropriate containers in a clean, temperature and humidity controlled environment where the records are safe from theft and, to the degree possible, natural or man-made disasters. If the program cannot provide a minimum preservation environment, it should reconsider whether it should even be in the historical records collecting business.

4. *First things first.* There needs to be a flavor of evenhandedness and balance in preservation work. In general, broad-scale and general preserva-

tion treatment of all the repository's materials (the sort of basic custodial responsibility outlined in number 3 above) should be in place or in process before more exacting, detailed work is carried out on particular collections.

5. *Continuum of preservation expertise.* There is an unsettled debate in the archival and preservation communities about how much preservation and conservation work can be carried out by archivists and records curators versus what must be left to trained professional conservators. In general, particularly for smaller historical records programs, the best advice is for the people in charge of the records to carry out preservation work as far as they are able; leave the exacting technical work, such as hands-on restoration and archival microfilming, to the experts.

6. *Different approaches for different formats.* Special formats such as photographs, microfilm, and computer disks require approaches and storage conditions that differ (sometimes slightly, sometimes greatly, depending on the format) from what is needed for paper.

The remainder of this chapter outlines ten approaches to preservation work; the appendices and several of the readings in the bibliography provide elaboration on the basic advice provided here.

UNDERSTAND THE THREE
FUNDAMENTAL FACTORS IN PRESERVATION

Preservation turns on the interplay of three factors. The first is *chemistry*, meaning the physical composition and make-up of the media used for records and for recording information about them. The most common material, paper, is a marvelous medium in many ways: it is relatively inexpensive to manufacture, easy to use, portable, and relatively durable. But paper will not last; it has within it the chemical seeds of its own destruction. Before the early nineteenth century, most paper was made by hand from cotton or linen rags; after the middle of the century, due to the increasing demand for paper, manufacturers switched to cheaper and more plentiful wood pulp, and the manufacturing process became mechanized. The result was paper that had a high degree of acidity, which causes paper to lose strength and become discolored and brittle. Most of the paper used for records during the past century and a half is recorded on this medium; therefore, most of the historical records in repositories today are in danger of relatively rapid decomposition and eventual loss. The second factor is *surroundings*. High temperatures accelerate the drying out and increasing brittleness of paper; high humidity may help break down its fibers and encourage mold and mildew growth. Pollution in the air can also accelerate damage. Poor storage conditions may expose records to the elements or to vermin and rodents, which can damage or destroy the records. The third factor is *people*. People, of course, create records and people can (and often do) destroy even those with enduring value, making them, in a sense, the ultimate preservation threat. People also determine the type of media used for records. In recent years, there has been a movement away from high-acid paper and toward longer-life, low-acid or "permalife" paper at least for some (still a small minority) of records. People affect the aging process through how they store and handle records.

DEVELOP AND FOLLOW A PRESERVATION PLAN

Preservation work, by definition and nature, tends to be open-ended and very demanding of resources unless management imposes limits and priorities. Documents cannot be saved forever but the work of saving as many as possible for as long as possible can absorb all the resources a program can reasonably be expected to commit to it, and more. For this reason, a plan is needed. The planning process involves evaluation of two areas, then formulation of the plan. The first area is to make a survey of the preservation-related physical aspects of the program's building and its records storage area. The survey should cover at least:

- Overall conditions of the building, including structural integrity and soundness, weight-bearing capacity, condition of the roof, and the heating and cooling system
- Environmental conditions where records are stored, particularly temperature, humidity, and cleanliness
- Physical makeup of the storage area, particularly size of rooms, storage shelving, and the use of containers
- Security, particularly the degree of protection against unauthorized entry, alarm systems, and the presence of smoke or fire detectors and fire suppression systems
- The quality of the staff's preservation-mindedness (see item number 3, below).

The second stock-taking area involves a survey of the existing collections. The objective is to determine rough quantities of records in various formats, to assess physical conditions, and to provide data for gauging preservation needs.

Figure 8.1 presents a model preservation survey checklist. The level of detail desired may make the task daunting; it is better to gather less data for the whole collection in the program than to go after too much information and wind up surveying only part of the holdings. "Although the idea of undertaking a collection survey may seem overwhelming, especially with extensive holdings and a

---

Preservation Survey

Collection/Record Group _____
Accession No. _____ Value _____
Estimated Use _____
Inclusive Dates _____ Dominant Dates _____
Size: Linear Feet _____ Items _____ Other Measure _____
Collection Copied _____ Format _____ Date _____
Other Form(s) of Publication _____
Survey Unit _____ Location _____
Name of Surveyor _____ Date of Survey _____

Type and Evaluation of Housings

 Primary Housings (physical and chemical condition, overfilled, underfilled):
 • archives box
 • records center box
 • drawer
 • other
 • none

 Secondary and Tertiary Housings (physical and chemical condition, fit):
 • folders
 • envelopes
 • sleeves
 • other
 • none

Types of Records: (specify quantity of records in each category)

	NONE	FEW	1/4	1/2	3/4	3/4-ALL
• loose paper						
• bound volumes						
• graphic materials						
• photographs						
• index cards						
• sound recordings						
• other						

Condition of Records (specify quantity of records in each category)

	NONE	FEW	1/4	1/2	3/4	3/4-ALL
• folded/rolled						
• brittle						
• tears						
• pressure-sensitive tape						
• acidic ink						
• mold						
• water damage						
• surface dirt						
• previous treatment/unstable						
• boards/case loose						
• boards/case detached						

Duplication Needs (specify quantity of records in each category)

	NONE	FEW	1/4	1/2	3/4	3/4-ALL
• impermanent media						
• faint text or image						
• colored media						
• fasteners						
• special formats						
• historical features						

General Observations:

Recommendations:
 (based on combined factors of value, use, and condition)
 Rehousing:
 Duplication:
 Treatment:
Estimated Time:
Priority: ____ high   ____ medium   ____ low   ____ none

Figure 8.1. Preservation Survey. A preservation survey form similar to this one can be developed to gather information needed to assess needs and prepare plans. From Mary Lynn Ritzenthaller, Preserving Archives and Manuscripts *(Chicago: Society of American Archivists, 1993), 11.*

small staff, it is possible to integrate data-gathering with ongoing archival functions," says the Society of American Archivists' manual. "For example, survey forms should be filled out whenever problems are noted during accessioning or processing activities, or before reshelving collections that have been used by researchers."[2] This advice is particularly sound because it indicates that analysis and planning are *ongoing* processes and that preservation needs ought to be considered at the time records are appraised and decisions are made about accessioning them.

Once the data is available, the planning needs to move ahead. There is no prescribed format or content, but the finished plan should address at least the following:

- *The preservation program's mission and vision* and how they relate to the overall mission and vision of the historical records program as a whole. Mission should indicate what the preservation work aspires to accomplish; vision should present the desired (and anticipated) state of affairs toward the end of the life of the plan.

- *The preservation program's philosophy*—a set of principles on how preservation work should proceed. The six principles outlined in the initial section of this chapter represent approximately the tenor and scope of what is needed here. The entire plan should represent a consensus of staff and management but it is essential that this particular section reflect that agreement. It can be likened to the rudder on a ship that guides the program through uncharted seas, unanticipated problems, occasional appearances of Murphy's Law, and the tendency in this business of work to exceed resources, no matter how carefully plans are drawn and budgets developed.

- *Responsibilities.* It should spell out the role of trustees and program leaders in supporting preservation; the duties of the preservation officer, if there is one; the obligations of staff who handle records and deal with researchers; and the constraints that researchers need to understand as they use the records. The statement of researchers' responsibilities translates to search room rules and the orientation interview; it is the intersection of preservation and researcher services.

- *Goals, objectives, and activities.* Like any viable plan, the preservation plan needs to include specifics, without at the same time being so specific that the program is straight-jacketed. The plan needs to cover: (A) steps that will be taken to improve the facility and the storage environment of the records; (B) training and development activities for staff in the area of preservation; (C) improvements in storing and housing of historical records; (D) reproduction, e.g., through archival microfilming; and (E) specific conservation and restoration work.

• *Issues that need discussion, analysis, or development of strategies.* This part of the plan represents problems to be solved rather than actions to be taken. It might include such questions as: How can the program integrate preservation into the program as a whole? How can it provide training in a timely, cost-efficient fashion? What role should consultants play in providing advice on how to handle particularly difficult preservation challenges?

• *Budget.* The plan needs to include an estimate of needed resources, particularly for relatively high-ticket items such as engaging consultants, hiring new staff, microfilming, or sending materials out for conservation work.

PUT SOMEONE IN CHARGE

Even small- to modest-sized programs have found it helpful to designate someone on the staff as the *preservation officer.* Doing so signals the underlying importance of preservation to the program, identifies a lead person for planning and coordination, and increases the likelihood that the work will get done. The preservation officer should have expertise and interest in preservation, as well as time enough to actually give attention to preservation work along with whatever other duties are assigned. However, the person does not have to be an expert in all phases and aspects of preservation and conservation work; for some areas, it is important only to have enough knowledge to understand that there is a problem and enough experience to know where to look for help. Nor should the person be charged with *all* the preservation responsibility; preservation-mindedness needs to permeate the program, with the preservation officer providing leadership, coordination, and advocacy. The preservation officer's list of responsibilities might include:

• Developing professional training and consciousness-raising initiatives for the rest of the staff. This boils down to an educational function that aims to let everyone know what preservation is, drive home its importance, show how it relates to other aspects of the program, publicize development activities such as professional seminars and conferences, develop and maintain reading materials, discuss selected topics, and monitor best practices and new developments in the field.

• Carrying out the survey of physical storage conditions and the survey of collections.

- Developing the preservation plan.
- Administering the plan, including advising colleagues in the program on their preservation-related responsibilities, assisting them in performing those responsibilities, fostering coordination between units, directly carrying out certain work, and handling contracts for repair and restoration of selected documents by an outside conservation laboratory.
- Ordering and monitoring the use of preservation and conservation supplies.
- Monitoring environmental and security conditions and calling for changes and improvements when needed.
- Coordinating disaster preparedness/response efforts.

MAINTAIN A BENIGN ENVIRONMENT

Controlling the storage environment is probably the single most important and effective preservation weapon in the historical records program's arsenal. Historical records should be stored in secure, fire-resistant stack areas, with temperature and humidity controls, fire detection and suppression systems, and controlled access. An optimal environment is almost certain to contribute to the long life of documents; a harmful environment practically guarantees accelerated deterioration. The environment is made up of several factors, and their optimal calibration depends on the nature of the historical records being stored. As a practical matter, most historical records programs store materials in several formats, with paper being the most common, so the environment needs to reflect what is best for the majority of the holdings. High temperatures accelerate chemical reactions; low temperatures can lead to too high relative humidity. Therefore, experts recommend maintaining a temperature around 68°F, give or take a few degrees. What needs to be avoided is either extreme heat or extreme cold, or, perhaps worst of all, rapid fluctuations that literally lead to expansion and contraction of paper fibers with predictable results. An optimal relative humidity level is around 45 percent, give or take a few percentage points. Again, being fairly consistent, even if it is a few points above or below optimal, is far preferable to cyclical ups and downs. Air quality is another important consideration; it is obviously related to both temperature and humidity. An ideal system includes air conditioning; next best is a high quality, carefully monitored and maintained air circulation and filtration system. Some elements to include in an overall approach to ensuring good air quality are:[3]

- A dedicated system rather than one that is shared with other parts of the building, e.g., rest rooms, kitchens, lounges, and other areas containing operations that can introduce pollution into the system.

- Sealed windows and doors that close tightly and are outfitted with gaskets.
- Positive air pressure within the controlled area, to prevent the introduction of contaminated air
- Even circulation of a constant volume of air throughout the stack area
- Filters in the air handling system to catch external pollutants
- Air intakes situated away from street traffic, loading docks, exhaust fans, and other potential sources of dirt and pollution
- Regular monitoring and replacement of air filters.

Good light is the friend of people who create and research in records, but it is an enemy of the records themselves. Exposure to light is one of many things that speeds up the deterioration of paper records and records on other media as well. Since people need light and historical records don't, and since they must coexist, obviously some compromises must be reached to accommodate both:

- Keep the lights off in stack areas except when people are working there or retrieving or returning records to the shelves.
- Do not construct stack areas where there are windows; or, if this can't be avoided, block or darken the windows.
- Where windows are present, such as in search rooms, and where there are fluorescent lights, minimize the flow of ultraviolet light, which is particularly harmful, through the use of UV filters.
- Avoid having records exposed for long periods of time to intense light, for instance, by researchers leaving them out on tables for longer than needed, or in exhibits that are in brightly lit areas. (UV filters on exhibit cases can help minimize damage; better yet is the practice of exhibiting facsimile copies, not originals).

Good housekeeping and good records preservation go hand in hand. The search room, processing area, and storage stacks should be regularly cleaned. Garbage should be removed every day; old furniture, dead equipment, and other debris should be taken away as soon as possible. Eating and drinking should not be allowed near the records; smoking, which is bad for people, harmful for records, and introduces a fire threat should be banned or banished to the outdoors.

USE APPROPRIATE CARTONS AND OTHER CONTAINERS

The physical housing of historical records helps determine how long they will last. The most common storage for loose paper records is to house them in paper folders, which are then placed in archival storage cartons that are specially manufactured for the purpose. Common manila folders and commercial quality cardboard boxes are *not* suitable for archival storage because they are too highly acidic, not strong enough, and will break down over time. Many programs use such materials because they are inexpensive (or even free, in the case of cardboard cartons which are sometimes procured at no cost from supermarkets or other stores), but this does a grave disservice to the historical records by accelerating their aging rather than helping slow it. The paper folders and paperboard cartons should be "acid-free." This assertion is based on the principle that any material brought into contact with historical records should be nondamaging and on the realization that acid from high-acid containers may actually harm records, even records that are themselves relatively high-acid. Certain plastic containers may work, but they are likely to be transparent or translucent and admit light, less likely to serve as a buffer against changes in temperature and humidity, and in general are not as suitable as paperboard for most applications.[4]

There are many different types of containers for historical records. Appendix 11 has suggestions for suppliers of cartons and other preservation supplies and services. Five types of enclosures are particularly important:

1. *Acid-free folders.* Folders are the first line of defense for loose paper records such as a series of letters. They are protective (need to be stiff enough to support the materials), help organize (a folder is well suited to holding a particular part of a series, such as all the correspondence filed under a certain alphabetical range), and provide access (folders can be easily labeled, even by simply writing on the tab with a pencil.)

2. *Acid-free storage cartons.* These cartons, sometimes informally called "archives cartons" or "archives boxes," provide clean, secure housing for folders, bound volumes, and other materials. They come in various sizes, are relatively inexpensive to purchase, are durable, and, because of their low acidity, help prolong the life of the records they house.

3. *Encapsulation.* Documents that consist of individual pages can be encapsulated between sheets of Mylar or some other chemically inert, transparent plastic. Encapsulation protects the document, permits viewing it without direct handling, and, like all good preservation treatments, is reversible.

4. *Metal or other storage cabinets.* Metal cabinets are commonly used to store certain historical records; for instance, specially constructed map cases store oversized maps, drawings, and prints. The cabinets should be in good shape, with a cured, baked-enamel finish, no paint cracking, and sturdy enough to support and protect the materials stored in them.

5. *Special containers for special formats.* Photographs, videotapes, computer records, and other special formats will require their own types of containers.

APPLY A HOLDINGS MAINTENANCE/
PHASED PRESERVATION/STAGED APPROACH

This strategy is tied to the fourth principle in the first section of this chapter, "First Things First." It proceeds on the assumptions that there is a basic obligation to preserve all of a program's holdings; that the program can't do all its preservation work at once; that some basic work on the majority of the collection is preferable to intensive work on some and total neglect of the rest; and that a pragmatic, gradualist approach is likely to work best in most cases. Actually, three distinct but related archival strategies are combined here. "Holdings maintenance" includes:

> replacing poor quality enclosures (or adding needed enclosures if they are not present), removing damaged fasteners, photocopying unstable records, enclosing weak or damaged materials in polyester film sleeves, and dusting the exteriors of bound volumes and boxes as well as shelves. . . . Such preservation activities are designed to prolong the useful life of entire collections, while at the same time eliminating or deferring the need for expensive conservation treatment.[5]

"Holdings maintenance" is a basic preservation activity—but it can be carried out along with arrangement and description. It is relatively quick, easy to do, has a lasting impact, and goes a long ways toward meeting reasonable preservation goals. Holdings maintenance fits in well with a broader "phased preservation" approach, defined as:

> An approach to preservation that emphasizes broad stabilizing activity to protect the entire holdings of a repository, rather than the concentration of resources solely on item level treatment. Such an approach includes, but is not limited to, preservation planning and surveys to establish priorities, disaster planning, controlling the storage environment, performing holdings maintenance, and selective treatment of materials.[6]

Phased preservation, in turn, is compatible with the third leg of this approach, what might be called *staged* preservation work. Staging has two parts, which need to be balanced. First, in general, preservation work ought to proceed more or less evenly over the entire collection, i.e., all materials are transferred to acid-free surroundings before more detailed, exacting work is done on any of them. But, second, there are clearly exceptions to be made to this even-handed approach, based on (A) conditions of the records; (B) importance of the records; and (C) researcher interest in and demand for the records.

STRIKE A BALANCE BETWEEN ROUTINE CONSERVATION WORK AND WORK DONE BY PROFESSIONAL CONSERVATORS

The program needs a settled approach to the conservation work that can and will be carried out by its own staff (presumably not professional conservators) and more exacting, technically demanding work that merits a professional conservator (who may be a staff member, a consultant, or a professional conservation laboratory). All conservation work should follow certain principles: it should not harm the document, it should not be invasive or change the document, and it should if possible be reversible. The following list represents the type of activities that a program should be able to handle with its own resources and staff:[7]

- Surface cleaning, including removing surface dirt, dust, and other materials, usually with a soft brush or soft eraser
- Humidification and flattening, where needed and appropriate; this requires some experience to know how much humidification is appropriate for particular formats, and how best to dry humidified materials
- Polyester encapsulation, which is basically sandwiching a sheet of paper between two layers of polyester and sealing it on all four sides
- Repairing simple, short tears, preferably through the use of long-fiber Japanese paper and a starch adhesive (leave longer tears to the conservator)

Activities best left to a professional conservator or outside conservation lab include:

- Fumigation and other aspects of pest management, which is necessary but must be performed by professionals because of the risk to people
- Deacidification, a process that decreases or removes the acid from paper; it is usually cost-effective and practical only if carried out in large quantities.
- Repairing extensive tears
- Other paper strengthening processes

USE REPRODUCTION FOR DISSEMINATION, SECURITY, AND PRESERVATION

Duplication of materials is a sound preservation tool as well as a means to increase security and support dissemination. Reproduction copying makes sense when: (A) the materials are particularly valuable for research and may be used in two or more locations at once; (B) they have severe and extensive preservation problems, making physical conservation work expensive and time-consuming; (C) they pose a security risk—they are susceptible to theft because of their intrinsic value, their signatures, some other feature, or because the program's security provisions are not at the desired level; or (D) some combination of these factors. The two most common approaches to reproduction for archival materials are (A) copying onto acid-free, long-lasting paper and (B) archival microfilming. Digital conversion of tangible records is being tried primarily as a dissemination tool, but the lack of clear standards means it can't be counted on to set any endurance records.

Microfilm, by contrast, is a reliable tool for preservation, dissemination, and space savings. Microfilming to archival standards reduces bulk by more than 90 percent in most cases (that is, the microfilm will take up less than 10 percent of the storage space of the originals), a boon to programs that send the originals to off-site storage (or, in rare instances, dispose of them altogether). Microfilm accurately and faithfully reproduces all the information in documents. When filming is done to exacting standards—the right film stock is used, quality control procedures are in place, identification targets are used to ensure authenticity, the film is properly processed, inspection procedures including checks for resolution (sharpness) and density (contrast between the writing and the background) are carried out—film can be counted upon to endure and serve as a surrogate for the original records. Microfilm has been around for more than a century and in active use for document reproduction for more than half a century, so there are clear guidelines and standards for historical records programs to follow.[8]

MAKE THE WELFARE OF THE RECORDS THE FIRST CONSIDERATION IN EXHIBITS

Professionally developed and mounted exhibits have long been regarded as an excellent means of displaying historical records, which is an important tool for fostering public historical appreciation and understanding. Exhibit techniques constitute a subfield of archival work and are beyond the scope of this book.[9]

From a preservation perspective, placing stellar historical documents on the public stage presents several problems: the documents may need to be repaired or physically strengthened before they are exhibited, exhibition mounting techniques need to be carefully applied to avoid harm to the documents, exposure to people means exposure to light (though this can be minimized through the use of subdued lighting and UV resistant glass), and being out in the open, even in a secure case, always means the risk of damage or theft. Therefore, unless there is an overwhelming countervailing objection, the best advice is to exhibit facsimiles rather than originals. If originals are to be exhibited, the program's conservation expert needs to work along with the exhibit developers to ensure that records preservation needs are addressed and that, after the exhibit, the documents return to serve another day.

PROMOTE USE AS THE ULTIMATE GOAL OF PRESERVATION

If historical records are so fragile, and if the world is fraught with so many perils, why not "preserve" them by locking them away in vaults? This notion may sound far-fetched, particularly if a program accepts the notion that *use* is the ultimate purpose of all archival work. But an inordinate fear of damage to the records, and an overdeveloped sense of curatorial responsibility, leads some programs to restrict or discourage research use of their holdings. Their motives are usually noble ones. Sometimes, the explanation is that the materials are just too old and fragile to bear handling; sometimes, that they are being held in storage until the program can perform preservation work on them, but it is not clear when that will happen! Programs need to be conscientious about preservation, but they also need to avoid taking in more materials than they can responsibly preserve and they must carry out reasonable preservation activities in a timely fashion so that the materials can be made available for research.

PREPARING FOR THE WORST

The final element of preservation, broadly conceptualized, is disaster planning and recovery. Disasters include primarily fire, water, wind, and earthquake damage, and they can, within the space of a few minutes, destroy or seriously damage the historical record treasures that have taken years or even centuries to accumulate. There is a tendency—perhaps part of human nature—to assume, or at least to hope, that disasters only took place long ago or far away, never at home, and that "it can't happen here!" Complacency is a great enemy

INTEGRATING PRESERVATION
AND ARCHIVAL ADMINISTRATION

Mary Lynn Ritzenthaller, one of the nation's foremost experts on preservation, has written eloquently about the need for preservation to be integrated with other archival functions in her Society of American Archivists' manual, *Preserving Archives and Manuscripts* (Chicago: Society of American Archivists, 1993), particularly chapter 8. She asserts:

> Preservation must be seen as integral to every activity in the archival repository. Each time a record or manuscript is handled, whether by archival staff in processing, scholars, or students in conducting research, or preparators mounting an exhibit, there is a potential for damage or loss. Every archival function must be carried out from a preservation perspective. This preservation concern or awareness can be developed, in part, by careful forethought—that is, thinking through all archival activities from a preservation standpoint and considering at each phase: What steps will be taken to accomplish this task? What are the potential dangers to the material? What staff members will be involved and what problems should they anticipate? Contingency plans should be developed for potential problems, and a clear chain of command established to expedite decision making and cope with emergencies. As a result of this approach, often termed preservation management, holdings will be less endangered and better cared for, and the repository will develop a reputation for being careful and conscientious with archival materials (p. 101).

Ritzenthaller's discussion shows how preservation-mindedness should inform every aspect of archival work. For instance, there are some preservation actions that can be taken during the provision of reference services:

- Dusting exteriors of boxes and bound volumes
- Placing fragile items in polyester sleeves
- Photocopying damaged documents
- Placing photos in polyester sleeves
- Adding spacer boards to underfilled boxes
- Replacing damaged folders/adding folders as required
- Removing and replacing damaging fasteners
- Noting presence of oversize materials and ensuring their safe access
- Counting items in folders containing valuable or sensitive materials
- Withholding records that will be damaged by use (p. 113).

of preservation. Survey after survey shows that even the most conscientious historical records custodians, dedicated professionals who spend their careers and much of their personal time collecting and servicing historical records, do not have plans for disasters—mainly because they assume "it can't happen here." Disaster preparedness has its own, extensive literature, which is worth pursuing not only because it tells how to prepare and respond but also because it describes actual disasters and their effects.[10] Disaster preparedness should include at least five elements:

1. *Assess threats.* It is helpful to carry out an assessment of possible threats; many programs do this as part of the survey of preservation needs, discussed earlier in this chapter. The assessment includes such things as identification of fire hazards; analysis of storage areas to determine, for instance, which are below grade and might be susceptible to flooding; checking the roof for structural integrity and signs of aging; checking electrical wiring for signs of aging, fraying, etc.; and assessing the risk of natural disasters such as earthquakes or tornadoes.

2. *Eliminate threats.* The best way to prepare for a disaster is, in effect, to minimize the chances of ever having one. Therefore, part of the work involves minimizing hazardous situations or eliminating them altogether. Some obvious examples: ban smoking in the building, remove hazardous and potentially explosive materials, and move the historical records from the basement to the first or second floor.

3. *Initiate proactive preventative measures.* This would include installation of intrusion alarms on the doors leading to the stacks, installation of smoke alarms, and installation of an effective fire suppression system.

4. *Develop a plan.* People who have experienced disasters in the past can attest that having a plan and ensuring that everyone is familiar with it are the keys to fast and effective responses in the event of a disaster. The plan should include:[11]

   - An introduction that states the purpose, indicates scope, and references other institutional documents (e.g., recovery plan for the parent institution)
   - Establishment of authority and assignment of responsibilities. This section should designate one person to be in charge of disaster recovery, establish decision-making channels, and indicate who is responsible for what, with particular attention to the roles of preservation officers, conservators, facilities managers, and security personnel.
   - A listing of disaster response activities, for instance, checking the building for further damage, documenting damage, gathering supplies, moving materials out of the damaged area, setting up a work area, carrying out air drying procedures, cleaning and restoring materials, etc.
   - Recovery procedures. This section spells out, in as much clear detail as possible, just what is to be done depending on the circumstances and damage. For instance, if freeze-drying is a priority option, the process should be spelled out.

- Additional information: phone tree for contacting staff, additional contacts (experts in particular areas), essential supplies and equipment, floor plans, and other information that may be needed for quick reference in the event of a sudden emergency.

5. *Talk about the issues.* Disaster prevention and response, like other aspects of preservation, should be everyone's concern. Therefore, it is essential to discuss the issue from various angles and perspectives, particularly: (A) raising the awareness of all staff members about the threat of disasters and making sure everyone takes initiative in spotting potential threats and advancing recommendations for ameliorating them; (B) involving everyone in the development of the plan, and, discussing it when it is completed, including doing a mental walk-through of critical parts of it.

Appendix 10 presents a checklist for evaluating the adequacy of security. Security-mindedness—planning to prevent and if need be react to disasters— are important archival obligations.

PRESERVATION OF HISTORICAL RECORDS: CHECKLIST

1. Does the program follow broad preservation principles that help set direction, priorities, and goals?
2. Is there a written preservation plan and procedures and someone designated to coordinate or carry out preservation-related activities?
3. Does the program have a supportive storage environment, including secure, climate-controlled stacks and appropriate storage containers?
4. Is there a systematic approach to preservation and conservation work, one that addresses the total preservation needs of all the program's holdings but also provides for intensive intervention for records with particular needs or outstanding research value?
5. Does the conservation portfolio include both general work by nonexperts and more exacting work by professional conservators?
6. Is reproduction, particularly microfilming, effectively used?
7. Does the program balance preservation needs against the need to get records out and available to users?
8. Does the program have a disaster prevention/preparedness/response plan in place?

9

ELECTRONIC ARCHIVES

ELECTRONIC ARCHIVAL RECORDS: CHALLENGES

Should electronic records—those created by, stored in, and transferred between computers—be treated differently from other records? Should *electronic archives* (or *digital archives*, as they are sometimes called) have a separate chapter in this book? Some archivists would answer *no*: a record is a record, what counts is informational content and not format, and valid archival principles apply in all cases. But others, while conceding that this might be true in theory or in an ideal world, recognize that electronic records require different treatment from that accorded traditional, *tangible* records in paper or microfilm format. Tangible records have been around for centuries and are relatively easy to understand and manage; electronic records have been around for a couple of decades and are relatively complicated and elusive. Paper records continue to increase in volume, but electronic records are growing at an even greater pace. Electronic records differ from their tangible counterparts; therefore, digital archives differ from *their* tangible counterparts. The table on page 140 summarizes some of the differences.

Archivists and records managers have relatively well developed strategies for dealing with records in traditional formats, but the growth in volume and complexity of electronic records has outdistanced the ability of records professionals to develop and apply solutions. Indeed, the fundamental work of defining what even constitutes a *record* in an electronic environment is a great chal-

TANGIBLE RECORDS	ELECTRONIC RECORDS
Record: fixed, "recorded," tangible	Record: fluid, embodies content, context, and structure
Originals usually distinguishable from copies	Originals usually indistinguishable from copies
Usually one original, few copies in few locations	Potential for many copies in many locations
Reading: no device needed (may need magnification for microfilm)	Reading: computer and software required
System dependence: none for paper; magnification device (reader) for microfilm	System dependence: hardware, software
Preservation: mostly addressing deterioration of format	Preservation: need to address deterioration of format, loss of content, and need for appropriate hardware and software
Longevity: predictable, based on experience	Longevity: unpredictable, not enough experience yet
Traditional archival principles, e.g., provenance, original order, are good fits	Some traditional archival principles apply; some need revision; some don't fit at all
Archivists can intervene effectively well along in the life cycle, including toward the end	Archivists need to be involved at beginning of life cycle to ensure that archival concerns are addressed
Archivists can carry out their work unilaterally or with assistance from others	Archivists need active cooperation from others, e.g., records managers, analysts, technical experts
Archival records come to the archives (custodial role)	Archival records may stay with originating office (archivists play advisory or oversight roles)

lenge. The work of the records manager and archivist is best done when electronic information systems are planned or under development; after that, it's difficult to intervene to identify records with enduring value and preserve them. Moreover, most electronic records suffer an inglorious fate: they are simply deleted from disks and hard drives, long before the records manager or archivist can do anything about them. Those that survive are difficult to appraise using traditional methods. Those that are appraised as having archival value are difficult to preserve; fundamentally, they are unpatterned electrons, likely to degrade or disappear with time.

Working with electronic records is difficult but the result may well be worth the effort from an archival standpoint: electronic records are compact, easily stored or transported, and may yield rich information through the use of computers and software designed to access their information. Flexibility of access and interactive search and retrieval potential are major assets. They are increasing in volume as computers are increasingly used in business activities and personal communication. E-mail may contain the greatest uncaptured outpouring of archival records in history! Moreover, computer records may be more important than paper source documents because they have more complete information, show the various stages and states of changing databases, and contain much information that, as a practical matter, is not printed out to paper. Many experts predict that, in the future, electronic records are likely to become the predominant format; paper and microfilm will still be important, but their status will be secondary to electronic records.

The research/development work in archival electronic records is like a runner suspended in mid-stride: off to a good start but nowhere near coming down on something solid and lasting. Most of the research and development work in the electronic records field has been carried out in large-scale government and university settings. The results are still being evaluated and tested. The National Archives and Records Administration has long had a program for accessioning clearly definable databases that have archival value, but its approaches to scheduling electronic records have been challenged in court and it is still working on a strategy for e-mail and other prolific electronic records that are now commonplace in government. The leading state archives are also trying to find solutions that will work. The records and archival communities are collectively moving forward together; solutions are in the offing but not yet available. Given the unsettled state of affairs, it is difficult to find ground to stand on. The Society of American Archivists suggests as a starting point a reassertion of the fundamental archival roles that must be carried out in the new environment as well as in the traditional one. These responsibilities include:[1]

- Manage cost-effective archival programs for the selection, retention, and use of both electronic and paper documentary materials.
- Ensure that an authentic and reliable record is created and available for use.
- Evaluate the universe of available documents and record-keeping systems to select those to preserve for future use.

- Preserve and document the context and arrangement of the materials retained for long-term use.
- Provide descriptive tools, such as registers, indices, and databases, to allow records-keepers, researchers, archivists, and others to locate and identify the information and evidence in archival holdings.
- Preserve information and evidence in a protective environment and in a format or media that will remain usable over time.
- Promote and facilitate the use of archives to explain the past, support accountability for the present, and provide guidance for the future.

STRATEGIC ISSUES

How should traditional collecting programs approach the issue of electronic archival records? There are at least six strategic issues that need to be addressed:

1. *In an electronic environment, how is "record" defined?* In the past, it has been easy to equate a record with its physical format; a letter, for instance, can be equated with the ink and the paper it is written on. This all-too-easy assumption that the record is the medium was never really valid; in reality, it was the *information* that counted all along. Moving to an electronic environment forces everyone to reconfront the issue, and this has led to a reconceptualization of what a "record" is. The best new definition is the one proposed by the International Council on Archives:

   > A record is recorded information that is produced or received in the initiation, conduct, or completion of an institutional or individual activity and that comprises content, context, and structure sufficient to provide evidence of activity, regardless of physical form or medium.[2]

   This is a good start; it is based on *information*, not *format*. But it does not indicate exactly what "recorded" means, and, like any definition, it needs to be explained, interpreted, and applied in any particular setting on a continuing and consistent basis.

2. *Where do electronic records fit in with the program's documentation/ collection/appraisal policies?* The program's approaches need to be tailored to the creating universe. For many programs, the universe is a hybrid one: most records are created through computers (that is, they start out as electronic records), but they are printed out (that is, they become paper records), and their retention as either electronic or paper (or both)

is a matter of personal or organizational policy (or whim). This is likely to change over time: electronic records will become more prevalent and will be considered the format of choice for both reference and storage, and paper, while still important, will come to be regarded as a *copy* of the record, which is created and maintained mainly for convenience. As the shift from paper to electronic records occurs, presumably there will be a corresponding shift from paper to electronic archival records. More and more archival records will need to be captured in electronic format—or not at all.

3. *How appropriate is a curatorial/custodial role?* Most collecting programs, by definition, collect, take custody of, and maintain historical records. That is their business. But should they take this approach in every case to archival *electronic* records? The answer may be *yes;* otherwise, the records will be lost. But for many programs, it may be *no.* Collecting programs that are inclined toward this approach have reached two underlying decisions: one, they cannot influence the creation of information systems (and therefore the creation of archival records) in all the offices and settings where potential archival records may be created; two, they lack the resources and expertise to take in and service electronic records that are being created with many kinds of software and will require hardware, software, and technical expertise to maintain. The best option may not be for collecting programs to take them but for the records to stay in the organizations and offices that created them, which presumably have the resources, technical expertise, computers and other equipment, and the incentive to maintain them. In this scenario, the historical records program moves to alternative roles: educator, technical advisor, and perhaps developer of access tools (see the section below on new roles for archival professionals). In fact, access becomes the new overriding goal; if the researcher has access to electronic records, particularly distance access over the Internet, it may not matter much where they are physically maintained.

4. *How effective and useful are available electronic records management tools and best practices?* The state of the art has not kept up with the state of the problem. The available tools, described briefly later in this chapter, are helpful but not yet equal to the task of preserving the electronic counterparts of tangible records. The tools are improving all the time; for instance, there is an increasing array of software for creating and managing electronic records. But success seems to be always on the horizon, something that may be close but never reached, or something that emerges gradually and incrementally—new software here, a better survey form there, a technical advance somewhere else that provides for more

RESEARCH AND DEVELOPMENT IN ELECTRONIC RECORDS

Many of the major electronic records research and development projects in the United States have been funded by the National Historical Publications and Records Commission. The Commission's newsletter, *Annotation*, and its Web site, *nara.gov/nhprc*, are good sources of information on progress and on available reports and other products. Or, write the Commission at National Archives and Records Administration, Washington, DC 20408.

Over the past few years, the records/archives community has developed a number of informal research/development agendas to help focus research efforts. One of the most recent and comprehensive statements was developed by the ARMA International Educational Foundation, *Research and Development Framework for Records and Information Management* (Prairie Village, Kans.: ARMA International Educational Foundation, 1998). The following excerpt from that statement provides an "Initial List of Research and Development Areas":

- How to survey, monitor, measure, and track changes in record-keeping needs and practices in modern offices, particularly in an electronic setting
- How to reconceptualize what constitutes a "record" in an electronic setting and state it in a concrete, understandable way, e.g., in a statutory definition in government or in regulations or directives for businesses
- How to further develop and apply the concepts of "record-keeping system" and "corporate memory" in institutional settings
- How to tie information management issues and concerns to the notion of information as a key strategic resource/asset that drives business, supports services, etc.
- How to tie records issues and concerns to the development of information policy in government and other institutions
- How to articulate, dramatize, and raise the visibility of records and information management and the work of professionals in this field
- How to deal with the records implications of home pages and Web sites, including their use to access records and their records management implications
- How to build effective partnerships and cooperation among information management professionals who have important influence on record creation and management, e.g., computer specialists, information technology experts, auditors, institutional counsel, program managers
- How to develop the most effective approaches to education and continuing professional development in this field.

longevity. Programs that begin to collect electronic records, therefore, will need to monitor developments, watch the results of research/development projects, follow developments in the journals and new books as they come out, and in general be part of the search for solutions.

5. *What are the program's own sources of expertise in electronic archives?* Given the scarcity of available publications and tools, the next strategic question is whether the program has expertise on staff, can make provision for staff to learn about electronic records issues, has resources to hire new staff, or can piece together the needed expertise through a combination of existing personnel and consultants. The electronic archives issues are sufficiently large and complex that a different type of expertise is needed from what is necessary for traditional programs. The expertise is needed in at least four areas: (A) program planning to accommodate electronic archives; (B) understanding of what constitutes a record in an electronic environment; (C) understanding of the various emerging tools, how they relate to each other, and how to apply and use them; and (D) how to preserve electronic archival records over the long term.

6. *Are there compromise, stopgap, or other expedient approaches?* Much of the work with electronic records in the near future, at least, may come in the form of *pragmatic compromises* with the ideal, simply settling on what works best from among the available options. For instance, many programs simply print out electronic archival records and store them in paper form. In effect, they relegate the computer to the role of word processor. Federal court decisions in the 1990s seemingly invalidated this approach for federal records; printing electronic records fails to capture many records, and, for those that it does, much of the contextual information (for instance, who got copies of e-mail) is lost and therefore the integrity and completeness of the record are undermined. However, the courts' opinions continue to be under appeal and review, meaning that looking to the courts for guidance will require monitoring of court cases and decisions as they are handed down. But print-to-paper is better than losing everything, or it may be regarded as a reasonable interim measure until electronic records policies can be developed and applied.

ELECTRONIC ARCHIVES: TEN ROLES FOR HISTORICAL RECORDS PROFESSIONALS

The broad question of how to identify, preserve, and make available archival electronic records is so complicated, shifting as technology shifts, and challenging that it has occasioned a reexamination of the role of archival professionals. Traditional, fairly well defined roles, including appraisal, custodial responsibilities, reference, and preservation, may well evolve into a new set of responsibilities. The new responsibilities are likely to include:

1. *Monitor.* The professionals who work in historical records programs will need to keep their eyes and ears open, attuned to the research/development, experimentation, and practical coping that is going on in the field to deal with electronic archival records. What is likely to happen is not the emergence of a single, all-purpose solution but, instead, the development of multiple approaches that constitute partial solutions.

2. *Educator.* Archival professionals have a rather daunting *teaching* job to do. They need to articulate to people with influence in the computer and software industries, program managers in business and government, and those technically proficient in the mysteries of computer systems that something very important is at stake: fundamentally, the survival of historical source material in digital form. Digital abundance should not mean the loss of history. This education must be done on a grand scale, for instance, reaching the computer industry; and also on a much smaller scale, day-to-day, office-by-office, individual-by-individual. Some of the work involves identifying patterns and providing insights so that people can understand what is happening. In this sense, archivists are similar to other information professionals. "We see the kinds of questions we handle changing and becoming more demanding," one expert has noted. "The information professional of the future will become the information sense maker."[3]

3. *Communicator.* Archivists cannot solve electronic records programs by themselves. The communication role is closely related to the educational/teaching role. People in the field need to communicate their concerns and objectives in terms that nonexperts can easily understand and grasp. Whatever the audience, the message needs to be tailored so that the audience can understand it and relate it to their concerns and work.

4. *Technical expert.* Historical records professionals will need to broaden their understanding of technical matters. They don't need to become experts in how computers work or all the features of the latest release of WordPerfect or Microsoft Windows. But they do need to understand the nature of electronic information systems, records and document management software, and access and retrieval tools.

5. *Partner.* It is now widely acknowledged that the best time for critical records-related decisions on the make-up of electronic information sys-

tems, and probably for the appraisal of records and the identification of those with archival value, is in the planning/setup stage. This fact requires the archivist to be present at the table when decisions are made—and to assert a right to come to the table if not invited. The archival expert needs to explain archival concerns, provisions for ensuring the clear creation and identification of records, and appraisal/selection criteria. But for this to work, it needs to be done in partnership with others at the table, particularly program managers, users of the system, and technical experts. A unilateral approach won't work; a willing partnership, with the archivist as a full partner, has much better prospects of resulting in the identification and saving of archival records.

6. *Overseer/standard setter.* This point is closely related to number 5. If electronic archival records remain with the offices or agencies of origin, then the role of the historical records expert may broaden to include establishing standards (or promoting adherence to established industry or professional standards), for instance, for forward migration of data as software and hardware change or for easy access to records. This will involve powers of persuasion—convincing programs why they need to do what the archivist recommends.

7. *Mediator.* Historical records programs have always played a *mediation* role that brings together researchers, finding aids/access tools, and the archival records themselves. That role will increase in importance and complexity as the number of electronic archives increase. Among other things, researchers will need an explanation of the make-up and content of electronic files, the software used, and of how to access them. Finding aids will in effect be built into the electronic files, but researchers will need help in using them.

8. *Distance communicator.* As noted in chapter 7, increasingly the place where researcher services specialist and researcher meet may not be the search room or over the phone; it may be in cyberspace. The rising use of Web sites and the probable increased volume of electronic archives are compatible, mutually reinforcing trends. Researchers will, understandably, expect to access electronic files in the archives right over the Internet, from their computers at home. Enabling them to do this—assuming the program permits it and can support it—will require a well developed set of instructions, help screens, interactive instructions, and other still-to-be-invented communications tools.

9. *Pragmatist.* Electronic archives work may require bending tradition, making compromises, experimenting, and finding new ways to make things work. American archival practice has always had a pragmatic in-

clination, one of the factors that accounts for its success. That trait will need to continue in play as each program finds its way into the electronic archival universe.

10. *Quick change expert.* Historical records programs tend to be places that value legacy and tradition and are not inclined to kick over the traces and bolt after new ideas. Those values have served in good stead over many years. But in the case of digital archives, the people working in those programs need to be receptive to new approaches and willing to have the program head in new directions if that is required to continue capturing the archival sources of history.

TOOLS FOR ARCHIVAL ELECTRONIC RECORDS

Once the decisions are made on the broad scale strategic issues noted above, and the program has decided what roles it wishes to play, consideration must be given to tools for management of archival electronic records. This is particularly critical if the program decides to launch a collecting/custodial initiative for electronic records. All of the tools are in flux, there are choices to be made as to how they are applied, and in any case their application requires action on the part of the originating individual or office more than on the part of the receiving/collecting program. Taken together, however, they constitute at least the outline of a viable approach to electronic records.

1. *Identify electronic records and differentiate them from nonrecords.* This process requires applying the definition noted above or deriving another definition and applying that one. Following that definition, capturing *content* is important but no longer sufficient. It is also necessary to provide for capturing *structure* (the arrangement and appearance of the content, including such things as fonts, page and paragraph breaks, relationships between fields, and links to other documents) and context (background information that illuminates the business environment and the technical environment in which the record was created). To rise to the level of record, electronic information needs to meet at least four conditions:[4]

   • Have information content that is (and continues to be) an accurate reflection of what actually occurred at a particular time in the function, activity, or transaction in question.

   • Be able to be reconstructed when required, so that each component part is brought together as a whole and presented in an intelligible way.

- Be able to be placed in context so that the circumstances of its creation and subsequent use by an agency or person can be understood in conjunction with its information content.
- Have been officially incorporated (either actively or passively) into an agency's or person's record-keeping system.

2. *Ensure that records are created, captured, and maintained as part of a record-keeping system.* In an electronic arena, it is next to impossible to identify records and zero in on those with archival value except in the context of a record-keeping system—an information system that is specifically designed with records issues in mind. Development of record-keeping systems entails investigation of documentation needs, analysis of business activity, identification of record-keeping requirements (see items 3 and 4, below), assessment of existing systems, identification of strategies, design of systems, implementation, and post-implementation review.[5] It requires a thorough understanding of the technology, the business of the organization, the documentation it needs to operate, and the documentation that is desirable for long-term research and other purposes. "Archivists have to change the nature and timing of their strategic intervention with records creators," observes one expert:

> We need to work "up front" with modelling and influencing organizational behaviour. We need to understand organizational culture, its functions, programmes, and activities and the type of essential evidence it requires to do its business and protect its legal and administrative obligations. . . . Our natural allies, who understand such risk analysis and risk management and the nature and purpose of evidence, and the risk of not having good records, are the senior managers, the auditors, the programme evaluators, the FOI [Freedom of Information], data protection, security, and privacy officers, the lawyers and legal advisors, the policy coordinators, and so on. In short, if we can reinvent our profession with such allies and help them to reinvent or reengineer their institutions towards creating, capturing, and maintaining reliable records, there are potential solutions possible for the electronic records crisis. . . .[6]

3. *Ensure that the record-keeping system includes functional specifications for the creation and maintenance of records.* The statement of functional specifications describes the requirements that are needed to ensure the creation of thorough, reliable, lasting records in record-keeping systems. The statements are a blend of guidelines and specification on policy, management, and technology that are intended to make sure that the essential traits of records—content, context, and structure—are present. There are several variations on the functional specifications and a growing array of software that, properly installed and used, can help ensure that the

specifications are met (see box). But the application of functional specifications, while very promising as an electronic records management tool, is still in its early stages. It requires technical expertise and partnership with records creators.

4. *Ensure that the record-keeping system includes metadata.* It is difficult to interpret, or evaluate the significance of, electronic records long after their creation unless the system captures and presents *metadata*, a database management term that originally literally meant "data about data" but whose meaning has been broadened over the past several years to include descriptive information about the origins of records, their uses, and the context in which they were created. It is the metadata that reveals much about the *context* and *structure* of the record, the two essential elements that, along with *content*, constitute the new definition of what a record is. The metadata required will vary depending on the institution and the need. One set of guidelines indicates that it should include:[7]

   - Data contained within the document . . . other than its intellectual content (for example, structure and layout); in many cases, much of this is implicit and tightly bound up with the document itself.
   - Information about the record and its relationships with other records in the assembly; for example, title, originator, classification and indexing, distribution.
   - Information about the use of the record: business activity, subsequent versions made, audit trail.

5. *Develop a form and approach for inventory and analysis of electronic records.* In order to make an informed decision on the fate of electronic records, the archivist needs descriptive information. This may be derived more or less automatically if the archivist is involved in the creation of record-keeping systems; the needed information is readily available and apparent during the design process. But in the case of already existing systems it will be necessary to gather and analyze descriptive information as best as possible from examination of the records themselves, interviewing people who designed and used the system, and checking the source documentation and outputs (if they are available). It is helpful to collect the following information:[8]

   - Name of the system, including commonly used name and formal name
   - Agency or organizational program supported by the system, including references to citations, directives, etc., if applicable
   - Purpose of the system; what it is intended to support or accomplish
   - Data input and sources
   - Outputs, e.g., reports, tables, charts, correspondence, etc.

FUNCTIONAL SPECIFICATIONS FOR ELECTRONIC RECORD-KEEPING AND RECORDS MANAGEMENT SOFTWARE

This is one of many areas in the world of records management and archives where the only appropriate description is: "under development." Historical records programs that are interested in this area are advised to keep in touch with developments as they unfold and particularly identify tools and approaches that seem practical and workable. Some examples of current tools:

Functional Requirements for Evidence in Recordkeeping (Pittsburgh: University of Pittsburgh, 1996). The University of Pittsburgh developed the most extensive set of functional specifications, based on examination of legal precedents, professional literature, best practices, and other sources. Their specifications are designed to ensure that records are created, captured, and maintained. *www.lis.pitt.edu/~nhprc/meta96.html.*

Model Guidelines for Electronic Records (Dover: Delaware State Archives, 1997, revisions ongoing) attempts to apply the Pittsburgh model using specific citations and other requirements in that particular state; it is, therefore, a good test of practical application. *www.lib.de.us/archives/g-lines.html.*

Models for Action: Practical Approaches to Electronic Records Management (Albany, N.Y.: Center for Technology in Government, 1998) takes the approach that provision for electronic records needs to be built into information systems as they are being designed to serve institutional business needs. It offers a sensible, practical set of guidelines but leaves plenty of room for customization and implementation. *www.ctg.albany.edu.*

Design Criteria Standard for Electronic Records Management Software (DOD Standard 5015.2-STD) (Washington: Department of Defense, 1997), presents specifications, endorsed by the National Archives and Records Administration, for software that will meet acceptable record-keeping requirements. *www.dtic.mil/c3/stdfb.html.*

Studies of Records Management Software. There are a few places to look for objective, practical evaluation of emerging records management software products. One of the best is *Doculabs*, an industry analysis firm offering practical, objective advisory services and testing for vendors and end-users. Its reports comparing and evaluating various software products are very useful. Contact Doculabs at 1201 W. Harrison Street, 3rd Floor, Chicago, IL 60607. *www. doculabs.com.*

- Informational content, including subject matter, geographical coverage, time span, update cycle, whether it contains micro or summary data, and other major characteristics of the system
- Hardware and software environment

- System manager(s), including name, address, phone number, etc.
- Location of code books, file layouts, and other documentation needed to understand the files
- Disposition authority (if established), including retention period, records retention and disposition schedule title and item number, etc.

6. *Establish a strategy for maintaining access to archival records.* One of the most important issues with electronic records is that they may be inaccessible in the future unless provision is made to ensure their continuing accessibility. To date, there is no single strategy that will do this. Options include maintaining the original hardware and software (costly and less than practical over long time periods), eliminate dependency on specific technology, eliminate inessential dependencies (for instance, software needed to add to files that have in fact been closed), and development and application of software that can emulate the original software.[9] Charles Dollar, whose writings on electronic records constitute a helpful blend of theory and practicality, recommends consideration of three strategies: (1) maintain electronic records processibility so that records can be read, interpreted, and transferred to a new technology platform; (2) migrate legacy systems that can be accurately read and interpreted by existing systems to new technology platforms; and (3) transfer electronic records that can be read and interpreted only by legacy systems to paper or microfilm (a practical approach when a technology solution is not available).[10]

7. *Develop criteria for appraisal of archival electronic records.* Most of the considerations and approaches discussed in chapter 5 apply to electronic records. The ultimate objective is to document certain functions or activities and to save records with enduring research value for various purposes related to the program's fundamental mission. The factor of the program's resources and capacity, introduced in that chapter, applies even more to electronic records where the ability to maintain the records and ensure access to them may constitute a major challenge. There are, however, some additional appraisal criteria to consider for electronic records:

   - *Huge quantity.* One consideration is the size of the records series; electronic records have an obvious advantage over paper in being much more compact. It may be practical for a program to accept a huge database in electronic format where its paper counterpart would be too large from a storage standpoint and too difficult to access from a research standpoint.
   - *Searchability.* Many electronic records can be searched easily by computers for particular names, dates, topics, etc. This is a plus when they are being appraised, and is one of the things that may give them an

edge over tangible records, which in most cases must be searched by hand or through existing indexes.

- *Manipulability*. Electronic records, being fluid, can be manipulated by the searcher to discover patterns and relationships. In effect, the computer, through the use of researcher-supplied software, performs an analysis on the electronic files to find the information or insights that the user needs.
- *Potential for correlations*. It is sometimes possible to have a computer match information in one set of electronic records with information in another set. For instance, names in one series of electronic records may be correlated with names in another series to make connections between the two.

Most of the programs that have thus far collected electronic archival records have been institutional archives, particularly government and universities. Programs that collect principally from the outside, the main audience for this book, have by and large not actively sought this material—yet. It is therefore difficult to generalize about the types of materials that ought to be collected. However, some or all of these should be considered good candidates:

- Correspondence files where the content has obvious research value and there is an automated indexing system, particularly if it can access key words or topics as well as sender/recipient.
- E-mail files if the system was used for substantial messaging about topics of importance to the collecting program, trivial material was deleted, the e-mail was organized into a record system, and there are effective search and retrieval capacities.
- Project files where all, or most, of the record material related to a particular project, initiative, problem, or other identifiable and well defined topic of interest, is available in one electronic filing system.
- Surveys, polls, and other studies of topics, people, groups, or localities where the collecting program has a subject interest.
- Socioeconomic data on people, groups, topics, or geographical areas that are in line with the program's collecting scope.
- Cartographic and environmental data about natural features on the surface, streams, highways, structures, community features, etc.

ELECTRONIC DOCUMENT IMAGING

The discussion to this point has pertained mostly to archival approaches to records that are in electronic form. There is, however, another angle: the digital conversion of tangible records, mostly through electronic imaging technology. This technology records and maintains information by using a laser beam to alter the light-reflective characteristics of an optical storage medium; the information is read by equipment that distinguishes between the presence and absence of reflected light. Special equipment is required and the work must be done to technical standards. Imaging has several advantages: it provides for density of storage, permits quick retrieval, presents the potential for duplication and transfer of the information, and, when applied through sophisticated equipment that is readily available in the market, makes for helpful indexing and easy retrieval of information. It is being used increasingly for records management applications, such as controlling incoming correspondence, documenting claims, and recording documents in county clerks' offices, where there is a high volume of records and retrieval time and access are important considerations.

Imaging has been less extensively applied to archival records to date, however, because there are no standards yet for longevity and therefore no solid assurance as to how long the information will last and be retrievable. Moreover, as is the case for records generated in electronic form originally, maintaining the functionality of the hardware and software, or migrating over time, constitute a major challenge. The process is relatively expensive and technically demanding. Of course, it is possible to maintain the original record in paper or micrographic form, but that may take away from the attractiveness of the use of the technology. Electronic imaging is on the rise, however, in part because of the interest in getting records into original form so that they can be accessed through Web sites. The best advice is to plan carefully, select records for application carefully, and continue to monitor developments in the field, particularly the development of standards.[11]

PRESERVING ARCHIVAL ELECTRONIC RECORDS

What about physical preservation of electronic records? There are now no standards for "archival" electronic media; that means that there is no guarantee that either the information on the media, or the media itself, will last indefinitely. In fact, much of the electronic information industry, broadly defined, is concerned with immediate uses of information and not concerned with durability or lasting value. Therefore, the assumption has to be that the media is not meant to survive for a very long time. A reasonable estimate for magnetic disks commonly used in computers today is that they can be expected to retain information in a viable, retrievable form for about ten years—

hardly archival! Therefore, electronic records need to be recopied from time to time to ensure the survival of the information. Archivists can take several steps to enhance longevity, including storage in a dust-and-dirt free environment at optimal temperature and humidity conditions. Fluctuations in either temperature or humidity should be avoided or at least minimized. Tapes and disks should be checked periodically for signs of deterioration and, if problems are detected, the materials should be recopied. Making backup copies of all electronic records, and storing the duplicates off-site, constitutes a sensible safeguard against loss.[12]

ELECTRONIC ARCHIVES: CHECKLIST

1. Does the program understand the similarities, and the differences, between traditional records and electronic records?
2. Has the program decided to accept, maintain, and make available electronic records?
3. If the program has made the determination to accept electronic records, has it also developed the technical and other expertise needed to service and maintain them?
4. Has the program considered the new roles that historical records experts need to play to encourage the systematic creation, identification, and preservation of electronic records?
5. Does the program monitor changes and developments in this area to identify model practices and approaches?

10

HISTORICAL RECORDS PROGRAMS
IN THE THIRD MILLENNIUM

TRENDS FOR THE NEXT DECADE

The first part of this concluding chapter attempts to anticipate issues and trends that will affect historical records programs in the opening years of the twenty-first century. The intention is not to predict the future with certainty, which is impossible, but rather to identify probable developments in a way that will help program directors plan for them. As is often the case with archival work, the fundamental challenge is to keep the best traditions and approaches, modify those that need changing, and invent new tools and approaches to fit new circumstances. This requires a creative blend of respect for traditional approaches, pragmatic adaptation, creativity, and strong leadership. Perhaps above all, it requires a willingness to support and roll along with *change*, which will be a constant companion in historical records work. The eight projected trends are summarized below.

1. *The quantity and importance of electronic records will continue to increase dramatically.* The new century is likely to be an electronic one as far as new records are concerned. Computers will continue to be used in the initial production of just about all significant records, as is already the case, but more and more records are likely to be maintained in electronic format only. Electronic records have several attractive traits, including ease of creation, speed of transmission, and compactness of storage,

which will increase their status as the storage and retrieval medium of choice. Paper will continue to be important, but increasingly as a convenience copy or as a duplicate and backup for the electronic version, which will come to be regarded as original, authentic, and commonplace. The archival community and other interested groups will continue to develop and explore potential solutions to the identification, preservation, and accessibility of electronic records of continuing value. There are likely to be multiple solutions, some of them pragmatic compromises that do not solve all of the issues or meet the goal of preservation of all archival electronic records. The challenge of electronic records is generally regarded as the greatest one that records managers and archivists will face in the coming years. If it is likened to a battle, the outcome—triumph in the sense of meaningful mastery of the problems and saving of records; defeat in the sense of most electronic archival records continuing to be lost; or some middling result in between—is by no means certain.

2. *Many services and interactions with customers will move to the Web.* Distance access to both finding aids and to copies of records themselves can be expected to increase. Large numbers of people, at least in the United States, will come to regard the computer, the Web, and the Internet as the mode of choice for accessing much of the information they need to do their work. Researchers as a group will expect more and more of what they seek to be available electronically from over the Internet. The Web may well become the first place to look for access to research information; hopefully it will not be the only place, but its importance as a source of information and a conduit to information is certain to increase dramatically. There is considerable evidence that young people, accustomed to using computers for sharing and getting information, will place their primary alliance on Web-based and mediated access. Historical records programs can be expected to respond by gravitating toward reference services on the Web via their home pages as a way of orienting researchers to their holdings and services, answering initial questions, and presenting finding aids and access tools (another reason that the advent of EAD, Encoded Archival Description, is so important). There will be a trend to accession records in electronic form, as noted in chapter 9, and also to make those records available in electronic form. Programs will also feel pressure to convert their existing paper holdings to a digital version so that they, too, can be made available. In fact, if there is any "megatrend" that is almost certain to sweep into historical records programs, it will be the move toward digital conversion to meet shifting researcher expectations and needs. This sounds like a good opportunity to

take advantage of the digital revolution, but it will also be a great challenge in terms of technical understanding, ensuring longevity, and costs
of both conversion and maintenance.

3. *There will be more care and attention to the issue of selection of historical
   records.* In part because of the vast advantages and frightening potential
   problems presented by electronic records, new approaches to the broad
   process of selection are likely to emerge. Appraisal and selection have always been at the heart of archival work, but the archival community as a
   whole has never been fully satisfied with either the processes or the results.
   The issue has always been: how to ensure the identification and survival of
   a rich, representative historical record, given limited time and resources
   and an overwhelming body of information? Five current trends are likely
   to expand and change the approach to selection. One, the number of institutional archival programs will increase, but as part of records management or broader information management programs. Institutions are re-
   discovering the value of good information management through the
   insights offered by the emerging phenomenon of knowledge management,
   which stresses the value of both implicit information (what employees and
   groups have in their minds) and explicit information (what is saved and
   recorded, including records). Information is being newly recognized as
   strategically important, essential for documentation, and important for corporate profits. The archival dimension—based on a realization that certain
   information has continuing value for historical and other research—should
   lead to more institutional archival programs, which will have the effect of
   documenting their companies and other organizations.

   Two, the relatively new notion of functional appraisal will catch on,
   leading to strategies that attempt to capture the macro documentation of
   certain functions and activities rather than trying to appraise series by series. Three, many appraisal decisions will in effect be made before records
   are actually created, when information systems are being set up; that is a
   logical extension of the concept of macro appraisal and also a practical necessity in electronic records systems where after-the-fact appraisal is likely
   to bring unsatisfactory results. Four, there will be more of a tendency to
   consider records along with other sources of information as a generic
   whole that constitutes documentation, particularly in a homogenized electronic environment where it is difficult to tell record from nonrecord.
   Five, actual research use will be better monitored and analyzed by programs and better used to inform the appraisal and selection process.

4. *Public understanding and appreciation of history and its sources will continue to be ambiguous.* To some degree, the health of historical records

programs depends on how well public history programs in historical societies and other settings are faring, and the welfare of public history programs depends on the public's interest in and support of history. Reading tea leaves may have as good a chance of predicting public support as analysis based on past and current trends. There are certainly disturbing signs of rootlessness and heedlessness in our highly mobile society, which sometimes seems to have abandoned traditional values and to care only about the present and the future, not the past. The state of teaching and learning history in the public schools is very discouraging. On the other hand, genealogical and family history are likely to continue on the upswing (the Web is a boon for genealogists who prefer working at home), and in some communities and social groups there is an almost palpable desire to reach back to their collective past for identification, inspiration, and guidance.

There are a few trends that seem likely to affect historical perception and interest. One, the presentation of historical events by television and movies appears to be a trend with a golden future, even if historians sometimes cringe at the way historical events are recreated and interpreted. Two, outdoor museums and "living history" settings seem to be destined for growth, though some may be obvious commercial ventures of "feel good" history that leaves out the sad and unsettling parts and where objectivity is secondary to selling T-shirts and souvenirs. Three, in part because of the changing demographic make-up of the population, there will continue to be a broad push to explore *everyone's* history, not just the history of the great and the elite. The recovery of the historical past of the American mosaic in all its splendor, complexity, and diversity will engender interest in study of historical records that have formerly been ignored, neglected, or marginalized.

Four, there will probably be more initiatives to bring historical records to the schools, based on the success that archival programs have had with this over the past few years, the natural appeal of historical records as teaching tools, and the fact that this can be done relatively inexpensively. If this indeed proves to be a trend that takes root and spreads, large numbers of young people will be exposed to historical records relatively early in their lives and will, presumably, be aware of them, and even appreciate them and use them, later on.

5. *Clearer standards will emerge for what constitutes a historical records or archival program.* This prediction, and numbers 6 and 7 below, are interrelated and mutually reinforcing. In years to come, more settled, precise, and comprehensive guidelines and standards as to what constitutes a his-

torical records program will come into existence. This book has attempted to set forth expectations for a minimally acceptable program and, in the future, there should be more literature along the same lines that goes beyond recommendations for archival *techniques* and instead describes the make-up, strategies, and administration of model *programs*. More case studies should also be available, documenting what actually works and what does not. As new programs are being planned, and as existing programs are reevaluated, there will be increased attention to recognized standards of procedure and attainment.

6. *More programs will meet minimum standards of organization and attainment.* If trend number 5 holds true, there will be clearer standards and more programs that meet them. The historical records landscape will change for the better as there are stronger programs that carry out their work in exemplary fashion. This does not mean that there will be hard-and-fast standards that everyone will have to meet as a condition of doing business. That approach would be counterproductive, would be met with resentment and resistance, and simply would not work. Instead, what is likely to happen is a growing recognition of what it takes to do historical records work well, to mount and maintain a program, and to meet the service expectations of researchers and others. Professional associations, e.g., American Association for State and Local History and the Society of American Archivists, can be expected to lead the way, through their publications, conferences, and in other ways.

7. *Programs will be marked by increasing professionalism.* A related trend will be the move to staff historical records programs with professional archivists. As noted earlier in this book, the archival profession is stressing professionalism, there are standards for certifying archivists, and a number of strong graduate archival education programs are turning out professionals with master's degrees who are admirably prepared to take up archival responsibilities. Over the years, as programs are more and more likely to meet reasonable program standards as noted in number 6, they will also be likely to employ qualified professionals to perform the work to meet both professional guidelines and the expectations of the parent institutions themselves.

8. *Statewide coordination efforts will bring more consistency and cooperation.* State archival programs acting directly and in their role as State Historical Records Coordinators cooperating with State Historical Records Advisory Boards have the momentum to continue as major players on the archival scene in the new century. The State Coordinators in most states carried out statewide assessment and reporting projects in the 1980s and statewide assessment and strategic planning projects in the 1990s. The

strategic plans had the effect of gathering real data upon which to base analyses and decisions, encouraging historical records programs in each state to think of themselves as part of a community with common interests, and of turning attention to the leadership role of the State Coordinators' offices. The process built relationships and connections and also produced strategic plans that hold out a vision, and also include goals and objectives, for each of the states that participated. The plans are not likely to be blueprints for what happens over the next decade—but they are likely to provide direction and inspiration, encourage a pulling together, and provide a focus for state leadership and resources.

AMERICA'S HISTORICAL RECORDS: TOWARD A NATIONAL AGENDA

The section above summarized what is *likely* to happen. This concluding section suggests some large-scale changes that *should* happen, at least in the opinion of the author, to strengthen historical records programs. It is presented for consideration by the records and archival community, state archival programs and Historical Records Advisory Boards, and federal agencies, particularly the National Historical Publications and Records Commission. These agencies are in a position to assert leadership, provide direction, and effect change over the long term. It also assumes that historical records, broadly defined, constitute a national treasure and, for that reason among others, merit national initiatives as well as state and local ones. Seven recommendations are presented.

1. *Advocate and support program leadership, development, and management.* The archival community is relatively strong in the area of techniques; it has a good understanding of what needs to be done to take care of historical records. What is much less well developed is a consensus on what makes up a successful historical records *program*. Four themes in particular need emphasis in professional development forums: (A) an assessment and planning process that should precede program start-up; (B) management in a time of continuing change; (C) management of human resources—people—whose time, talents, and energies will be as essential to program success in the future as they have been in the past; and (D) advocacy for the program. Also needed are more case studies of successful programs and what factors account for their good fortune. Efforts in this area could take the form of planning/development grants, publications, seminars, and other professional development forums.

2. *Develop better means of sharing program information and materials.*
Even though the archival community has an excellent track record of
sharing, there is substantial room for improvement, for instance, in sharing manuals on historical records program practices among state archival
programs, or sharing of internal procedures materials that they have developed themselves among historical records programs. Thousands of
programs in the United States are performing roughly the same kind of
work every day; there is a great deal to be learned, time to be saved, and
mistakes to be avoided, through sharing of program materials. Three
areas in particular are good candidates for sharing: (A) effective policies
and procedures that work well for accomplishing the work, e.g., processing manuals, registration forms, security regulations; (B) model practices
that have proven their worth in meeting leading edge issues and problems
such as management of electronic records or the development of Web-
based services; and (C) case studies in program development and management. The Web provides a seemingly easy way of sharing; what are
needed are protocols, more incentives to share, and a coordinating mechanism. The State Historical Records Coordinators' Steering Committee
has begun to develop plans to support broader information sharing. These
efforts, and others like them, deserve heightened support.

3. *Provide for continuing survey and assessment.* The state surveys and
strategic plans of the 1990s provided extensive baseline data for planning
and action. Now a mechanism is needed to keep our collective finger on
the pulse through periodic surveys that update the data. Surveys will provide state and federal agencies with macro-views of the state of development and needs; they will provide individual historical records program
managers with data against which to compare their own programs. Future
survey and assessment efforts should: (A) be carried out periodically, on a
regular basis, e.g., every five or ten years; (B) repeat at least some of the
questions every time in order to meaningfully measure change; (C) con-
solidate state surveys into a national profile each time; and (D) produce
summary reports for each state, and nationally, that highlight and dramatize findings and are customized for public distribution and attention.

4. *Develop a research/development framework.* The historical records field
needs a broadly agreed-upon agenda that identifies the areas that most
need sustained research and the development of analysis and recommendations for action. Currently, there are partial agendas, e.g., for electronic
records, but none exists for the field as a whole. An agenda would be helpful, for instance, in helping grant funding agencies set priorities and allocate funds, in guiding graduate students to topics for master's theses or

doctoral dissertations, and in suggesting topics for sessions at professional conferences. The agenda would need to include, but should not be totally devoted to, research and development in the implications of digital technologies, particularly techniques for identifying and managing archival electronic records.

5. *Develop more and better ways to spread the word.* Historical records, valuable though they are, will continue to be underappreciated and underutilized unless more imaginative ways can be found to let the public know about what the records are and why they matter. Work in this area might include: (A) more work with the news media to increase use of historical records for background research on news stories and features and to secure increased coverage of historical records issues per se; (B) negotiating for hyperlinks to historical records programs from frequently-visited specialty sites; (C) campaigns to increase teaching and study of local and state history in the schools; (D) development of courses, particularly at the high school and college levels, on historical awareness and understanding and on the role of information in our society, with the intention of including some coverage of historical records as courses are planned; and (E) develop closer ties with groups that are natural users of historical records, e.g., historians, genealogists, attorneys, and title searchers, and get them to communicate the value and importance of historical records to their colleagues and professional organizations.

6. *Revisit the role of professional associations.* Professional associations in the historical records field, broadly defined, as well as in the local history field, are sensing opportunities and the need to change. In part, it is a matter of time and demographics: younger people have different expectations and needs from a professional identity than people who are older. In part, it is a matter of technology broadening the range of information delivery options but also changing (almost always, increasing) expectations that information will be readily and easily available. Some ways that changed approaches may help meet challenges in the future: (A) find ways to deliver more services over the Internet; (B) develop mechanisms for interassociation collaboration; (C) continue to define and articulate what it means to be an archival professional; (D) help develop guidelines for program building and management, as noted above; (E) find ways to deliver more services over the Internet; and (F) help to raise the visibility of the field.

7. *Revisit the role of the federal government in historical records affairs.* The National Archives and Records Administration has done an exemplary job as custodian of the national government's archival records and its funding

arm, the National Historical Publications and Records Commission, has funded hundreds of individual projects and fostered the development of informal state networks with the State Historical Records Coordinators and State Historical Records Advisory Boards at their centers. The opening years of the twenty-first century will be an opportune time for fresh examination of a number of issues: (A) What are the best approaches to strengthen the role of the Coordinators and the Boards so that they, in turn, can best serve the needs of their states' historical records community? (B) How should Board-supported initiatives be funded? (C) Should federal historical records grant funding be increased and, if so, how should increases be applied? (D) What should be the relationship among federal funding agencies that have an interest in historical records, e.g., National Historical Publications and Records Commission, National Endowment for the Humanities, Institute for Museum and Library Services, and the National Parks Service? (E) How can federal research into electronic records, particularly that carried out by the National Archives and Records Administration, contribute to the solution of archival electronic records issues in general?

CONCLUSION: THE ROAD AHEAD

Historical records work will continue to be exciting and rewarding, for at least three reasons. One, the attractive combination of history and service will continue to be near the heart of archival work, no matter what the setting or circumstances, and the rewarding feeling of working with people to help perpetuate the record of the past will retain its magnetic appeal. If anything, the stakes are greater than in the past. Two, the business of program building, certainly a worthy challenge in the twentieth century, will continue to be an absorbing calling in the twenty-first. Keeping programs growing and changing will require well developed leadership and management skills, energy, and devotion. There will, however, continue to be an immense reward in terms of satisfaction with presenting the past and the present to the future. Three, information technology, which is sometimes compared to historic transformational forces such as the invention of the printing press or the internal combustion engine, will certainly continue to change everything. There will be destruction of the old at the same time that there is potential for building anew, which makes for an exciting employment environment to say the least! There has never been a better, more promising time to be engaged in historical records work.

Appendix I

CODE OF ETHICS FOR ARCHIVISTS

The archival code of ethics provides guidelines that ensure objectivity, balance, and fairness in archival work. It indicates areas where programs need to set policies to avoid problems and misunderstandings or to resolve them if they arise. Society of American Archivists, *Code of Ethics for Archivists*, adopted by SAA Council in 1992. Available at *www.archivists.org*. Reprinted with permission of the Society of American Archivists.

CODE OF ETHICS FOR ARCHIVISTS

Archivists select, preserve, and make available documentary materials of long-term value that have lasting value to the organization or public that the archivist serves. Archivists perform their responsibilities in accordance with statutory authorization or institutional policy. They subscribe to a code of ethics based on sound archival principles and promote institutional and professional observance of these ethical and archival standards.

Archivists arrange transfers of records and acquire documentary materials of long-term value in accordance with their institution's purposes, stated policies, and resources. They do not compete for acquisitions when competition would endanger the integrity or safety of documentary materials of long-term value, or solicit the records of an institution that has an established archives. They cooperate to ensure the preservation of materials in repositories where they will be adequately processed and effectively utilized.

Archivists negotiating with transferring officials or owners of documentary materials of long-term value seek fair decisions based on full consideration of authority to transfer, donate, or sell; financial arrangements and benefits; copyright; plans for processing; and conditions of access. Archivists discourage unreasonable restrictions on access or use, but may accept as a condition of acquisition clearly stated restrictions of limited duration and may occasionally suggest such restrictions to protect privacy. Archivists observe faithfully all agreements made at the time of transfer or acquisition.

Archivists establish intellectual control over their holdings by describing them in finding aids and guides to facilitate internal controls and access by users of the archives.

Archivists appraise documentary materials of long-term value with impartial judgment based on thorough knowledge of their institutions administrative requirements or acquisitions policies. They maintain and protect the arrangement of documents and information transferred to their custody to protect its authenticity. Archivists protect the integrity of documentary materials of long-term value in their custody, guarding them against defacement, alteration, theft, and physical damage, and ensure that their evidentiary value is not impaired in the archival work of arrangement, description, preservation, and use. They cooperate with other archivists and law enforcement agencies in the apprehension and prosecution of thieves.

Archivists respect the privacy of individuals who created, or are the subjects of, documentary materials of long-term value, especially those who had no voice in the disposition of the materials. They neither reveal nor profit from information gained through work with restricted holdings.

Archivists answer courteously and with a spirit of helpfulness all reasonable inquiries about their holdings, and encourage use of them to the greatest extent compatible with institutional policies, preservation of holdings, legal considerations, individual rights, donor agreements, and judicious use of archival resources. They explain pertinent restrictions to potential users, and apply them equitably.

Archivists endeavor to inform users of parallel research by others using the same materials, and, if the individuals concerned agree, supply each name to the other party.

As members of a community of scholars, archivists may engage in research, publication, and review of the writings of other scholars. If archivists use their institution's holdings for personal research and publication, such practices should be approved by their employers and made known to others using the same holdings. Archivists who buy and sell manuscripts personally should not compete for acquisitions with their own repositories, should inform their employers of their collecting activities, and should preserve complete records of personal acquisitions and sales.

Archivists avoid irresponsible criticism of other archivists or institutions and address complaints about professional or ethical conduct to the individual or institution concerned, or to a professional archival organization. Archivists share knowledge and experience with other archivists through professional associations and cooperative activities and assist the professional growth of others with less training or experience. They are obligated by professional ethics to keep informed about standards of good practice and to follow the highest level possible in the administration of their institutions and collections. They have a professional responsibility to recognize the need for cooperative efforts and support the development and dissemination of professional standards and practices.

Archivists work for the best interests of their institutions and their profession and endeavor to reconcile any conflicts by encouraging adherence to archival standards and ethics.

CODE OF ETHICS FOR ARCHIVISTS AND COMMENTARY

The code is a summary of guidelines in the principal areas of professional conduct. A longer Commentary explains the reasons for some of the statements and provides a basis for discussion of the points raised.

I. The Purpose of a Code of Ethics

The Society of American Archivists recognizes that ethical decisions are made by individuals, professionals, institutions, and societies. Some of the greatest ethical problems in modern life arise from conflicts between personal codes based on moral teachings, professional practices, regulations based on employment status, institutional policies and state and federal laws. In adopting a formal code of professional ethics for the Society, we are dealing with only one aspect of the archivist's ethical involvement.

Codes of ethics in all professions have several purposes in common, including a statement of concern with the most serious problems of professional conduct, the resolution of problems arising from conflicts of interest, and the guarantee that the special expertise of the members of a profession will be used in the public interest.

The archival profession needs a code of ethics for several reasons: (1) to inform new members of the profession of the high standards of conduct in the most sensitive areas of archival work; (2) to remind experienced archivists of their responsibilities, challenging them to maintain high standards of conduct in their own work and to promulgate those standards to others; and (3) to educate people who have some contact with archives, such as donors of material, dealers, researchers, and administrators, about the work of archivists and to encourage them to expect high standards.

A code of ethics implies moral and legal responsibilities. It presumes that archivists obey the laws and are especially familiar with the laws that affect their special areas of knowledge; it also presumes that they act in accord with sound moral principles. In addition to the moral and legal responsibilities of archivists, there are special professional concerns, and it is the purpose of a code of ethics to state those concerns and give some guidelines for archivists. The code identifies areas where there are or may be conflicts of interest, and indicates ways in which these conflicting interests may be balanced; the code urges the highest standards of professional conduct and excellence of work in every area of archives administration.

The code is compiled for archivists, individually and collectively. Institutional policies should assist archivists in their efforts to conduct themselves according to this code; indeed, institutions, with the assistance of their archivists, should deliberately adopt policies that comply with the principles of the code.

II. Introduction to the Code

Archivists select, preserve, and make available documentary materials of long-term value that have lasting value to the organization or public that the archivist serves. Archivists perform their responsibilities in accordance with statutory authorization or institutional policy. They subscribe to a code of ethics based on sound archival principles and promote institutional and professional observance of these ethical and archival standards.

Commentary: The introduction states the principal functions of archivists. Because the code speaks to people in a variety of fields—archivists, curators of manuscripts, records managers—the reader should be aware that not every statement in the code will be pertinent to every worker. Because the code intends to inform and protect non-archivists, an explanation of the basic role of archivists is necessary. The term documentary materials of long-term value is intended to cover archival records and papers without regard to the physical format in which they are recorded.

III. Collecting Policies

Archivists arrange transfers of records and acquire documentary materials of long-term value in accordance with their institutions purposes, stated policies, and resources. They do not compete for acquisitions when competition would endanger the integrity or safety of documentary materials of long-term value, or solicit the records of an institution that has an established archives. They cooperate to ensure the preservation of materials in repositories where they will be adequately processed and effectively utilized.

Commentary: Among archivists generally there seems to be agreement that one of the most difficult areas is that of policies of collection and the resultant practices. Transfers and acquisitions should be made in accordance with a written policy statement, supported by adequate resources and consistent with the mission of the archives. Because personal papers document the whole career of a person, archivists encourage donors to deposit the entire body of materials in a single archival institution. This section of the code calls for cooperation rather than wasteful competition, as an important element in the solution of this kind of problem.

Institutions are independent and there will always be room for legitimate competition. However, if a donor offers materials that are not within the scope of the collecting policies of an institution, the archivists should tell the donor of a more appropriate institution. When two or more institutions are competing for materials that are appropriate for any one of their collections, the archivists must not unjustly disparage the facilities or intentions of others. As stated later, legitimate complaints about an institution or an archivist may be made through proper channels, but giving false information to potential donors or in any way casting aspersions on other institutions or other archivists is unprofessional conduct.

It is sometimes hard to determine whether competition is wasteful. Because owners are free to offer collections to several institutions, there will be duplication of effort. This kind of competition is unavoidable. Archivists cannot always avoid the increased labor and expense of such transactions.

IV. Relations with Donors, and Restrictions

Archivists negotiating with transferring officials or owners of documentary materials of long-term value seek fair decisions based on full consideration of authority to transfer, donate, or sell; financial arrangements and benefits; copyright; plans for processing; and conditions of access. Archivists discourage unreasonable restrictions on access or use, but may accept as a condition of acquisition clearly stated restrictions of limited duration and may occasionally suggest such restrictions to protect privacy. Archivists observe faithfully all agreements made at the time of transfer or acquisition.

Commentary: Many potential donors are not familiar with archival practices and do not have even a general knowledge of copyright, provision of access, tax laws, and other factors that affect the donation and use of archival materials.

Archivists usually discourage donors from imposing conditions on gifts or restricting access to collections, but they are aware of sensitive material and do, when necessary, recommend that donors make provision for protecting the privacy and other rights of the donors themselves, their families, their correspondents, and associates.

In accordance with regulations of the Internal Revenue Service and the guidelines accepted by the Association of College and Research Libraries, archivists should not appraise, for tax purposes, donations to their own institutions. Some archivists are qualified appraisers and may appraise records given to other institutions.

It is especially important that archivists be aware of the provisions of the copyright act and that they inform potential donors of any provision pertinent to the anticipated gift.

Archivists should be aware of problems of ownership and should not accept gifts without being certain that the donors have the right to make the transfer of ownership.

Archivists realize that there are many projects, especially for editing and publication, that seem to require reservation for exclusive use. Archivists should discourage this practice. When it is not possible to avoid it entirely, archivists should try to limit such restrictions; there should be a definite expiration date, and other users should be given access to the materials as they are prepared for publication. This can be done without encouraging other publication projects that might not conform to the standards for historical editing.

V. Description

Archivists establish intellectual control over their holdings by describing them in finding aids and guides to facilitate internal controls and access by users of the archives.

Commentary: Description is a primary responsibility and the appropriate level of intellectual control should be established over all archival holdings. A general descriptive inventory should be prepared when the records are accessioned. Detailed processing can be time-consuming and should be completed according to a priority based on the significance of the material, user demand and the availability of staff time. It is not sufficient for archivists to hold and preserve materials: they also facilitate the use of their collections and make them known. Finding aids, repository guides, and reports in the appropriate publications permit and encourage users in the institution and outside researchers.

VI. Appraisal, Protection and Arrangement

Archivists appraise documentary materials of long-term value with impartial judgment based on thorough knowledge of their institution's administrative requirements or acquisitions policies. They maintain and protect the arrangement of documents and information transferred to their custody to protect its authenticity. Archivists protect the integrity of documentary materials of long-term value in their custody, guarding them against defacement, alteration, theft, and physical damage, and ensure that their evidentiary value is not impaired in the archival work of arrangement, description, preservation, and use. They cooperate with other archivists and law enforcement agencies in the apprehension and prosecution of thieves.

Commentary: Archivists obtain material for use and must insure that their collections are carefully preserved and therefore available. They are concerned not only with the physical preservation of materials but even more with the retention of the information in the collections. Excessive delay in processing materials and making them available for use would cast doubt on the wisdom of the decision of a certain institution to acquire materials, though it sometimes happens that materials are acquired with the expectation that there soon will be resources for processing them.

Some archival institutions are required by law to accept materials even when they do not have the resources to process those materials or store them properly. In such cases archivists must exercise their judgment as to the best use of scarce resources, while seeking changes in acquisitions policies or increases in support that will enable them to perform their professional duties according to accepted standards.

VII. Privacy and Restricted Information

Archivists respect the privacy of individuals who created, or are the subjects of, documentary materials of long-term value, especially those who had no voice in the disposition of the materials. They neither reveal nor profit from information gained through work with restricted holdings.

Commentary: In the ordinary course of work, archivists encounter sensitive materials and have access to restricted information. In accordance with their institution's policies, they should not reveal this restricted information, they should not give any researchers special access to it, and they should not use specifically restricted information in their own research. Subject to applicable laws and regulations, they weigh the need for openness and the need to respect privacy rights to determine whether the release of records or information from records would constitute an invasion of privacy.

VIII. Use and Restrictions

Archivists answer courteously and with a spirit of helpfulness all reasonable inquiries about their holdings, and encourage use of them to the greatest extent compatible with institutional policies, preservation of holdings, legal considerations, individual rights, donor agreements, and judicious use of archival resources. They explain pertinent restrictions to potential users, and apply them equitably.

Commentary: Archival materials should be made available for use (whether administrative or research) as soon as possible. To facilitate such use, archivists should discourage the imposition of restrictions by donors.

Once conditions of use have been established, archivists should see that all researchers are informed of the materials that are available, and are treated fairly. If some materials are reserved temporarily for use in a special project, other researchers should be informed of these special conditions.

IX. Information about Researchers

Archivists endeavor to inform users of parallel research by others using the same materials, and, if the individuals concerned agree, supply each name to the other party.

Commentary: Archivists make materials available for research because they want the information on their holdings to be known as much as possible. Information about parallel research interests may enable researchers to conduct their investigations more effectively. Such information should consist of the previous researcher's name and address and general research topic and be provided in accordance with institutional policy and applicable laws. Where there is any question, the consent of the previous researcher should be obtained. Archivists do not reveal the details of one researcher's work to others or prevent a researcher from using the same materials that others have used. Archivists are also sensitive to the needs of confidential research, such as research in support of litigation, and in such cases do not approach the user regarding parallel research.

X. Research by Archivists

As members of a community of scholars, archivists may engage in research, publication, and review of the writings of other scholars. If archivists use their institution's holdings for personal research and publication, such practices should be approved by their employers and made known to others using the same holdings. Archivists who buy and sell manuscripts personally should not compete for acquisitions with their own repositories, should inform their employers of their collecting activities, and should preserve complete records of personal acquisitions and sales.

Commentary: If archivists do research in their own institutions, there are possibilities of serious conflicts of interest—an archivist might be reluctant to show to other researchers material from which he or she hopes to write something for publication. On the other hand, the archivist might be the person best qualified to research an area represented in institutional holdings. The best way to resolve these conflicts is to clarify and publicize the role of the archivist as researcher.

At the time of their employment, or before undertaking research, archivists should have a clear understanding with their supervisors about the right to research and to publish. The fact that archivists are doing research in their institutional archives should be made known to patrons, and archivists should not reserve materials for their own use. Because it increases their familiarity with their own collections, this kind of research should make it possible for archivists to be more helpful to other researchers. Archivists are not obliged, any more than other researchers are, to reveal the details of their work or the fruits of their research. The agreement reached with the employers should include in each instance a statement as to whether the archivists may or may not receive payment for research done as part of the duties of their positions.

XI. Complaints About Other Institutions

Archivists avoid irresponsible criticism of other archivists or institutions and address complaints about professional or ethical conduct to the individual or institution concerned, or to a professional archival organization.

Commentary: Disparagement of other institutions or of other archivists seems to be a problem particularly when two or more institutions are seeking the same materials, but it can also occur in other areas of archival work. Distinctions must be made between defects due to lack of funds, and improper handling of materials resulting from unprofessional conduct.

XII. Professional Activities

Archivists share knowledge and experience with other archivists through professional associations and cooperative activities and assist the professional growth of others with less training or experience. They are obligated by professional ethics to keep informed about standards of good practice and to follow the highest level possible in the administration of their institutions and collections. They have a professional responsibility to recognize the need for cooperative efforts and support the development and dissemination of professional standards and practices.

Commentary: Archivists may choose to join or not to join local, state, regional, and national professional organizations, but they must be well-informed about changes in archival functions and they must have some contact with their colleagues. They should share their expertise by participation in professional meetings and by publishing. By such activities, in the field of archives, in related fields, and in their own special interests, they continue to grow professionally.

XIII. Conclusion

Archivists work for the best interests of their institutions and their profession and endeavor to reconcile any conflicts by encouraging adherence to archival standards and ethics.

Commentary: The code has stated the best interests of the archival profession—such as proper use of archives, exchange of information, and careful use of scarce resources. The final statement urges archivists to pursue these goals. When there are apparent conflicts between such goals and either the policies of some institutions or the practices of some archivists, all interested parties should refer to this code of ethics and the judgment of experienced archivists.

Appendix 2

BASIC ELEMENTS OF
HISTORICAL RECORDS PROGRAMS

All viable historical records programs should develop the core or essential elements that are needed to ensure that they give responsible, conscientious care to the records in their charge. This appendix describes a desirable set of basic elements. The elements are described in general terms and should be flexibly interpreted to fit a given program setting. Taken together, however, they are meant to define a framework of minimally acceptable attainment for historical records programs. *Source:* New York State Archives and Records Administration, *Basic Elements of Historical Records Programs*, Brochure (Albany: NYS Archives and Records Administration, 1989).

ADMINISTRATIVE ELEMENTS

These elements are the foundations of the program and determine its basic directions.

1. Operating Authority and Mission Statement

Every historical records program should have a law, charter, or other legal document that defines its authority, purpose, and program setting. There should also be a mission statement that describes why the program was initiated; its relationship to the parent agency's basic work and goals; what geographical area, groups, activities, developments, experiences, or other topical areas it aims to document;

what types of records or information it aims to collect; and what types of research groups or interests it exists to serve and to support. The mission statement provides the basis for the structural framework for the rest of the program.

2. Adequate, Continuing Financial Support

Every program needs a continuing source of funding in order to plan activities and operate responsibly on a continuing basis. For most historical records programs, this should mean a regular budget item that is part of the parent agency's budget. This steady, reliable source of support may be supplemented by grants and other outside funding to carry out additional program activities, beyond the essentials.

3. Secure Storage and Other Facilities

Historical records are invaluable cultural and informational resources. Collecting, maintaining, and making them available carries responsibilities to preserve and protect. Programs need secure, fireproof storage facilities. Temperature and humidity controls are essential; air conditioning is highly desirable. These atmospheric controls help extend the life of fragile paper and other records. There should also be enough room, equipment, and other facilities for staff to carry out work on the records. Also essential is a search room large enough to accommodate researchers who use the materials and providing for surveillance and other anti-theft measures.

4. Sufficient, Qualified Staff

Every program needs at least one person who, by training and experience, knows how to administer historical records in line with commonly accepted professional and archival guidelines and practices in core archival functions: appraisal, arrangement and description, preservation, reference services, and public programs. Beyond this minimal expectation, additional professional and support staff probably will be needed, depending on the size and nature of the program, to carry out the operational elements described below.

5. Planning and Balanced Program Administration

Successful historical records program administration presupposes at least a general planning process that proceeds from the mission statement and addresses, on a continuing basis, the questions of "What do we want to accomplish?" and "How can we make sure we will accomplish these things?" Planning enables those responsible for programs to establish direction and maintain control, encourages effective marshaling of staff and other resources, and helps ensure forward movement toward defined goals rather than merely reacting to everyday pressures and problems. A plan, based on program self-analysis of the type explained in the manual *Strengthening New York's Historical Records Programs*, should define overarching goals, intermediate objectives to reach them, and more discrete activities to move to the objectives. It should provide for a balance—some resource and activities devoted to each operational element of the program rather than excessive preoccupation with some elements and neglect of others.

OPERATIONAL ELEMENTS

These elements define and make up the historical records program's day-to-day operations. They encompass the actual work of dealing with historical records.

6. A Systematic Approach to Appraisal and Selection of Records

Historical records programs should have a systematic approach to selection of records that is based on three considerations. The first might be characterized as *documentation objective*. What does the program aim to document, and how does its work relate to work of other repositories or programs that seek to document the same or closely related geographical area or topical field? The second is *collection policy*. This should be consistent with both the documentation objective and the program's mission statement; it defines the sorts of records the program is most interested in retaining or collecting and generally how it will operate to accomplish this. The third is *appraisal*. This refers to the process of systematically analyzing each given set of potentially valuable records to determine which, if any, have enough continuing research value to warrant making them part of the repository's collection.

7. Appropriate Finding Aids and Provisions for Access

Historical records should be arranged and described in accordance with standard professional archival canons. In general, records should be arranged and described, at least in summary fashion, as soon as possible after they are collected in order to make them available for research. The repository should maintain a summary of its holdings and produce more detailed finding aids to assist repository personnel in working with researchers and to assist the researchers themselves in locating desired records. The MARC AMC (Machine Readable Cataloging for Archives and Manuscripts Control) format is now widely accepted as the standard approach to archival description and is used in the New York statewide historical records database and by most of New York's leading repositories. Where appropriate, descriptive information should be sent for entry into a state or national database. Repositories need to be open for research on a regular basis.

8. Preservation of the Records and/or Their Information

Every program has a basic custodial responsibility to preserve the records in its charge. This means appropriate environmental, anti-fire, and security provisions, as noted above. It means requiring careful use by researchers and provisions to prevent theft. It should also include basic conservation and handling provisions such as storage in acid-free folders and cartons. Many programs use microfilming or other reproduction methods to ensure that the information in the records is reproduced onto a medium that is longer-lasting than the original (paper) medium.

9. Promoting Use

Programs that collect, arrange, describe, and make available their records have, in effect, only done part of their jobs. The fact is that most historical records in New York are underutilized or not used at all by researchers whose information needs could be met through historical records. Historical records programs need to devote some time and resources to providing information directly to researchers on their holdings, the research potential of those holdings, and program services. This can be done through distribution of materials that describe holdings and emphasize research potential; through talks to researcher groups; through provision of material for their newsletters, journals, or other publications; and in other ways.

10. Continuing Campaign for Public Awareness

A historical records program needs one final dimension: efforts to reach out to and inform the concerned public about the importance and usefulness of the historical records the program holds and about the program itself. These efforts do not only encourage greater appreciation of historical records. In the long run, they also bring attention to the program, appreciation of its work, and indirectly, greater support for that work.

Appendix 3

SAMPLE SELF-ASSESSMENT GUIDE FOR HISTORICAL RECORDS PROGRAMS

Please note: This *Guide* was produced for historical records programs in Georgia. Please do not contact the Georgia grants project staff noted on pp. 182–83 or fill out the form on page 183.

Source: The Georgia Historical Records Advisory Board, *A Self-Assessment Guide for Historical Repositories* (The Georgia Historical Records Advisory Board, 1999).

CONTENTS

Element 9: Facilities
Element 10: Trained Staff
Element 11: Disaster Preparedness Plan
Element 12: Arrangement
Element 13: Description
Element 14: Access Policy
Element 15: Reference Service
Element 16: Duplication and Reformatting of Historical Records
Element 17: Cooperative Programs
Element 18: Outreach
Element 19: Advocacy
Element 20: Consultants
Summary
Collection Survey

ACKNOWLEDGMENTS

In December 1997, National Historical Publications and Records Commission (NHPRC) awarded the Georgia Historical Records Advisory Board (GHRAB) a one-year planning grant to identify the minimum qualifications for an active, effective historical records program; to generate self-assessment tools for repositories; to prepare to provide group training and individualized coaching focused on bringing historical organizations up to a minimum level; and to lay the foundation for a regrant project which the Commission also funded.

The Board assembled a planning committee of professional archivists to help identify preferred practices for Georgia's historical repositories, develop a self-assessment form and resource manual, and advise the Board on a proposed grant program for historical organizations. Planning Committee members included:

Brenda Banks, Georgia Department of Archives & History
Virginia Cain, Emory University
Steve Engerrand, Georgia Department of Archives & History
Susan Potts McDonald, Emory University
Kaye Minchew, Troup County Archives
Alice Taylor-Colbert, Shorter College Museum & Archives
Frank Wheeler, Georgia Historical Society
Julia Marks Young, Georgia State University

The resulting self-assessment, *Saving Georgia's Documentary Heritage*, is based on existing archival guidelines, such as those reflected in the Society of

American Archivists' *Evaluation of Archival Institutions: Services, Principles, and Guide to Self Study* (1982). The format and some content were derived from *Strengthening New York's Historical Records Programs: a Self-Study Guide* (1988), developed by the New York State Archives and Records Administration. Additional resources included *Care of Historical Records* by the Society of Georgia Archivists and Georgia Historical Society (1996) and the Archival Fundamentals Series by the Society of American Archivists.

Our thanks to all of our colleagues for their contributions to this project.

Anne Smith
Project Coordinator
October 1, 1998

INTRODUCTION

Purpose of the Self-Assessment Form

This self-assessment form is designed to assist all governing boards, directors, and staff members (paid and volunteer) in strengthening their organization and its work in preserving Georgia's documentary heritage.

The Georgia Historical Records Advisory Board (GHRAB) is aware of the importance of historical records to individuals and society and the need for able stewards to care for these records. GHRAB also recognizes that all organizations can benefit from additional planning, training, and funding. To encourage these beneficial activities, the Board developed this form and an information resources manual. The Board will also support training opportunities and offer grant funds for historical repositories over a two-year period, October 1, 1998, to September 30, 2000.

Completing the self-assessment form will allow your staff, volunteers, and governing board to identify your organization's areas of strength and areas that need additional attention and development. With this knowledge, your repository can establish reasonable goals for improvement and develop short term and long range plans.

Identification of needs is the first step in seeking assistance in the form of training or funding. In addition to using this information to apply for a GHRAB grant, you will find the results will support in-house planning and applications to other funding sources.

Definitions

For purposes of this self-assessment form, the term "repository" is used to mean a library, historical society, archives, or similar organization. It is any organization that houses and cares for historical records. "Archival program" is used to refer to the work of your organization—preserving and providing access to historical materials.

How to Use This Form

Each element of preferred practice is defined, and reasons for its importance are stated. Please read carefully and answer each question as appropriate, i.e. yes, no, not applicable (N/A) or, if you don't know the answer, check D/K.

Please answer each question to the best of your knowledge. *Do not worry if the answer is "no" or "don't know." These answers will not prevent your organization from obtaining a GHRAB grant!*

After you have answered the questions for each element of preferred practice, complete the summary sheet at the end of the booklet. This summary will allow you to identify areas that need improvement and to establish priorities. You will also find a collection survey form to help you establish the size of your collection.

If your assessment indicates a need for training, you may wish to take advantage of workshops offered by the Society of Georgia Archivists, the Georgia Historical Society, the Georgia Department of Archives and History and GHRAB. If your organization would benefit from grant funds for a specific project, you may wish to develop a grant proposal. We hope this self-assessment will be a helpful tool for all Georgia organizations with responsibility for historical records.

The Grant Staff are happy to assist you in all activities related to this project. Please contact us for help with completing your self-assessment form, applying for a grant, or obtaining information about educational offerings. If you have any questions or would like assistance, please contact:

Anne P. Smith
Historical Repositories Grant Project Coordinator
Georgia Historical Records Advisory Board
c/o Georgia Department of Archives & History
330 Capitol Avenue, SE
Atlanta, GA 30334
404 657-4530
404 657-8427 fax
asmith@sos.state.ga.us

or

Jill Swiecichowski
Historical Repositories Grant Project Archivist
Georgia Historical Records Advisory Board
Georgia Department of Archives & History
330 Capitol Avenue, SE
Atlanta, GA 30334
404 651-6794
404 657-8427 fax
jill@sos.state.ga.us

REPOSITORY INFORMATION

REPOSITORY NAME: _____

ADDRESS: _____
_____
_____

TELEPHONE: _____
FAX: _____
E-MAIL: _____

ASSESSMENT PARTICIPANTS (name & title):

_____

_____

_____

_____

_____

CONTACT PERSON:

_____
         Name   Title

DATE ASSESSMENT COMPLETED: _____

ELEMENT I: LEGAL AUTHORITY

What is legal authority?

Legal authority is written authorization for the repository to collect, preserve, and make available historical records. This authorization may take many forms including articles of incorporation, enabling legislation, city or county ordinances, or a statement of authorization from a parent organization such as a college or university.

By-laws, constitutions, or institutional policies may supplement a repository's legal authority. The organization may be governed or directed by a government official, board of trustees, or university president or provost.

Why is legal authority important?

- It provides the legal basis for the repository's operation.
- It makes it possible for the organization to participate in fund-raising and related activities.
- It inspires donor confidence.
- It implies a long-term commitment on the part of an organization.

Self-Assessment Questions

	YES	NO	N/A	D/K
1. Does your repository have a written statement that authorizes its establishment and continued existence? *(If no, proceed to the next element)*	—	—	—	—
2. In the case of a parent organization, does the statement of authority clearly outline the repository's relationship to the parent organization and the repository's placement in the organizational structure?	—	—	—	—
3. Do you have written documentation (bylaws, policies and procedures, etc.) that clearly states the position(s) with authority to make commitments on behalf of the repository?	—	—	—	—
4. Is your organization in compliance with local, state, and federal regulations regarding its operation and fund-raising?	—	—	—	—

ELEMENT 2: FINANCIAL RECORDS

What is an adequate financial record-keeping system?

An "adequate financial record-keeping system" is one that allows the repository to accurately track income and expenditures, prepare budgets and reports on the repository's finances. "Adequate finances" implies resources sufficient to ensure at least the basic arrangement, description, and physical preservation of and access to the repository's historical records. It is important to keep track of the repository's financial status in order to ensure that resources are available and used appropriately. Provisions should be made for an annual audit or review of the financial records. Designation of an individual(s) authorized to sign checks, accept gifts, and enter into contracts is essential.

Why is a financial record-keeping system important?

- A careful accounting of finances enables a repository to set priorities and plan its activities, including acquisitions, preservation activities, processing, and public programming.
- Grant funding, often administered by state and federal agencies, is awarded to financially stable organizations with reliable record-keeping systems.
- Usually repositories rely upon a number of sources for operating funds. Public taxes, grants, membership fees, donations, sales, rentals and money-raising events may contribute to the operating budget. It is essential that a proper record-keeping system exist to cope efficiently with these sources of income and to ensure compliance with state and federal laws.

Self-Assessment Questions

	YES	NO	N/A	D/K
1. Does your repository have its own budget?	—	—	—	—
2. Does your repository have specific funds allocated for its operation? *(If no, proceed to the next element)*	—	—	—	—
3. Is your repository able to prepare financial reports on a regular basis?	—	—	—	—
4. Are the financial records of the repository audited or examined as appropriate by an independent firm on a regular basis?	—	—	—	—

	YES	NO	N/A	D/K
5. Is there a clear distinction between basic, ongoing responsibilities that need to be supported by the repository's regular operating budget and special projects that might be appropriate for outside funding?	—	—	—	—
6. Does your repository have a budget for capital expenditures in addition to regular operating expenses?	—	—	—	—

ELEMENT 3: MISSION STATEMENT

What is a mission statement?

A mission statement is a definition of the repository – what the repository is and what it does. It should be a brief statement, usually no more than a paragraph in length, which explains:

- why the repository exists. (What are its aims and objectives?)
- what the repository collects—what groups, activities, or experiences the repository documents.
- what groups or interests the repository serves.

Why is it important?

- A mission statement explains the repository's reason for collecting, holding, or even deaccessioning certain types of records.
- It is a clear and unambiguous statement that serves as a guide for planning, setting goals and objectives.
- It clarifies the repository's role to present and future members of the governing board, staff, volunteers, funding agencies, and the general public.

Self-Assessment Questions

	YES	NO	N/A	D/K
1. Does your archival repository have a written mission statement? *(If yes, proceed to question 4)*	—	—	—	—
2. Does your parent organization have a written mission statement? *(If no, proceed to the next element).*	—	—	—	—

	YES	NO	N/A	D/K
3. Is the parent organization's mission statement detailed enough to direct the work of the archival repository?	—	—	—	—
4. Has your mission statement been reviewed within the past 5 years by the repository's governing body?	—	—	—	—
5. Have changes occurred which suggest that your current mission statement may need to be revised?	—	—	—	—
6. Does your mission statement clearly reflect the repository's current functions and collecting focus?	—	—	—	—
7. Is your mission statement realistic in terms of the physical and financial capacity of the repository?	—	—	—	—

ELEMENT 4: ACQUISITION/COLLECTION DEVELOPMENT POLICY

What is an acquisition or collection development policy?

A written acquisition policy is a formal statement that guides the repository's selection of materials to be added to its collections. The resources of any repository are limited, and the repository cannot collect all materials. Only materials that are relevant and valuable to the mission of the repository should be acquired, and a written policy is essential in achieving this goal. The policy also provides a basis for cooperation with other repositories thus avoiding duplication of efforts.

Why do you need a written acquisition policy?

- It helps the repository manage its resources more productively by adhering to its mission.
- It allows the repository to focus on those materials it is committed to preserving and prevents acquiring materials it has no need for, no room for, and no staff time/ funds to process and maintain.
- It provides a clear definition of desired materials thus encouraging donations.
- It provides a firm reason not to accept inappropriate materials offered by donors and reserves space for additional appropriate collections.

Self-Assessment Questions

	YES	NO	N/A	D/K
1. Does your repository have a written acquisition policy? (If no, proceed to the next element)	—	—	—	—
2. Has the policy been reviewed in the last 5 years?	—	—	—	—
3. Is the policy consistent with the mission of the repository?	—	—	—	—
4. Is the policy realistic in terms of the repository's ability to care for the materials it acquires?	—	—	—	—
5. Does the policy contain statements regarding:				
• its purpose?	—	—	—	—
• the types of activities supported by the collection? (research exhibits, outreach, publications, etc.)?	—	—	—	—
• the clientele served by the collection (scholars, students, genealogists, etc.)?	—	—	—	—
• the priorities of the collection (i.e. strengths and weaknesses, geographic and subject areas collected)?	—	—	—	—
• the limitations of the collection (what you do not collect)?	—	—	—	—
• cooperative agreements with other archival repositories regarding collecting?	—	—	—	—
• resource sharing?	—	—	—	—
• your deaccessioning policy?	—	—	—	—
• procedures for monitoring the progress and reviewing the policy?	—	—	—	—
6. Is the policy known and understood by staff (paid and volunteer)?	—	—	—	—
7. Is the policy known and understood by:				
• the repository's membership?	—	—	—	—
• the repository's governing body?	—	—	—	—
• the general public?	—	—	—	—

ELEMENT 5: DEED OF GIFT

What is a deed of gift?

A deed of gift is a legal instrument that documents the formal act of donation of material to a repository. Specifically, it transfers the legal title of ownership of an item(s) from the donor to the repository. This title transfer should include both the physical and intellectual property rights.

Why is a deed of gift important?

- It secures the legal title of physical and intellectual property rights.
- It informs the repository of any legality regarding the administration or use of donated materials.
- It protects the repository and its staff from legal problems that may arise regarding ownership and rights to historical records, including access, publication, and possible deaccession.

Self-Assessment Questions

	YES	NO	N/A	D/K
1. Does your repository currently use a deed of gift form? *(If no, proceed to the next element)*	—	—	—	—
2. Has this form been reviewed within the past five years?	—	—	—	—
3. Has this form been reviewed by legal counsel?	—	—	—	—
4. Does the form contain:				
• donor's name, address, and signature?	—	—	—	—
• repository's name, address, and representative's signature?	—	—	—	—
• date of the transfer of title?	—	—	—	—
• description of the material transferred by the deed?	—	—	—	—
• designation of copyright ownership?	—	—	—	—
• any restrictions regarding use and names of those who can impose/lift such restrictions?	—	—	—	—
• names of those authorized to dispose of unwanted materials?	—	—	—	—

ELEMENT 6: DEPOSIT AGREEMENT

What is a deposit agreement?

A deposit agreement is a legal document that places material in the custody of a repository without transferring the legal title to the materials. There are many reasons to accept or not to accept deposits and a policy should be established after careful review of all these reasons. If the repository does accept material deposited for safekeeping, a written agreement should document the status of the materials. (Note: Deposit agreements are used for materials that are placed within a repository for safekeeping and access. Loans of materials for exhibit purposes are discussed under Cooperative Programs.)

Why is a deposit agreement important?

- It informs the repository of any legality regarding the administration or use of donated materials.
- It protects the repository and its staff from legal problems which may arise regarding ownership and rights to historical records, including care, access, publication, and use.
- It provides a basis for recovering costs associated with caring for the collection.

Self-Assessment Questions

	YES	NO	N/A	D/K
1. Does your repository accept deposits? *(If no, proceed to the next element.)*	—	—	—	—
2. Does your repository currently use a deposit agreement form? *(If no, proceed to the next element)*	—	—	—	—
3. Has this form been reviewed within the past 5 years?	—	—	—	—
4. Has this form been reviewed by legal counsel?	—	—	—	—
5. Does the form contain:				
• the depositor's name, address, and signature?	—	—	—	—
• repository's name, address, and representative's signature?	—	—	—	—
• the date of the deposit and the time span for deposit?	—	—	—	—
• a description of the material deposited?	—	—	—	—

	YES	NO	N/A	D/K
• a description of any restrictions regarding use?	—	—	—	—
• description of repository's responsibility for processing?	—	—	—	—
• a statement regarding the repository's responsibility in case of loss or damage?	—	—	—	—
• the name(s) of depositor's representative(s) with authority to make decisions regarding its disposition?	—	—	—	—
• a procedure for withdrawal of materials by the depositor?	—	—	—	—
• a procedure for return of materials by the repository?	—	—	—	—
6. Are any costs to the depositor clearly identified?	—	—	—	—

ELEMENT 7: ARCHIVAL APPRAISAL

What is archival appraisal?

Appraisal is the technique of analyzing the historical, legal, administrative, fiscal, and intrinsic value of records and deciding whether to retain and preserve them. (This is different from a monetary appraisal for tax purposes, which must be carried out by a qualified individual other than the archivist or the donor.) Archivists generally weigh the value of records by evaluating the possible present and future uses of the information found in the records. Appraisals should be consistent with the repository's acquisitions policy. Appraisals should also take into account the current condition of the materials and the availability of expertise and funding to address any preservation problems.

Why is archival appraisal important?

Archival storage space and processing are costly. Using good appraisal techniques allows the repository to save the most important records. Records of limited value should not be permanently retained in an archive.

Self-Assessment Questions

	YES	NO	N/A	D/K
1. Does your repository have a written set of appraisal guidelines? (*If no, proceed to question 4*)	—	—	—	—

	YES	NO	N/A	D/K

2. Are your appraisal guidelines based on generally accepted records appraisal guidelines?   ___   ___   ___   ___

3. Are your appraisal guidelines consistent with your acquisition/collection development policy?   ___   ___   ___   ___

4. Does your repository have a staff person with experience in archival appraisal?   ___   ___   ___   ___

5. Does your repository ever use outside appraisal consultants to evaluate questionable materials?   ___   ___   ___   ___

6. When materials are appraised as not appropriate for your repository, do you refer the materials to other repositories that may collect in that area?   ___   ___   ___   ___

ELEMENT 8: ACCESSION RECORDS

What are accession records?

Accession records are documents that record information about each new acquisition. These records are the basic documents for all subsequent control. The records usually consist of an accession register, which records the accession in chronological order and assigns the accession number, and accession forms, which record basic information about the materials. The accession number is a unique number that permanently identifies the materials.

Self-Assessment Questions

	YES	NO	N/A	D/K

1. Does the repository have written accession procedures for historical records deposits, donations, and purchases?   ___   ___   ___   ___

2. Does the repository maintain an accession register or log?   ___   ___   ___   ___

3. Does the repository use accession forms? (*If no, proceed to question 5*)   ___   ___   ___   ___

	YES	NO	N/A	D/K

4. Are the accession forms adequate to record
   the following:
   - accession number?
   - date received?
   - statement of provenance (origin)?
   - description of material?
   - date range of material?
   - quantity/size of collection?
   - condition of material?
   - location within repository?
   - notation of any restrictions?
   - status of accession, i.e. gift, deposit,
     purchase, etc.?
   - donor/depositor information?
   - copyright owner?
   - relationship to previously accessioned
     materials?
5. Is a record of accessions maintained on a
   permanent basis?

ELEMENT 9: FACILITIES

What are adequate facilities?

Adequate facilities are those which provide a clean, stable, and secure physical environment. Records exposed to high levels of heat, relative humidity, light, and dirt degrade more quickly than records stored in conditions that are cool, dry, dark, and clean. A clean environment and controlling temperature, relative humidity and light can dramatically increase the longevity of records. Good air circulation is important to help prevent mold.

Appropriate environmental conditions are important for all areas but are especially critical for the storage areas. Ideally, reference service will be provided in an area separate from the storage area. Storage areas should be secured to prevent access by unauthorized personnel. Fire and security protection with 24-hour monitoring is recommended for the facility.

Why are adequate facilities important?

- Unsuitable environmental conditions are a primary cause of damage to records.

- Suitable storage conditions slow deterioration and help prevent damage to records.
- Proper facilities instill donors with confidence that their gifts will receive appropriate care.
- Adequate facilities allow the repository to satisfy its mission to preserve historical records.

Self-Assessment Questions

	YES	NO	N/A	D/K
1. Does your repository possess temperature and relative humidity controls that enable it to maintain overall adequate environmental conditions (i.e. consistent temperature 68°F +/- 2°F and relative humidity 40% +/- 5%)?	—	—	—	—
2. Are these conditions monitored on a regularly scheduled basis?	—	—	—	—
3. Is there a regular schedule for pest inspection and control?	—	—	—	—
4. Is there a regular cleaning schedule for record storage areas?	—	—	—	—
5. Are storage areas protected from daylight and other sources of light?	—	—	—	—
6. Are materials permanently stored in containers (boxes, folders) made of chemically stable materials?	—	—	—	—
7. Are records stored away from overhead pipes and air conditioning units?	—	—	—	—
8. Are records stored at least four inches off the floor?	—	—	—	—
9. Are all storage areas equipped with smoke and/or heat detectors?	—	—	—	—
10. Is the fire alarm system monitored by a security firm/central office on a 24 hour basis?	—	—	—	—
11. Is there a fire suppression system?	—	—	—	—
12. Is access to storage areas limited to staff only?	—	—	—	—
13. Is the repository equipped with a security system that is monitored on a 24-hour basis?	—	—	—	—

	YES	NO	N/A	D/K
14. Is your facility insured?	—	—	—	—
15. Is the collection insured?	—	—	—	—

ELEMENT 10: TRAINED STAFF

What is a trained staff?

A trained staff includes at least one person who possesses, through training and experience, professional competence in basic archival principles and procedures. Although this is normally a paid employee, it may also be a volunteer. This person should guide the repository's functions of appraisal, arrangement and description, preservation, and reference service. The repository should also have sufficient staff to supply services appropriate for its holdings and the needs of its researchers.

Why is a trained staff important?

- Awareness and implementation of appropriate practices and procedures enhance the care of historical records.
- A qualified archivist can provide basic training for volunteers and others.
- Professional staffing improves the repository's credibility and image in the community.
- Trained staff improve funding opportunities since many grant awards require that a repository have at least one professional staff member.

Self-Assessment Questions

	YES	NO	N/A	D/K
1. Does your repository employ, or have as a volunteer, an archivist with professional training and experience?	—	—	—	—
2. If your repository does not have a qualified archivist, is it making plans to hire an archivist or recruit a qualified volunteer?	—	—	—	—
3. Does your repository utilize volunteer workers?	—	—	—	—
4. Are there enough experienced staff members to train and supervise volunteers?	—	—	—	—
5. Does your repository have a planned training program for volunteers?	—	—	—	—

	YES	NO	N/A	D/K

6. Are staff members familiar with the archival
   code of ethics endorsed by the Society of
   American Archivists?

7. Are staff members able to attend
   conferences, workshops, and other training
   opportunities?

ELEMENT 11: DISASTER PREPAREDNESS PLAN

What is a disaster preparedness plan?

A disaster preparedness plan is a written document, kept current, that helps a repository protect its holdings in case of natural or man-made disasters. Disasters range from a fire or flood to a leaking water pipe. The plan describes procedures, responsibilities, and appropriate responses for specific problems. It also identifies individuals, supplies, and resources available in case of emergency.

Why is a disaster preparedness plan important?

- A plan helps the repository identify potential hazards that can be corrected and prevent or minimize damage from natural disasters that cannot be avoided.
- It enables the repository to respond quickly and appropriately to emergency situations.
- Planning increases awareness by staff, volunteers, and governing board members of good maintenance practices that may prevent disasters.
- Coordinating planning with fire and police departments helps insure appropriate responses to the special concerns of a historical repository.

Self-Assessment Questions

	YES	NO	N/A	D/K

1. Does your repository have a written disaster
   plan?
   (*If no, proceed to the next element*)

2. Is your plan up-to-date and reviewed on a
   regular basis?

3. Are staff members required to read and be
   familiar with your disaster plan?

	YES	NO	N/A	D/K
4. Have all staff members been trained in emergency procedures such as the use of fire extinguishers, first aid, etc.?	—	—	—	—
5. Are copies of your plan maintained off-site and readily available in case of emergencies?	—	—	—	—
6. Are your volunteers and governing board members familiar with your plan?	—	—	—	—
7. Are your local police and fire departments aware of your particular needs in case of emergency?	—	—	—	—
8. Does your plan include a list of what to save first?	—	—	—	—
9. Are emergency supplies available in-house as identified in your plan?	—	—	—	—

ELEMENT 12: ARRANGEMENT

What is arrangement?

Arrangement is the process of putting materials into order following accepted archival principles, particularly those of provenance and original order. The principle of provenance deems that records of different creators or donors should not be intermingled. The "creator" is an organization or individual who created, accumulated, and/or maintained and used the records in the conduct of business or personal life. Records are best understood when the original order of the materials is maintained.

The process of arrangement usually includes identifying, foldering, organizing, boxing, and shelving the materials. The primary intent is to achieve physical control over your holdings. There are five basic levels of arrangement—repository, record group/collection, series (subseries), file unit (folder, volume, reel, etc.), and item.

Why is arrangement important?

- Maintaining original order provides valuable information on how and why the records were originally created.
- It provides staff and users with a way to locate materials within the collection or record group.
- It ensures that information needed for the preparation of collection descriptions is available.

Self-Assessment Questions

	YES	NO	N/A	D/K

1. Does your repository have a written procedure for arranging materials?
2. Does your repository take into consideration the principles of provenance and original order when arranging its materials?
3. When transferring materials to your repository, do you try to maintain their original order?
4. When processing, if the original order has been lost and you must reconstruct it or impose a new order, do you document that you have tried to reconstruct it, or simply that it was lost?
5. If nontextual or oversized records must be removed from the collection, do you make note of where they can be found?

ELEMENT 13: DESCRIPTION

What is description?

Description is the process of analyzing and recording information about the materials. A collection description includes a biographical sketch or a history of the organization that created the records, information about their contents, physical characteristics, the reason they were created, relationship to other records, and ways in which they can be found and used. The description provides the basic level of access for potential users.

Why is description important?

- It provides a researcher with an indication of what types of documents and subjects are contained in a collection, thus saving time and unnecessary handling of materials.
- It gives a sense of how the materials can best be used.
- It supplies a history of the materials.

Self-Assessment Questions

	YES	NO	N/A	D/K

1. Does your repository create collection descriptions to aid researchers?

	YES	NO	N/A	D/K

2. Do your descriptions follow a consistent format for describing the records? ___ ___ ___ ___

3. Do your descriptions contain the following information:
   - creator? ___ ___ ___ ___
   - title statement? ___ ___ ___ ___
   - date span? ___ ___ ___ ___
   - physical description/volume? ___ ___ ___ ___
   - historical or biographical note? ___ ___ ___ ___
   - scope and content note? ___ ___ ___ ___
   - restrictions? ___ ___ ___ ___

4. Are the elements in your descriptions consistent with the descriptive elements found in the MARC format? ___ ___ ___ ___

5. Have any of your descriptions been entered into an in-house OPAC (online public access catalog)? ___ ___ ___ ___

6. Does your repository post collection information on a web site? ___ ___ ___ ___

7. Are any descriptions of your records available in a national bibliographic utility such as the Research Libraries Information Network (RLIN) or the Online Computer Library Center (OCLC)? ___ ___ ___ ___

ELEMENT 14: ACCESS POLICY

What is an access policy?

An access policy is a written statement that describes the repository's rules and procedures for providing public access to its collections. The policy should take into consideration the type of records that are contained in the repository, the mission of the repository, and the desires/needs of its users. Records should be made available to all users on an equal basis. Staff and researchers should carefully observe any restrictions on access.

Why is an access policy important?

- It protects the rights and privacy of record creators and the sensitivity/confidentiality of records.

- It helps repository staff communicate and enforce restrictions on access to researchers.
- It can help provide security for records that may be fragile, highly sensitive, or extremely valuable.
- It reassures donors/creators that their materials will be properly protected and used in the repository.

Self-Assessment Questions

	YES	NO	N/A	D/K
1. Does your repository have a written policy on collection access?	___	___	___	___
(*If no, proceed to the next element*)				
2. Does the policy state who may use the facility?	___	___	___	___
3. Has your repository taken steps to ensure compliance with the Americans with Disabilities Act?	___	___	___	___
4. Have the records on restrictions to collections been well maintained?	___	___	___	___
5. Are restrictions on access to collections reviewed on a regular basis to determine if they are still necessary?	___	___	___	___
6. Does the staff consistently and equitably enforce restrictions on collection access?	___	___	___	___
7. Is the copyright law posted for users to see?	___	___	___	___

ELEMENT 15: REFERENCE SERVICE

What is reference service?

Reference service is providing information to users about the repository's records, making materials available for research, and providing copies of records when appropriate. When performed by trained staff with knowledge of the organization's collections and effective research techniques, this service makes research materials more accessible to the public.

Why is reference service important?

- It makes research materials more accessible to the public.
- It helps the staff monitor the condition of materials.
- Good service enhances the organization's public image and reinforces the repository's goals of preserving and providing access to historical information.

- Skilled reference service combined with detailed descriptions protects materials from unnecessary or inappropriate use.

Self-Assessment Questions

	YES	NO	N/A	D/K
1. Does your repository have regularly scheduled reference hours?	—	—	—	—
2. Are your reference hours posted?	—	—	—	—
3. Are researchers made aware of any fees associated with using your records or duplicating materials?	—	—	—	—
4. Is a trained staff member available for regular consultation during reference hours?	—	—	—	—
5. Do you ask researchers to register and/or complete a research application?	—	—	—	—
6. Does your repository maintain forms which track what materials are used by researchers?	—	—	—	—
7. Does your repository have written procedures regarding the handling of its materials?	—	—	—	—
8. Are researchers made aware of procedures for requesting and using materials?	—	—	—	—
9. For service and security purposes, is a staff member always present when records are being used?	—	—	—	—
10. Are collection descriptions easily accessible to researchers?	—	—	—	—
11. Does your repository answer written requests for information?	—	—	—	—
12. Does your repository answer telephone requests for information?	—	—	—	—
13. Does your repository answer e-mail requests for information?	—	—	—	—
14. Are statistics on reference use kept?	—	—	—	—
15. Are users able to have materials photocopied?	—	—	—	—
16. Are users allowed to photocopy materials for themselves?	—	—	—	—
17. Do you have methods of reproducing photographs?	—	—	—	—
18. Do you have forms for reproduction requests?	—	—	—	—

	YES	NO	N/A	D/K
19. Does your repository reserve the right to refuse to copy material when there are risks to the material?	—	—	—	—
20. Do you have a policy on publication of materials from your collections?	—	—	—	—
21. Is the federal copyright law posted and strictly observed?	—	—	—	—

ELEMENT 16: DUPLICATION AND REFORMATTING OF HISTORICAL RECORDS

What are duplication and reformatting?

Duplication and reformatting refer to the reproduction of information in another format or medium. Sometimes, the preservation of the information in historical records is more important than preserving the documents themselves. Duplication or reformatting of materials may be considered in circumstances such as poor physical condition of records, or the desire to provide access to documents at other repositories.

Microfilming materials or photocopying records onto alkaline paper are two common techniques for preservation and access. Digitizing records is an option for increasing access but not for preservation.

Why is the duplication and reformatting of historical records important?

Duplication or reformatting may be used to:

- protect material by reducing wear and tear on original.
- increase the availability of archival records through sale and/or loan.
- protect information from disasters by storing the original or a copy in an off-site location.
- save space in some instances such as microfilm versus maintaining original newspapers.

Self-Assessment Questions

	YES	NO	N/A	D/K
1. Does your repository currently photocopy materials for preservation purposes?	—	—	—	—
2. Has your repository staff compiled a list of materials that are candidates for duplication or reformatting?	—	—	—	—

	YES	NO	N/A	D/K
3. Does your repository own a microfilm reader?	—	—	—	—
4. Does your repository own a microfilm reader-printer?	—	—	—	—
5. Has your repository had any of its materials microfilmed? *(If no, proceed to question 8)*	—	—	—	—
6. Did your vendor adhere to national standards for preservation microfilming?	—	—	—	—
7. Has your repository invested in duplicate copies of microfilm so the original (security) copy can be stored at an off-site location in case of disaster?	—	—	—	—
8. Has your repository digitized materials for access?	—	—	—	—
9. Does your repository have the equipment and staff needed to provide access to digitized materials?	—	—	—	—

ELEMENT 17: COOPERATIVE PROGRAMS

What are cooperative programs?

Cooperative programs involve two or more repositories working together to increase or improve their services. Cooperative programs could include loans of materials, exchanging or temporarily sharing staff for special projects, developing multi-repository disaster-preparedness plans, jointly purchasing supplies or equipment, joint applications for grant projects or consultants, sharing a facility, or working together in advocacy and public outreach efforts. Mission statements and acquisition policies that minimize competition enhance cooperative programs.

Why are cooperative programs important?

- Combining resources with another repository frequently helps both organizations meet their goals.
- Joint efforts may provide access to additional staffing, physical, or financial resources.
- Working with another repository may provide access to experience or expertise not available within the repository.

Self-Assessment Questions

	YES	NO	N/A	D/K
1. Does your mission statement and collection policy encourage cooperation with other repositories?	—	—	—	—
2. Has your repository participated in a cooperative program?	—	—	—	—
3. Has your repository considered cooperating with another institution with similar holdings to create descriptions and access to the materials?	—	—	—	—
4. Does your repository loan materials to other organizations? (*If no, proceed to the next element.*)	—	—	—	—
5. Does your repository have a written policy on loans?	—	—	—	—
6. Has your loan policy been reviewed within the past five years?	—	—	—	—
7. Does your repository use a loan form that clearly describes the materials, loan period, and responsibilities of both organizations?	—	—	—	—
8. Are materials adequately insured and protected by the borrowing institution?	—	—	—	—
9. Does your repository keep adequate records of loans and review these records on a regular basis?	—	—	—	—

ELEMENT 18: OUTREACH

What is outreach?

Outreach is the provision of services or programs that promote awareness of the nature and importance of preserving our documentary heritage. Outreach can take many forms including reference service; exhibits focusing on archival collections; written reports, brochures, newsletters, etc.; repository guides; on-line public access catalogs or bibliographic networks; workshops, lectures, field trips, or repository orientations for key groups such as students, genealogists, scholars, etc.; donor contacts and web sites.

Why is outreach important?

- It raises public awareness and promotes understanding of the importance of historical records and historical records programs.
- It helps build a strong local base of support for the archival program.
- It encourages increased use of the repository and its collections.
- It aids in identifying new sources of archival records.
- It enhances the repository's image.

Self-Assessment Questions

	YES	NO	N/A	D/K
1. Does your repository offer any public programs such as workshops, lectures, etc.?	—	—	—	—
2. Do you have exhibits focusing on your archival materials?	—	—	—	—
3. Is your repository open to the public on a regular schedule?	—	—	—	—
4. Does your repository publish brochures?	—	—	—	—
5. Does your repository publish a newsletter?	—	—	—	—
6. Are published repository guides available to the public?	—	—	—	—
7. Is your repository's catalog available through an on-line public access catalog or a bibliographic network?	—	—	—	—
8. Does your repository have a web site?	—	—	—	—
9. Does your repository target key groups of researchers?	—	—	—	—
10. Does your administrative staff contact potential donors of materials?	—	—	—	—

ELEMENT 19: ADVOCACY

What is advocacy?

Another form of outreach, advocacy refers to the efforts made by a repository's governing board or administrative staff to secure financial and other support for their programs. Advocacy efforts might include letter writing campaigns, personal contacts, public meeting, or special publications. These efforts may be directed towards the general public; local, state, and federal governing bodies; or funding agencies.

Why are advocacy efforts so important?

- They increase public support for historical records programs.
- They educate the public on archival issues.
- They help the public and resource allocators understand why historical records are important.
- They increase financial support.
- They promote cooperation between repositories and allied groups.

Self Assessment Questions

	YES	NO	N/A	D/K
1. Does your repository participate in advocacy campaigns in support of historical records issues?	—	—	—	—
2. Has your repository cooperated with other organizations in support of historical records issues?	—	—	—	—
3. Have you joined or are you familiar with state or national associations and organizations which campaign on the behalf of archival issues?	—	—	—	—
4. Does your repository have an ally in the community with effective advocacy influence?	—	—	—	—

ELEMENT 20: CONSULTANTS

What is a consultant?

An archival consultant is an individual with specialized training and experience in the theoretical and practical aspects of archival work. Archival consultants can be very helpful in providing guidance and specific services for your repository.

For smaller organizations with limited staff, a consultant can be hired to provide services such as arranging and describing records, training volunteers, helping establish professional standards, developing policies and procedures, or evaluating the facility. The consultant may provide advice and assistance in developing a plan of action to address identified needs. Consultants may also be hired to discuss the feasibility of starting an archive within an established organization.

Why are archival consultants important?

- They can provide professional expertise to a repository with limited, untrained, or volunteer staff.
- They can help steer a repository on the right path by helping develop a coherent plan of action.
- They can serve as a long-term source of current information (particularly with regard to technology) when an ongoing relationship is established.
- They can save personnel costs by providing skills that are only required for a brief period.

Self-Assessment Questions

	YES	NO	N/A	D/K
1. Do you know how to locate a qualified archival consultant?	—	—	—	—
2. Has your repository ever hired an archival consultant? *(If no, proceed to the summary)*	—	—	—	—
3. Did your repository check your consultant's references?	—	—	—	—
4. Was there a written contract that clearly stated the repository's expectations of the consultant?	—	—	—	—
5. Was a follow-up visit provided or ongoing relationship established with the consultant?	—	—	—	—
6. Did the consultant provide a final written report?	—	—	—	—

SUMMARY

For each element, review your responses and determine if you are generally satisfied with your repository's current status or if this is an area that needs improvement and check the appropriate box. If this is an area that needs to be addressed as soon as possible, check the priority box. After completing the summary, list your priority elements in the appropriate order at the bottom of the form.

# ELEMENTS	ACCEPTABLE	NEEDS IMPROVEMENT	PRIORITY
1. Legal Authority			
2. Financial Records			
3. Mission Statement			
4. Acquisition/Collection			
5. Deed of Gift			
6. Deposit Agreement			
7. Appraisal			
8. Accession Records			
9. Storage Facilities			
10. Trained Staff			
11. Disaster Preparedness			
12. Arrangement			
13. Description			
14. Access Policy			
15. Reference Service			
16. Duplication & Reformatting			
17. Cooperative Programs			
18. Outreach			
19. Advocacy			
20. Consultants			
TOTALS			

PRIORITIES FOR IMPROVEMENT:

1. _____
2. _____
3. _____

COLLECTION SURVEY

A complete assessment of your archival program includes identifying the size and contents of your collections. It is difficult to "measure" your collections exactly; however, the following may be helpful in estimating.

If your collection is unorganized, estimate roughly how much space the historical records would occupy if they were in boxes or on shelves.

Do not count an item or group of materials more than once. For instance, if you know the number of photographs and the linear feet they occupy, give one or the other but not both.

Use the following approximations, if necessary, to estimate total number of linear feet:

1 Hollinger box/document case (approx. 12" x 5" x 10")	=	0.5 lin. ft.
1 Records center carton (approx. 15" x 12" x 10")	=	1 lin. ft.
1 Transfer carton (approx. 24" x 12" x 10")	=	2 lin. ft.
1 Filing cabinet drawer	=	2 lin. ft.

I. Size—Total Collection

1. *Paper records* (including unpublished, handwritten or typescript materials such as loose correspondence, letter books, office files, scrapbooks, ledgers, and other similar materials.) _____ lin. ft.

2. *Other materials* (estimate number of items or number of linear feet for each of the following.)

Photographs (include slides & negatives)	____ photos	or	____ lin. ft.
Microfilm	____ reels	or	____ lin. ft.
Oversize paper (maps, blueprints, etc.)	____ items	or	____ lin. ft.
Motion picture film	____ reels	or	____ lin. ft.
Videotapes	____ items	or	____ lin. ft.
Audiotapes	____ items	or	____ lin. ft.
Computer media (disks, CD's)	____ items	or	____ lin. ft.

3. Volumes (published books, journals, etc.) ____ items

4. Artifacts ____ items or ____ items

II. Processed Materials ____ items or ____ lin. ft.
   (arranged, described, finding aids available)

III. Unprocessed Materials ____ items or ____ lin. ft.

Appendix 4

COOPERATIVE APPROACHES TO HISTORICAL RECORDS PROGRAMS

Cooperative approaches, which may involve coordinated collecting and resource sharing, can help improve the administration of historical records overall. This appendix presents some study questions that can help promote discussions among repositories. *Source:* State Archives and Records Administration, *Strengthening New York's Historical Records Programs: A Self-Study Guide,* prepared by Richard J. Cox (Albany, N.Y.: State Archives and Records Administration, 1989), 127–44.

WHY COOPERATE?

1. Does the historical records program have a statement of mission and a strategic plan that can assist it in identifying potential cooperative activities?
2. Has the program ever cooperated with another historical records repository? Has the program ever considered participating in a cooperative venture with another repository?
3. Are there other historical records programs in the locality with which cooperation would be possible?
4. Could any elements of the historical records program be best accomplished or supported by cooperative ventures?

5. Could the program save money or more efficiently use other resources in some areas of its work by cooperating with other historical records repositories?
6. Has the program explored types of cooperation effectively used by other repositories?
7. Has outside expertise been sought to suggest areas where cooperation could be applied?

COOPERATION IN APPRAISAL AND ACQUISITION OF HISTORICAL RECORDS

8. Has the historical records program considered potential areas of competition, overlap, and cooperation in the formulation of its acquisition policy?
9. Does the program's written acquisition policy support the adequate documentation of the repository's main areas of geographical, topical, and institutional interests?
10. Has the program identified its potential to participate in cooperative ventures?
11. Does the program seek the advice of records users and other outside expertise to help it identify and select records having enduring value?
12. Is the program adequately disseminating results of its work in order to encourage opportunities for cooperation?

COOPERATION IN PRESERVATION

13. Could the historical records program obtain regular assistance from a professional conservator by combining its resources with other repositories?
14. Could the program more effectively carry out an ongoing survey and condition analysis of its facility by cooperating with other historical records repositories to obtain the aid of a professional conservator?
15. Could the program develop a more effective disaster-preparedness plan by joining with neighboring historical records repositories, libraries, and museums?
16. Could the program obtain or improve preservation training for its staff by cooperating with neighboring repositories?

17. Has the program explored other cooperative preservation methods such as the joint purchasing of acid-free storage supplies or the pooling of resources for establishing a preservation microfilming program?

18. Has the program examined the availability of regional service agencies in preservation?

19. Has the repository's governing board and staff read the recent report of the New York Document Conservation Advisory Council, *Our Memory at Risk,* and considered ways of meeting its recommendations through cooperative preservation projects?

COOPERATION IN REFERENCE AND ACCESS

20. Has the historical records program participated in any cooperative efforts in reference and access?

21. Could the program enhance its services to researchers by cooperating with other historical records repositories in areas such as the joint hiring of trained archivists?

22. Could the program expand its research constituency through cooperative ventures like joint finding aids, descriptive brochures, workshops, and other public programs?

23. Has the repository cooperated with the Historical Documents Inventory project or entered information on its holdings directly into an automated descriptive network like RLIN?

COOPERATION IN BASIC ADMINISTRATION FUNCTIONS

24. Has the historical records program participated in any cooperative efforts in areas of basic administration?

25. Has the program taken advantage of services offered by cooperative agencies in their region, such as one of the historical service consortia or library research councils?

26. Do the program's strategic plan and related documents adequately identify areas in which the repository potentially could benefit by cooperative approaches to obtain expertise, reduced costs, or more efficient use of available resources?

27. Would the repository benefit from any of the following?
    A. Joint hiring and sharing of consultants or regular staff
    B. Temporary exchanges of staff for special projects

    C. Cooperative purchasing of equipment
    D. Cooperative purchasing of supplies
    E. Sharing of facilities for storage of historical records holdings and for staff work

28. Has the program considered merging with another institution in the same region that has a similar mission and programs?

COOPERATION IN TRAINING AND PROFESSIONAL DEVELOPMENT

29. Has the historical records program cooperated with other repositories to develop or to sponsor training and professional development opportunities for its staff?

30. Has the program worked with other repositories to encourage local colleges and universities, professional associations, or state agencies to offer educational courses that would strengthen the work of its staff?

31. Has the program participated with other repositories in the hiring of consultants for the purpose of staff training and development?

32. Does the program encourage its staff to exchange information with other repositories for administering historical records?

33. Has the program considered providing for access to literature on historical records administration through cooperation with other repositories and organizations?

COOPERATION IN PUBLIC PROGRAMMING

34. Does the historical records program regularly obtain information about statewide policy and legislative proposals affecting local historical records programs?

35. Has the program cooperated with other historical records repositories and allied groups on behalf of historical records issues?

36. Is the program aware of the Coalition for New York's Documentary Heritage and other existing advocacy groups?

37. Are there potential areas of cooperation for advocacy and outreach with other historical records programs in the locality?
    A. Monitoring and influencing legislation
    B. Letter-writing and other advocacy campaigns on behalf of a specific historical records issue

    C. Pooling resources for mailings and the production and distribution of promotional materials?

    D. Cosponsoring public forums about historical records issues

38. Could some of the repository's public programs be strengthened and made more effective by cooperation with other historical records repositories?

    A. Brochures, leaflets, and other promotional or educational materials

    B. Orientation programs

    C. Special events and exhibits

    D. Ongoing press releases and media contact

Appendix 5

HISTORICAL RECORDS PROGRAM PLAN

This hypothetical plan, from the fictitious Chesapeake County Historical Society, is presented as an illustration of the make-up of planning documents. It attempts to outline conditions and issues, to convey strategies, and to indicate the work to be performed while still allowing for flexibility.

CHESAPEAKE COUNTY HISTORICAL SOCIETY
DEPARTMENT OF HISTORICAL RECORDS
STRATEGIC PLAN
JANUARY 1, 2000

Introduction

The Chesapeake County Historical Society, chartered in 1893, encourages the preservation of the evidence of the county's historical development, collects artifacts and historical records relating to the history of the county and contiguous areas, and fosters an understanding and appreciation of history among the residents of the county, particularly young people in the schools. The Society has its own strategic plan, *Future Legacy: Planning for Saving History in Chesapeake County*, approved by the Trustees in 1997. Additional information on the Society and its priorities is found in its annual report, which, along with other information, is available from its Web site, *www.chesahist.org*.

This Strategic Plan for the Department of Historical Records was developed during 1999 through an extensive discussion and analytical process that included studies and proposals from staff working groups, several meetings with the Historical Records Advisory Committee, questionnaires for researchers, and two open meetings with customer groups at the Society's office in Chesapeake City. It is meant to indicate what the Department expects to do over approximately the next half decade. It was approved by the Director of the Society and the Trustees in December 1999. This Strategic Plan is consistent with the 1997 plan approved for the Society as a whole.

The Department of Historical Records was established in 1947 with a general charge to collect historical records relating to the county. Over the years, its mission, vision, and goals have been modified several times. The current plan represents revised directions as the Department enters the new century. It reflects a preliminary agreement developed in 1999 among the major businesses and collecting entities in the county for the systematic documentation of major institutions and historical themes.

Mission

The mission of the Chesapeake County Historical Society Department of Historical Records is to foster the systematic historical documentation of the people and institutions of the county, primarily through direct collection of records of enduring value, and to actively encourage and support their use by researchers whose work holds promise to illuminate county history.

Vision

Adequate documentation to reconstruct and understand the historical development of Chesapeake County will be created, identified, preserved, made available, and actively used by researchers.

Goals

The following statement of goals indicates in general terms *what the program intends to accomplish* during the next half decade.

1. Implement the 1999 county-wide documentation/collection agreement, emphasizing the four areas where the Historical Society is designated as the lead institution: (A) history of ethnic groups, particularly minorities; (B) history of transportation; (C) history of agriculture; and (D) history of the fishing industry.

2. Actively identify, appraise, and collect historically valuable records, particularly in the four areas identified in (1), so that the holdings grow by approximately 20 percent annually, and including electronic records where appropriate.

3. Arrange and describe all holdings to the series level within two months after accessioning; carry out more detailed work on holdings of particular research importance.

4. Carry out basic preservation work on all holdings but employ microfilm as the preservation/dissemination tool of choice and microfilm at least 20 percent of holdings.

5. Continue public and educational programs, stressing seminars based on research done in the Department's holdings and traveling exhibits.

6. Mount and begin delivering services over a Web site, coordinated with the Society's existing site.

STRATEGIES

This statement of strategies indicates in general terms *how the program intends to accomplish the goals* it has set.

1. *Customer responsiveness and service excellence.* One of the hallmarks of the program will continue to be its stress on service and responsiveness. In approaching its work, it will be guided by the fundamental assumptions that the program exists to serve people, that the ultimate goal of its work is use of its holdings, and that it has an obligation to provide prompt, responsive service that satisfies its various customer groups.

2. *County-wide cooperation.* The program does not operate unilaterally or in isolation. It will continue to actively cooperate with other programs, particularly in documentation and collecting efforts, and including especially the State Historical Society, the county library system, the historical societies in Ocean Beach, Berne, Chesapeake City, and Whitney, and the archival programs at Chesapeake County Community College, Calvin State College, and Johnson College.

3. *Enhancing resources.* It will actively develop new sources of support, including beginning a fund-raising effort for selected topics, developing a volunteer program, and developing an internship program for students from the graduate archival education program at the University of Maryland.

4. *More visibility.* One of the ways of advancing the program on all fronts is to increase its visibility and the understanding and appreciation of the Society's administration, trustees, potential donors, and others. Therefore,

the program will focus on its newsletter, annual report, and Web site development as multiple means of reaching a broader audience with a more imaginative and convincing array of messages.

5. *Digital proficiency.* The Program's leadership and staff recognize that more and more records of lasting value are created only in digital form, that this means a gradual rise in electronic archives, and that the program needs to increase its capacity to deal with this change. Therefore, there will be emphasis on staff training and development, monitoring professional developments, keeping up with the literature, learning from other programs, cooperating with institutions that are creating electronic archival records, and learning by doing.

6. *Individual and team initiative and empowerment.* The Department will continue its policy of encouraging, supporting, and rewarding initiative on the part of individuals and teams and of empowering people to accomplish the work.

7. *Personnel development.* The Department recognizes a need for continued development of professional personnel, particularly in the area of electronic records and digital archives, and will therefore urge and support staff in taking courses, actively engaging in professional activities, and organizing discussions and seminars at the Society.

Program Goals for 2000

This section describes the work that the Department intends to accomplish during the first year of the strategic plan, i.e., 2000.

1. Implement the inter-institutional county-wide documentation plan by serving as secretariat for the working group, scheduling and organizing bimonthly meetings, and developing proposals, and developing and beginning the implementation of plans for documentation and collecting in the areas where the Society has assumed lead responsibility.

2. Revise and refine the collecting policy in light of the documentation plan and appraise and collect approximately 200 cubic feet of materials, including the archival records of the Chesapeake County Grange, the Waterfront Fishermen's Association, and the Wright Family records.

3. Arrange and describe new accessions and eliminate the arrangement/description backlog through work on the following materials: Cortland Company records, Susquehanna Steamship Company records, Chesapeake County Chamber of Commerce files, several small collections of church records, and the Miscellaneous Genealogy file.

4. Carry out repair and restoration work on the county survey and map collection, including extensive cleaning, mending tears, and encapsulation, using an outside conservation firm for most of the work.

5. Have the following collections microfilmed to archival specifications, using an outside vendor: Allen Daniel Collection, Susanna Vultaggio literary materials, Mary Nealon diaries, Robert Evans clippings scrapbooks, and the Greek-American Benevolence Society records.

6. Provide reference services to approximately 100 researchers in the search room, approximately 200 more via phone and letter, and about 1000 over the Web site.

7. Develop a home page and Web site for the Department, taking into account available resources, researcher priorities, and increased reference demand.

8. Develop three historical exhibits, on (A) The People of Chesapeake; (B) Steam and Electric Interurban Railroads; and (C) Farm, Factory, and Fishing. The first one will travel to selected schools and other sites; the second will be at the Society's exhibit center; and the third will be shown at the annual Chesapeake County Fair.

9. Organize and host a seminar, in cooperation with the State Archives and the State Historical Society, on the topic of Recovering Our Past: Strategies and Approaches for Research in Historical Records.

10. Continue sound program administration, including staff and team empowerment, quarterly staff meetings, individual work plans and frequent meetings between supervisors and employees, monitoring of work on this annual work plan and development of next year's plan, sharing of financial and other information, and professional development opportunities.

Appendix 6

GUIDE TO DONATING PERSONAL OR FAMILY PAPERS TO A REPOSITORY

Historical records programs need to provide guidance to people who are considering donating their own records, or the records of their family, to the repository. This brochure indicates the advantages of turning over historical records, identifies issues, and discusses the mechanics. Society of American Archivists, *A Guide to Donating Your Personal or Family Papers to a Repository*, Pamphlet (Chicago: Society of American Archivists, 1994, second printing 1997). Also available at *www.archivists.org*. Reprinted with permission of the Society of American Archivists.

A GUIDE TO DONATING YOUR PERSONAL OR FAMILY PAPERS TO A REPOSITORY

For millennia, written records have provided essential clues to the past. Through letters, diaries, and unpublished writings of many types, and also through the audible and visual records of recent times, researchers have been able to study and understand much about the history of particular families, communities, businesses, and organizations, the history of specific events and broader societal trends, and the history of the United States in general.

Letters, diaries, photos, and other material collected over the years give vital and unique information regarding your life or the history of your family. And while these papers obviously matter to you, they may be important to your community, state, or nation, too. Whether or not members of your family attained a degree of fame, they have contributed to the heritage of a certain place and time. When you donate your personal or family papers to a manuscript repository, your family history becomes a part of your community's collective memory.

WHAT IS A REPOSITORY AND WHAT CAN IT DO FOR YOU?

Manuscript repositories—also called archives, historical societies, and special collections libraries—carefully preserve collections of written, visual, and audible material created by private citizens both past and present. Such repositories ensure that these personal and family papers will be available for research by generations to come.

A manuscript repository is run by professionals—archivists, curators, or librarians—whose first priority is the preservation of historical materials. They can discuss with you the historical value of your papers, and advise you on which repository would be best for your papers. In addition, once you donate papers the staff will continue to work with you as you locate or identify other materials to donate.

If your personal or family papers are deemed appropriate for a repository's collections, and you agree to donate those papers, you stand to gain many benefits. A repository can provide the papers with environmentally-controlled, secure storage and can oversee their proper handling and use. Equally important, it can provide research access to the contents of the papers, both to you and to the scholarly public. In future years, researchers—including students, professors, genealogists, journalists and many others—may thus find your papers both interesting and of value to their work.

WHAT TO PRESERVE?

Most repositories accept donations of as little as a single item and as large as dozens of boxes. Material need not be organized; it need not be "old"; and it need not relate to a famous individual, event, or organization in order for it to be historically significant. Generally, however, repositories are more interested in a coherent body of material rather than individual items; photos, tapes, and films should be identified. Repositories usually ask that historical material itself not be mailed or dropped off without first consulting with the staff; a repository must evaluate all material offered and ask the donor to sign a donation agreement.

DO YOU NEED TO "CULL" THE PAPERS OR REORGANIZE THEM?

Archivists are experts in identifying materials that should be transferred to a repository or manuscript library. Because the research value of records may be diminished if items are removed or if the records are rearranged, donors are encouraged to contact the repository staff before weeding, discarding, or reorganizing their papers and records.

EXAMPLES OF HISTORICALLY VALUABLE MATERIAL

While it is important that the archives staff be permitted to survey papers or records in order to determine which materials have enduring historical value, listed below are types of materials that are often valuable to a researcher. These lists, which are suggestive and not definitive, illustrate the wide range of documentation often useful for historical and administrative research.

Among the types of materials in personal and family papers of interest to researchers are:

- letters
- memoirs/reminiscences
- diaries
- scrapbooks/photo albums
- professional papers
- genealogical information
- speeches/lectures
- business records
- subject files
- legal documents
- minutes/reports
- brochures and flyers
- photographs (labeled)
- films/videos/audio tapes (labeled)

Also of interest are files relating to the individual's civic, business, religious, political, and social activities.

Churches, political organizations, businesses, economic interest groups, community groups, voluntary associations, professional associations, and other collective enterprises all produce records which document their purpose, policies, and activities. An individual or family may hold the records of such a business or organization, and this material, too, may be significant. In addition to papers and records, some archives (or their affiliated museums or libraries) also collect artifacts, art, books, maps, and music.

WILL A REPOSITORY TAKE EVERYTHING YOU OFFER?

Although a repository cannot accept everything that may be offered (whether because of staff and space constraints or because the papers are not within the collecting mission of the particular institution), it welcomes the chance to review material; if it is not appropriate for one repository, there may be another one to which it could be referred. Some material, though, may be of more sentimental than historical value, and should be kept by the individual or family itself.

DONATING PERSONAL OR FAMILY PAPERS TO A REPOSITORY

Archivists can best assist you if you make an appointment in advance. If you are unsure how to contact a repository in your area, you may wish to begin by speaking with someone at your state historical society or state archives. The Society of American Archivists can also provide you with suggestions.

DONATIONS

Most archives can only invest materials and labor in the preservation of items which they own. Therefore, most archives accept donations of individual or family papers, but will not accept such material on deposit or on loan. Donors are asked to sign a donation agreement, which formally signifies that the papers become the actual property of the archives.

ACCESS TO COLLECTIONS

Once material is donated to a repository, it does not circulate—in order to insure that it is preserved as long as humanly possible. Access to donated papers is governed by the repository's written policies regarding availability, photo duplication, and publication. A prospective donor should become familiar with such policies and discuss any special needs or concerns with the curator before completing the donation agreement.

RESTRICTIONS ON ACCESS

Sensitive material that may exist in individual or family papers should not be removed by the donor. Instead, the donor should discuss with the archivist the possibility of restricting part of the collection to protect the privacy of the donor or others. While archives desire to make all papers freely accessible to researchers, they normally will agree to reasonable and equitable restrictions for limited periods of time.

COPYRIGHT

Assignment of copyright is often complex, and you should work with the repository staff to clarify issues of copyright ownership. Generally, copyright belongs to the creator of writings and other original material (such as photos and music), but can be legally transferred to heirs or others. Moreover, ownership of copyright is separable from ownership of the physical item (the letter or photo). Curators often ask donors to donate not only the physical papers but also any copyright in them that the donor might own. This request is made to make it easier for researchers to use quotations from the papers in their work.

CONDITIONAL GIFTS

A repository usually is not able to promise that donated materials will be placed on exhibit or used in some other specific fashion as a condition of accepting the gift.

MONETARY APPRAISALS FOR TAX DEDUCTIONS

In certain circumstances, it may be possible for a donor to take a tax deduction for the donation of a manuscript collection to a repository. Donors are encouraged to speak with their tax accountants or attorneys about this possibility. Curators cannot give tax advice, nor are they permitted to appraise the monetary value of a collection. The curator may be able to provide donors with a list of local manuscript appraisers who can (for a fee) make monetary appraisals for the donor. It is up to the donor to arrange for and bear the cost of any such appraisal, although the repository will make the collection available to an appraiser hired by the donor.

MONETARY DONATIONS

Most repositories are non-profit organizations. Preparing papers for use by researchers is the most expensive operation in a repository. Although such grants are rarely a prerequisite for the acceptance of a collection, donors who are able to assist repositories by making grants toward the arrangement, cataloging, and conservation of their donations of papers are encouraged to do so.

© 1994. The Society of American Archivists.

This brochure was prepared by the Manuscripts Repositories Section of the Society of American Archivists. Grateful acknowledgement for permission to borrow from their respective brochures is made to the Nebraska State Historical Society, the Bentley Historical Library of the University of Michigan, and the Minnesota Historical Society.

Last updated: January 22, 1997.

Appendix 7

GUIDE TO DEEDS OF GIFT

Repositories and donors both need guidance on how to execute deeds of gift that transfer custody of records to the repository and outline any conditions on the transfer. This pamphlet provides helpful information on how to proceed. Society of American Archivists, *Deeds of Gift: What Donors Should Know* (Pamphlet: Society of American Archivists, 1998). Available at *www.archivists. org.* Reprinted with permission of the Society of American Archivists.

DEEDS OF GIFT: WHAT DONORS SHOULD KNOW

Donors of historical materials are individuals or organizations that give materials to manuscript repositories, archives, historical societies, or special collections libraries. Donated materials often include papers and records documenting personal lives and family history, or the history of organizations, such as businesses and religious groups. Repositories are administered by professional archivists, curators, or librarians, who are responsible for assembling these materials, preserving them, and making them available for study. The relationship between you, as a donor, and a repository must be based on a common understanding of your wishes and the ability of the repository to carry out its mission and responsibilities. Potential donors and repository representatives should review the materials being offered for donation and discuss repository policies and procedures for the care and use of donated materials. If both parties agree that the repository is an appropriate place for preservation of the materials, they complete and sign a deed of gift.

The deed of gift is a formal, legal, agreement that transfers ownership of, and legal rights in, the materials to be donated. Executing a deed is in the best interests of both donor and repository. After discussion and review of the various elements of the deed, it is signed by both the donor or donor's authorized agent, and an authorized representative of the repository. The signed deed of gift establishes and governs the legal relationship between donor and repository and the legal status of the materials.

Various elements are essential to a deed of gift; others may be specific to the repository to which the materials are donated. The typical deed of gift identifies the donor, transfers legal ownership of the materials to the repository, establishes provisions for their use, specifies ownership of intellectual property rights in the materials, and indicates what the repository should do with unwanted materials. If you have any questions about the language of the deed of gift, ask for an explanation from the repository representative or from your attorney.

If you created and/or collected the materials you are donating, all that is needed in this section is your full legal name. If you are acting on behalf of someone else who created and/or collected the materials, include information on your relationship to that person or entity. You might note, for example, sister, niece, son, or business agent. If you are not the creator of the materials, the repository may ask you to explain how you have the authority to donate them. The repository will provide its full name as the recipient.

This is generally a summary, such as "John Doe Personal Papers," or "Records of the First Baptist Church of Detroit," and is written by the repository staff in consultation with you. The repository may wish to be more specific in describing the materials, or append a more detailed listing of the materials to the agreement.

In this section, the donor formally agrees to transfer legal ownership and physical custody of the materials, including future donations, to the repository. The deed will specify a point in time (usually upon signing the deed or upon physical transfer of the material to the repository) when the materials become the legal property of the repository. It will manage and care for them, employing the best professional judgment of its staff and according to accepted professional standards and its mission and objectives.

Repositories prefer to accept materials through transfer of ownership. The cost of storing, preserving, and making collections available for research is so high that repositories generally can only afford to do so for materials they own.

As the professional staff of the repository reviews the materials you donated, there may be reason to reformat some or all of them. Long-term preservation of fragile materials, for instance, is a primary reason for microfilming or copying papers for use by researchers. Unless you note to the contrary in the gift agreement, when you transfer legal ownership of your materials to the repository, you agree that the staff may make reformatting decisions. The repository representative will discuss with you the means by which your collection can be transported to the repository.

An essential mission of repositories is to make their collections open and available for research use. They are able to do this because most donors do not limit access to the materials they donate. There may be instances, however, when a donor or repository feels it is appropriate to restrict access to all or a portion of the materials for a limited and clearly stated period of time.

If the materials you donate contain student records, income tax records, medical records or legal case files relating to third parties (that is, to individuals other than you or your immediate ancestors, or to organizations other than the one whose records are being donated), federal or state privacy laws may apply. If you know that such materials exist, bring this to the attention of the repository representative. If such materials are discovered by the repository during cataloging, the repository representative will discuss them with you.

If your concerns go beyond these types of materials, explain them to the representative, and be as specific as possible when you discuss the papers or records you want to restrict. If needed, the representative will work with you to arrive at language regarding the restriction that is acceptable to you and which can be enforced by the repository.

When you sign the gift agreement, you transfer legal ownership of the actual materials you want to donate. Ownership of intellectual property rights (primarily copyright, but including trademarks and patent rights) may also be legally transferred by the deed of gift. Copyright generally belongs to the creator of writings or other original material (such as photographs and music). Donors are encouraged to transfer all rights they possess in and to the materials donated to the repository; this assists researchers in their scholarship by making it easier to quote from documents. If you wish to retain all or a portion of the intellectual property rights you own, you may include such a provision in the deed of gift, but you and the representative should agree upon a date after which the rights will be transferred to the repository. You are not able to transfer ownership of rights to the works of others found in the materials you donate. These works might include such items as letters written to you by others.

In the course of arranging and describing the materials you donate, the repository's staff will retain substantive materials of permanent historic value and separate out those materials that are routine, duplicative, or outside the collecting scope of the repository. The repository needs guidance in dealing with these separated materials. You may choose to have the repository dispose of them in the manner they deem appropriate. This usually includes shredding or disposing of duplicates or materials of no historical significance, and transferring out-of-scope materials to another unit within the repository or to another repository. You may, however, prefer to have the separations returned directly to you. You should discuss your options with the repository's representative and arrive at an agreement that can be stated in the deed of gift.

Repositories vary widely in the kinds of materials they collect, the users they serve, and the facilities in which they preserve materials and make them available for research. As a result, a repository may require or permit the deed of gift to contain language related to a wide range of other issues. If you have any questions or concerns about what is or is not included in a deed of gift, it is important that you raise these with the repository representative prior to signing the agreement. Although it is possible that a repository may not be able to accommodate a specific request, it is best to ensure that all relevant issues are discussed.

It is important to sign the deed of gift as soon as you and the representative have discussed and agreed upon its provisions. Few repositories will accept a collection without a signed deed of gift. If necessary, the deed of gift can be amended if both sides concur. Amendments should be signed and dated by both the donor and the repository representative.

The deed of gift confirms a legal relationship between the donor and repository that is based on trust and common understanding. This relationship ensures that the materials you have donated, which help illuminate our past and its influence upon us, are preserved and made available to future generations.

This brochure was prepared as a joint project of the Manuscript Repositories and Appraisal and Acquisitions Sections of the Society of American Archivists. Christine Weideman served as principal author.

©1998 by the Society of American Archivists. All rights reserved.

Appendix 8

EXAMPLES OF HISTORICAL RECORDS DESCRIPTIONS

Archivists are increasingly using standard, or at least consistent, approaches to describing historical records. This appendix presents some helpful examples, including illustrating the use of MARC tags, the preferred format for archival description. Source: New York State Archives and Records Administration, *Guidelines for Arrangement and Description of Archives and Manuscripts* (Albany, N.Y.: State Archives and Records Administration, 1995), 25–33.

EXAMPLES OF DESCRIPTIVE RECORDS

The following examples show descriptions for various of kinds of archival and manuscripts materials. After each example is a second version of the description showing the use of MARC AMC fields. Container lists or folder lists also exist for most of the descriptions. Those are not shown here since the format of such lists will vary depending on each series or collection, and no specific guidelines are necessary for their preparation. These examples are based on actual descriptions created by a variety of repositories, but some changes may have been made for the purpose of illustration.

ACCESSION LEVEL RECORDS

Columbia University. Teachers College.
Scrapbooks, [ca. 1887–1952]

45 linear ft.

Summary: Scrapbooks contain clippings relating to Teachers College and its predecessor organization, the Industrial Education Association (founded 1884)

Indexing terms:

Industrial Education Association (New York, N.Y.)

Teachers colleges—New York (N.Y.)

Scrapbooks.

MARC Record Version

035		≠a(NIC)NYNE588–97–0025
110	2	≠Columbia University.≠bTeachers College.
245	00	≠kScrapbooks,≠f[ca. 1887–1952]
300		≠a45 linear ft.
520		≠aScrapbooks contain clippings relating to Teachers College and its predecessor organization, the Industrial Education Association (founded 1884).
610	20	≠aIndustrial Education Association (New York, N.Y.)
650	0	≠aTeachers College≠zNew York (N.Y.)
655	7	≠aScrapbooks.≠2ftamc
851		≠aColumbia University.≠bTeachers College. Milbank Memorial Library, Special Collections,≠cNew York, NY.NYNE592 800 0145

Vassar College, Board of Trustees.

Minutes.

6 linear ft.

Arranged chronologically.

Minutes from Board meetings and some committee meetings, 1861–1957, and transcriptions of wills leaving bequests to Vassar College.

Restricted.

Administrative transfer from the Office of the Trustees, 6/15/1963.

Indexing terms:

Vassar College Administration.

Women's colleges New York (State) Poughkeepsie.

MARC Record Version

110	2	≠aVassar College,≠bBoard of Trustees.
245	00	≠kMinutes.
300		≠a6 linear ft.
351		≠aArranged chronologically.
520		≠:aMinutes from Board meetings and some committee meetings, 1861–1957, and transcriptions of wills leaving bequests to Vassar College.
506		≠aRestricted.
541		≠aOffice of the Trustees,sd6/15 / 1963.
610	20	≠aVassar College≠xAdministration.
650	0	≠aWomen's colleges,≠zNew York (State)≠xPoughkeepsie.

MANUSCRIPT COLLECTION DESCRIPTIONS

Frederick A. DeZeng, 1756–1838.

Papers, 1781–1849.

.25 linear ft.

Baron DeZeng, a Hessian officer who became a naturalized American citizen, was the first manufacturer of window glass in the United States.

Summary: Letters and documents, 1781–1831, to, from, and about DeZeng, and letters, 1843–1849, to DeZeng's son, William Steuben DeZeng. Subjects include the Onondaga Nation, Shakers, the Ontario Glass Company, and personal and family matters. Correspondents include Governor George Clinton, General Philip Schuyler, and William H. Seward.

Use of this collection requires advance notice.

Inventory available.

Indexing terms:

DeZeng family.

Ontario Glass Company.

Onondaga Indians.

Windows.

Glass manufacture—New York (State)

Glass manufacture—Canada Ontario.

Hessians—United States.

Shakers.

Ontario (Canada) InduStries.

New York (State) Industries.

DeZeng, William Steuben, 1793–1844.

Clinton, George, 1739–1812.

Schuyler, Philip John, 1733–1804.

Seward, William Henry, 1801–1872.

MARC Record Version

100	1	≠aDeZeng, Frederick A.,≠d1756–1838.
245	00	≠a Baron Frederick DeZeng Papers,sf1781–1849.
300		≠a.25 linear ft.
545		≠aBaron DeZeng, a Hessian officer who became a naturalized American citizen, was the first manufacturer of window glass in the United States.
520		≠aLetters and documents, 1781–1831, to, from, and about DeZeng, and letters, 1843–1849, to DeZeng's son, William Steuben DeZeng. Subjects include the Onondaga Nation, Shakers, the Ontario Glass Company, and personal and family matters. Correspondents include Governor George Clinton, General Philip Schuyler, and William H. Seward.
506		≠aUse of this collection requires advance notice.
555	0	≠aInventory available.
696	34	≠aDeZeng family.
610	10	≠aOntario Glass Company.
650	0	≠aOnondaga Indians.
650	0	≠aWindows.
650	0	≠aGlass manufacture≠zNew York (State).
650	0	≠aGlass manufacture≠zCanada;≠zOntario.
650	0	≠aHessians≠zUnited States.
650	0	≠aShakers.
651	0	≠aOntario (Canada)≠xIndustries.
651	0	≠aNew York (State)≠xIndustries.
700	10	≠aDeZeng, William Steuben,≠d1793–1844.
700	10	≠aClinton, George,;≠d1739–1812.
700	10	≠aSchuyler, Philip John,≠d1733–1804.
700	10	≠aSeward, William Henry,≠d1801–1872.

Metcalf, George R., 1914–

Papers, 1956–1971.

2 linear ft.

Writer, state senator, president of the National Committee Against Discrimination in Housing.

Summary: Collection comprises material for Metcalf's books, BLACK PROFILES (13 biographies of prominent black Americans living and deceased), and UP FROM WITHIN: TODAY'S BLACK LEADERS (a biographical sequence of emerging black personalities and their contributions to the black revolution in America). Material consists of clippings, correspondence, typescripts, transcribed interviews, notes and miscellaneous printed material, and one taped interview with Metcalf on a variety of topics including urban rehabilitation. Material in collection is about Martin Luther King, Jr., Malcolm X, Roy Wilkins, Shirley Chisolm, W.E.B. Du Bois, Rosa Parks, Thurgood Marshall, Medgar Evers, Jackie Robinson, Eldridge Cleaver, Whitney Young, Jr., Harriet Tubman, Edward Brooke, Julian Bond, James H. Meredith, Andrew Brimmer, and others.

Permission required to quote from transcribed interviews.

Finding aids: Partial inventory.

Indexing terms:

King, Martin Luther,Jr., 1929–1968.

X, Malcolm, 1925–1965.

Wilkins, Roy, 1901–

Chisolin, Shirley, 1913–

Du Bois, W. E. B. (William Edward Burghardt), 1868–1963.

Parks, Rosa, 1913–

Marshall, Thurgood, 1908–

Evers, Medgar Wiley, 1925–1963.

Robinson, Jackie, 1919–1972.

Cleaver, Eldridge, 1935–

Young, Whitney M.

Tubman, Harriet, 1820?–1913.

Brooke, Edward, 1919–

Bond, Julian, 1940–

Meredith, James Howard.

Black nationalism—United States.
Afro-Americans—Civil rights.
Afro-American athletes.
Afro-American judges.
Civil rights workers—United States.
Interviews.
Afro-American authors.

MARC Record Version

100	1	≠aMetcalf, George R.,≠:d1914–
245	00	≠kPapers,≠f1956–1971.
300		≠a2 linear ft.
545		≠aWriter, state senator, president of the National Committee Against Discrimination in Housing.
520		≠aCollection comprises material for Metcalf's books, BLACK PROFILES (13 biographies of prominent black Americans living and deceased), and UP FROM WITHIN: TODAY'S BLACK LEADERS (a biographical sequence of emerging black personalities and their contributions to the "black revolution" in America). Material consists of clippings, correspondence, typescripts, transcribed interviews, notes and miscellaneous printed material, and one taped interview with Metcalf on a variety of topics including urban rehabilitation. Material in collection is about Martin Luther King, Jr., Malcolm X, Roy Wilkins, Shirley Chisolm, W.E.B. Du Bois, Rosa Parks, Thurgood Marshall, Medgar Evers, Jackie Robinson, Eldridge Cleaver, Whitney Young, Jr., Harriet Tubman, Edward Brooke, Julian Bond, James H. Meredith, Andrew Brimmer, and others.
540		≠aPermission required to quote from transcribed interviews.
555	0	≠aPartial inventory.
600	10	≠aKing, Martin Luther,≠cJr.,d1929–1968.
600		≠aX, Malcolm,≠d1925–1965.
600	10	≠aWilkins, Roy,≠d1901–
600	10	≠aChisolm, Shirley,≠d1913–
600	10	≠aDu Bois, W.E.B.≠q(William Edward Burghardt), ≠d1868–1963.
600	10	≠aParks, Rosa,≠d1913–
600	10	≠aMarshall, Thurgood,≠d1908–

600	10	≠aEvers, Medgar Wiley,≠d1925–1963.
600	10	≠aRobinson, Jackie,≠d1919–1972.
600	10	≠aCleaver, Eldridge,≠d1935–
600	10	≠aYoung, Whitney M.
600	10	≠aTubman, Harriet,≠d1820?–1913.
600	10	≠aBrooke, Edward,≠d1919–
600	10	≠aBond, Julian,≠d1940–
600	10	≠aMeredith, James Howard.
650	0	≠aBlack nationalism≠zUnited States.
650	0	≠aAfro-Americans≠xCivil rights.
650	0	≠aAfro-American athletes.
650	0	≠aAfro-American judges.
650	0	≠aCivil rights workers≠zUnited States.
655	7	≠aInterviews.≠2ftamc.
656	7	≠aAfro-American authors.≠21csh.

ARCHIVAL SERIES DESCRIPTIONS

Cornell University. Crew.

Records, 1871–1973.

4.6 cubic ft., 1 phonograph record, 1 tape recording, 1 videocassette.

Summary: Includes varsity and freshman crew rosters; Coach Charles Court-ney's diary and journals of distances rowed, weather conditions, and other in-formation; regatta programs; scrapbook; map; correspondence with Todd Jess-dale; minutes of the Sprague Boat Club; photographs, photograph albums, and glass negatives of crew events, Ithaca; New York views, and the Cayuga Lake Inlet; a phonograph record and cassette copy concerning a 1946 regatta at Lake Washington; material pertaining to John L. Collyer and Donald E. Maclay; and a videocassette of the 1957 Cornell crew victory at Henley.

Finding Aids: Box list.

Indexing terms:

Collyer, John L.

Courtney, Charles.

Jessdale, Todd.

Maclay, Donald E.

Cornell University—Athletics.

Sprague Boat Club.

Regattas.

Rowing.

Ithaca (N.Y.)

Cayuga Lake.

Diaries.

Glass plate negatives.

Journals.

Maps.

Photoprints.

Scrapbooks.

MARC Record Version

110	2	≠aCornell University.,≠bCrew.
245	00	≠kRecords,≠f1871–1973.
300		≠a4.6 cubic ft.,≠bl phonograph record, 1 tape recording, 1 videocassette.
520		≠aIncludes varsity and freshman crew rosters; Coach Charles Courtney's diary and journals of distances rowed, weather conditions, and other information; regatta programs; scrapbook; map; correspondence with Todd Jessdale; minutes of the Sprague Boat Club; photographs, photograph albums, and glass negatives of crew events, Ithaca, New York views, and the Cayuga Lake Inlet; a phonograph record and cassette copy concerning a 1946 regatta at Lake Washington; Material pertaining to John L. Collyer and Donald E. Maclay; and a videocassette of the 1957 Cornell crew victory at Henley.
555	0	≠aBox list.
600	10	≠aCollyer, John L.
600	20	≠aCourtney, Charles.
600	10	≠Jessdale, Todd.
600	10	≠aMaclay, Donald E.
610	20	≠aCornell University≠xAthletics.
610	20	≠aSprague Boat Club.
650	0	≠aRegattas.
650	0	≠aRowing.
651	0	≠aIthaca (N.Y.)
651	0	≠aCayuga Lake.

655   7   ≠aDiaries.≠2ftamc.
655   7   ≠aGlass plate negatives.≠2ftamc.
655   7   ≠aJournals.≠2ftamc.
655   7   ≠Maps.≠2ftamc.
655   7   ≠aPhotoprints.≠2ftamc.
655   7   ≠aScrapbooks.≠2ftamc.

Associated Colleges of Upper New York.

Records, 1946–1954.

2.3 linear ft.

Organized in two series as follows: I. Associated Colleges of Upper New York, 1946–1954; II. Metropolitan Survey, 1946–1949.

Historical note: To educators in New York State, the close of World War II heralded the return of an anticipated one hundred thousand veterans seeking the college level education provided by the G.I. Bill of Rights. To alleviate the overcrowded conditions facing colleges and universities, the State of New York created a temporary educational entity entitled Associated Colleges of Upper New York (ACUNY). ACUNY was chartered in 1946 by the Board of Regents of New York. Four temporary two-year colleges were established to absorb the influx of students and provide qualified veterans with the first two years of their college education. The colleges were Sampson College (1946, now known as SUNY at Champlain), and Middletown College.

The Board of Trustees of ACUNY consisted largely of presidents of private and public colleges in New York State. New York University was represented by Harold O. Voorhis, Vice President and Secretary. Voorhis acted as chairman of the Metropolitan Survey, 1946–1947, a study by ACUNY to determine the need of an emergency college to serve veterans in New York City.

Summary: The records consist of correspondence, minutes, reports, memoranda, financial records, surveys, press releases, and newspaper clippings relating to the administration of ACUNY. The Metropolitan Survey is well documented. Also included is printed matter such as administrative handbooks, facility bulletins, student handbooks, guidebooks, and brochures of the colleges of ACUNY.

Unpublished finding aid is available (folder level control).

Indexing term:

Allen, John.

Chase, Harry Woodburn, 1883–.

Day, Edmund Ezra, 1883–.

Dewey, Thomas E. (Thomas Edmund). 1902–1971.

Gilbert, Amy.

Kastner, Elwood.

Knowles, Asa Smallidge, 1901–1956.

Louttit, Chauncey McKinley, 1901–1956.

Miller, J. Hillis (Joseph Hillis), 1928–

Morse, Frederick A.

Rondileau, Adrian, 1912–

Voorhis, Harold Oliver, 1896–

Associated Colleges of Upper New York.

Cornell University.

Rutgers University.

Mohawk College.

Sampson College.

Middletown College.

State University of New York—Champlain

Colleges and Universities—Administration.

Higher education—New York State.

Veterans—Education—New York State.

World War, 1939–1945—Veterans.

MARC RECORD VERSION

110	2	≠aAssociated Colleges of Upper New York.
245	00	≠aAdministrative subject and correspondence files,≠f1946–1954.
300		≠a2.3 linear ft.
351		≠aOrganized in two series as follows: I. Associated Colleges of Upper New York, 1946–1954; II. Metropolitan Survey, 1946–1949.
545		≠aTo educators in New York State, the close of World War II heralded the return of an anticipated one hundred thousand veterans seeking the college level education provided by the G.I.

Bill of Rights. To alleviate the overcrowded conditions facing colleges and universities, the State of New York created a temporary educational entity entitled Associated Colleges of Upper New York (ACUNY). ACUNY was chartered in 1946 by the Board of Regents of New York. Four temporary two-year colleges were established to absorb the influx of students and provide qualified veterans with the first two years of their college education. The colleges were Sampson College (1946, now known as SUNY at Champlain), and Middletown College.

545 ≠bThe Board of Trustees of ACUNY consisted largely of presidents of private and public colleges in New York State. New York University was represented by Harold O. Voorhis, Vice President and Secretary. Voorhis acted as chairman of the Metropolitan Survey, 1946–1947, a study by ACUNY to determine the need for an emergency college to serve veterans in New York City.

520 ≠aThe records consist of correspondence, minutes, reports, memoranda, financial records, surveys, press releases, and newspaper clippings relating to the administration of ACUNY. The Metropolitan Survey is well documented. Also included is printed matter such as administrative handbooks, facility bulletins, student handbooks, guidebooks, and brochures of the colleges of ACUNY.

541 ≠aHarold O. Voorhis, ≠bOffice of the Vice President and Secretary, 16 College Lane, Poughkeepsie, NY ≠6cAdministrative transfer, ≠d1975.

555	8	≠aUnpublished finding aid is available≠(folder level control).
600	10	≠aAllen, John.
600	10	≠aChase, Harry Woodburn,≠d1883–
600	10	≠aDay, Edmund Ezra,≠t1883–
600	10	≠aDewey, Thomas E.≠q(Thomas Edmund),≠d1902–1971.
600	10	≠aGilbert, Amy.
600	0	≠aKastner, Elwood.
600	10	≠aKnowles, Asa Smallidge,≠d1901–1956.
600	10	≠aLouttit, Chauncey McKinley,≠4d1901–1956.
600	10	≠aMiller, J. Hillis≠q(Joseph Hillis),≠d1928–
600	10	≠aMorse, Frederick A.
600	10	≠aRondileau, Adrian,≠d1912–
600	10	≠aVoorhis, Harold Oliver,≠d1896–
610	20	≠aAssociated Colleges of Upper New York.
610	20	≠aCornell University.

610	20	≠aNew York University.
610	20	≠aRutgers University.
610	20	≠aMohawk College.
610	20	≠aSampson College.
610	20	≠aMiddletown College.
610	20	≠aState University of New York≠zChamplain.
650		≠aColleges and Universities≠xAdministration.
650		≠aHigher education≠zNew York State.
650		≠eaVeterans,,≠xEducation≠zNew York State.
650		≠aWorld War, 1939–1945≠xVeterans.

Appendix 9

CHECKLIST FOR ACCESS AND REFERENCE SERVICES

The exact makeup of access policies and reference services will depend on the program's size, setting, researcher traffic, and goals. The list of questions below is intended to assist programs in developing appropriate services. It is taken from a 1989 SAA study manual; the questions are still helpful but the list is limited because it lacks questions about researcher services via the Web. *Source:* Paul H. McCarthy, ed., *Archives Assessment and Planning Workbook* (Chicago: Society of American Archivists, 1989), 45–47. Reprinted with permission of the Society of American Archivists.

ACCESS POLICIES AND REFERENCE SERVICES

Principles

The archives must provide opportunity for research in the records it holds. The archives should be open for research use on a regular and stated schedule. It should provide adequate space and facilities for research use and should make its records available on equal terms of access to all users who should abide by its rules and procedures. Any restrictions on access should be defined in writing and should be carefully observed. The archives should provide information about its holdings and instruct users in their use. Staff members familiar with the holdings and capable of making informed decisions about legal and ethical considerations affecting reference work should be available to assist readers. The archives should report its holdings to appropriate publications so that potential users may know of their existence. The archives should assist users by providing reproductions of materials in its possession whenever possible.

Questions

YES	NO	N/A	
—	—	—	1. Does the archives maintain hours of service on a regular and posted schedule?
—	—	—	2. Are the number of hours reasonably adequate for anticipated use?
—	—	—	3. Does the archives have a written policy on access?
—	—	—	4. Is the access policy equitable and consistent with the SAA Statement on Access?
—	—	—	5. Does the policy clearly define who may use the facility?
—	—	—	6. Are the records of restrictions well-maintained, clear, and easily and equitably administered?
—	—	—	7. Is there a systematic procedure for periodic review of restrictions and prompt opening of materials after restrictions expire?
—	—	—	8. Is there an adequate plan for deciding whether an unprocessed or partially processed collection shall be made available for research?
—	—	—	9. Is the policy regarding loans equitable and easily administered?
—	—	—	10. Are loaned records adequately protected?
—	—	—	11. Does the archives keep adequate records of materials loaned?
—	—	—	12. Does the archives provide for readers written guidelines containing information about policies affecting research use, such as access policies, rules for the use of materials, security rules, sample citations, photocopy policies, copyright provision, and other specific information?

YES   NO   N/A

—   —   —   13. Are the rules and procedures adequate to control and protect materials, provide a proper atmosphere for research, and yet not unduly impede access to materials?

—   —   —   14. Is space provided for researchers (the reading room) adequate?

—   —   —   15. Is the reading room appropriately equipped for the records to be examined?

—   —   —   16. Is it adequately staffed?

—   —   —   17. Is staff supervision and surveillance sufficient to provide necessary assistance and to prevent theft or damage, including potential dangers from copying documents?

—   —   —   18. Does the archives answer written requests for information about its holdings?

—   —   —   19. Does the archives answer telephone requests for information about its holdings?

—   —   —   20. Are there appropriate guides to the archives?

—   —   —   21. Does the archives make finding aids available to readers?

—   —   —   22. Does the archives regularly report holdings and new accessions to new catalogues such as NUCMC and/or enter descriptive information about record groups and collections into on-line catalogues and databases?

—   —   —   23. Are the records of reference service adequate to permit analysis of reference needs, to provide protection in case of theft or abuse, and to permit planning for and evaluation of reference services?

—   —   —   24. Does the archives have a policy on informing readers of parallel research?

—   —   —   25. Is an adequate reference collection accessible?

—   —   —   26. Does the archives provide copying services to researchers?

—   —   —   27. Is the copying service convenient and are its charges/fees appropriate?

YES	NO	N/A	
___	___	___	28. Are records adequately protected from harm during copying?
___	___	___	29. Does the archives refuse to provide copies when the copy process risks damage to the original?
___	___	___	30. Are staff members who deal with researchers well-informed about laws affecting research, especially copyright, privacy, and freedom of information laws?
___	___	___	31. Do staff members inform users of the implications of these laws for their research as appropriate?

Appendix 10

REPOSITORY SECURITY CHECKLIST

Security is a paramount concern in a historical records repository. It is impossible to anticipate and provide for every eventuality but it is possible to address many potential threats and problems. The following extensive checklist suggests many questions that it is helpful to ask as part of analysis and planning to ensure optimal security. From Timothy Walch, *Archives and Manuscripts: Security* (Chicago: Society of American Archivists, 1977), 30, reprinted in Mary Lynn Ritzenthaller, *Preserving Archives and Manuscripts* (Chicago: Society of American Archivists, 1993), 67.

REPOSITORY SECURITY CHECKLIST

____ Is there a repository security officer?
____ Is there a procedure to check all applicants' backgrounds before hiring?
____ Is the repository ensured against theft by employees?
____ Is access to stack and storage areas on a need-to-go basis?
____ How many employees have master keys and combinations to vaults and other restricted areas?
____ Is an employee assigned to the reading room at all times?
____ Do employees recognize the seriousness of the theft problem and the need for vigilance in the reading room?
____ Have employees been instructed in the techniques of observation?

____ Have employees been told what to do if they witness a theft?

____ Has contact been made with the crime prevention unit of the appropriate law enforcement agency?

____ What type of personal identification is required of patrons?

____ Are patrons interviewed and oriented to collections prior to use of collections?

____ Has there been an effort to apprise patrons of the need for better security?

____ What are patrons allowed to bring into the reading room?

____ Is a secure place provided for those items not allowed in the reading room?

____ Do call slips include the signature of patrons? What other information is included? How long are call slips retained?

____ How much material are patrons allowed to have at any one time?

____ Are archival materials stacked on trucks near the patrons' seats or kept near the reference desk?

____ Has the reading room been arranged so that all patrons can be seen from the reference desk?

____ Do patrons have access to stack areas?

____ Are patrons allowed to use unprocessed collections?

____ Are patrons' belongings searched when they leave the reading room?

____ Do accession records provide sufficient detail to identify missing materials?

____ Are archival materials monetarily appraised as part of routine processing?

____ Are particularly valuable items placed in individual folders?

____ Are manuscripts marked as part of routine processing?

____ Do finding aids provide sufficient detail to identify missing materials?

____ Does the insurance policy cover the loss of individual manuscript items?

____ Does the insurance policy reflect the current market value of the collections?

____ What is the procedure for the return of archival materials to the shelves? Are folders and boxes checked before they are replaced?

____ Are document exhibit cases wired to the alarm system?

____ Are all exterior doors absolutely necessary?

____ Are there grills or screens on the ground floor windows?

____ Are doors and windows wired to a security alarm? If located in a library or building with easy access, does the repository have special locks and alarms to prevent illegal entry?

___ Is a security guard needed to patrol the repository after closing?

___ Are fire and alarm switch boxes always locked?

___ Are security alarm boxes always secured, tamper-proof, and away from the mainstream of traffic?

___ Does the repository have a vault or very secure storage area?

___ Is a master key system necessary?

___ Does the repository have special key signs to prevent addition, removal, or duplication of keys?

___ Is after-hours security lighting necessary?

___ Does the repository have a sprinkler system or other suitable fire suppression system?

___ Does the repository have adequate fire extinguishers in accessible locations?

___ Does the repository have a low temperature alarm in the event of heat failure to prevent frozen pipes?

___ Are manuscripts and records stored in areas near water pipes or subject to flooding?

___ Does the repository have written procedures for fire alarms, drills, and evacuations?

Appendix II

SELECTED LIST OF VENDORS OF ARCHIVAL SUPPLIES AND SERVICES

The following is a list of vendors of supplies and services. It is not meant to imply any endorsement but is included as a helpful starting point. From Anne P. Smith and Jill Swiecichowski, compilers, *Preferred Practices for Historical Records Repositories: A Resource Manual* (Atlanta: Georgia Historical Records Advisory Board, 1999), Section 30. Reprinted with permission of the Georgia Historical Records Advisory Board.

SELECTED LIST OF VENDORS FOR SERVICES AND SUPPLIES

Appearance on this list does not constitute an endorsement of these vendors.

Abbey Publications
7105 Geneva Drive
Austin, TX 78723
512-929-3993
512-929-3995 FAX

Abbey pH pens, newsletters
Archival Products - LBS
2134 East Grand Avenue
P.O. Box 1413
Des Moines, IA 50305
800-526-5640
Boards, pam-binders, stainless steel staples, photocopy replacement service

Archivart Division
Heller & Usdan, Inc.
7 Caesar Place
Moonachie, NJ 07074
800-804-8428
Paper products: boards, folders, papers, boxes

Belfort Instrument Company
727 South Wolfe Street
Baltimore, MD 21231
410-342-2626
410-342-7028 FAX
Hydrothermographs

Bookmakers
6001 66th Avenue
Suite 101
Riverdale, MD 20737
301-459-3384
301-459-3384 FAX
General supplies for preservation

Cole Palmer Instrument Company
625 East Bunter Court
Vernon Hills, IL 60061
800-323-4340
Psychrometers, hydrothermographs and supplies

Conservation Resources International, Inc.
8000-H Forbes Place
Springfield, VA 22151
800-634-6932
703-321-0629 FAX
Paper and plastic products, stainless steel staples

Gaylord
Box 4901
Syracuse, NY 13221-4901
800-448-6160
800-272-3412 FAX
General supplies for preservation, including pH pens

Hollinger Corporation
P.O. Box 610
3810 South Four Mile Run Drive
Arlington, VA 22206
800-634-0491
703-671-6600
Paper products: boards, folders, papers, boxes

Humidal
P.O. Box 610
Colton, CA 92324
909-825-1793
Temperature/relative humidity cards (catalog # 6203-LCC)

Image Permanence Institute
Rochester Institute of Technology
70 Lomb Memorial Drive
Rochester, NY 14623-5604
716-475-5199
716-475-7230 FAX
A-D indicator strips

Keepsafe Systems, Inc.
570 King Street West
Toronto, Ontario MV5 1M3
416-703-4696
Anoxic supplies, barrier film

Light Impressions
439 Monroe Avenue
Rochester, NY 14607-3717
800-828-6216
716-271-8960
716-442-7318 FAX
General supplies for preservation

Metal Edge, Inc.
6340 Bandini Blvd.
Commerce, CA 09440
800-862-2238
800-822-6937 FAX
General supplies for preservation

Plastic Reel Corporation of America
Brisbin Avenue
Lyndhurst, NJ 07071
201-935-5100
White cotton gloves, plastic storage containers

Qualimetrics
1165 National Drive
Sacramento, CA 95834
800-247-7234
Hydrothermographs, psychrometers, UV meters

TALAS
213 West 35th Street
9th Floor
New York, NY 10001-1996
212-736-7744
General supplies for preservation, blue wool strips, soft white brushes

Thomas Scientific
99 High Hill Road at I-295
Swedesboro, NY 08085
609-467-2000
Stainless steel double-door microspatula

3M Company
3M Center
St. Paul, MN 55154
800-328-0067
Polyester film, double-sided tape

UFP Technology
2175 Partin Settlement Road
Kissimmee, FL 34744
407-933-4880
Foam book supports

University Products
P.O. Box 101
South Canal Street
Holyoke, MA 01041
800-628-1912
General supplies for preservation, including pH pen

Appendix 12

SUGGESTED READINGS

This appendix discusses selected publications that are recommended for further reading. It is selective and does not cover everything. The best continuing roundup of new literature is found in the reviews in the *American Archivist* and in the Society of American Archivists' annual *Professional Resources* catalog, which includes SAA publications as well as important works in the field issued by other publishers.

BASIC WORKS

As noted in chapter 2, the best place to begin understanding what archivists do and the nature of archival work is the Society of American Archivists' "Archival Fundamentals" manual series. Lewis Bellardo and Lynn Lady Bellardo, *A Glossary for Archivists, Manuscript Curators, and Records Managers* (1992) defines archival terms. F. Gerald Ham, *Selecting and Appraising Archives and Manuscripts* (1992) explains the selection process. Frederic M. Miller, *Arranging and Describing Archives and Manuscripts* (1990) covers physical arrangement, intellectual access, and finding aids. James O'Toole, *Understanding Archives and Manuscripts* (1990) is the best starting point for an explanation of what archivists do and why they do it. Mary Jo Pugh, *Providing Reference Service for Archives and Manuscripts* (1991) describes services to researchers. Mary Lynn Ritzenthaler, *Preserving Archives and Manuscripts* (1993) covers the basics of preservation. Thomas Wilsted and William Nolte, *Managing Archival and Manuscript Repositories* (1991) introduces management techniques.

Very helpful basic manuals and books on archival programs include Beth Yakel, *Starting an Archives* (Chicago: SAA, 1994), which simplifies and clarifies the procedure for beginning a program; Gregory S. Hunter, *Developing and Maintaining Practical Archives* (New York: Neal-Schuman, 1997), a very usable volume with considerable practical advice and checklists, presented in easily understood language; and Richard Cox, *Managing Institutional Archives: Foundational Principles and Practices* (Westport, Conn.: 1992), aimed at business and other institutions; Judith Ellis, ed., *Keeping Archives*, 2d ed. (Port Melbourne, Victoria, Australia: Australian Society of Archivists, 1993), the most comprehensive single-volume presentation of archival principles and techniques, with considerable applicability to the American scene; Gregory Bradsher, ed., *Managing Archives and Archival Institutions* (Chicago: University of Chicago Press, 1989), which has some essays of continuing value despite its date; Faye Phillips, *Local History Collections in Libraries* (Littleton, Colo.: Libraries Unlimited, 1995), a comprehensive manual for integrating local history collections in libraries; and Bruce W. Dearstyne, *The Archival Enterprise: Modern Archival Principles, Practices, and Management Techniques* (Chicago: American Library Association, 1993).

Four journals are particularly helpful for keeping up with archival affairs: *American Archivist*, published by the Society of American Archivists, the most important publication in the field; *Archival Issues*, published by the Midwest Archives Conference; *Provenance*, issued by the Society of Georgia Archivists; and *Archivaria*, the very impressive journal of the Association of Canadian Archivists.

RECORDS MANAGEMENT

The most popular book on records management is Mary F. Robek, Gerald F. Brown, and David O. Stephens, *Information and Records Management: Document-Based Information Systems*, 4th ed. (New York: Glencoe, 1995). Other useful overviews include Betty Ricks, Ann J. Swafford, and Key E. Gow, *Information and Image Management: A Records System Approach* (Cincinnati: South-West Publishing Company, 1992); Susan Z. Diamond, *Records Management: A Practical Approach*, 3rd ed. (New York: Amacom, 1995); Ira Penn, Gail Pennix, and Jim Counsen, *Records Management Handbook*, 2d ed. (Brookfield, Vt.: Gower, 1994); and Bruce W. Dearstyne, *Managing Government Records and Information* (Prairie Village, Kans.: ARMA International, 1999). The world's first records management standard, Standards Australia, *Australian Standard: Records Management*, 6 parts (Sydney: Standards Australia, 1996), provides very helpful guidance well beyond that nation.

PROGRAM ANALYSIS AND PLANNING

Several publications provide questionnaires that help analyze needs, identify resources, point to model practices, and in general form the basis for program planning. Paul H. McCarthy, ed., *Archives Assessment and Planning Workbook* (Chicago: Society of American Archivists, 1989) provides an excellent overview of the fundamentals of an archival program, helpful checklists, and planning worksheets. The New York State Archives and Records Administration's *Strengthening New York's Historical Records Programs: A Self-Study Guide*, prepared by Richard J.Cox (Albany, N.Y.: State Education Department, 1989), describes program elements, presents study questions, and also presents model policy statements. The best current publications are two manuals prepared for use in Georgia, Anne Smith, *Saving Georgia's Documentary Heritage: A Self-Assessment Guide for Historical Repositories* (Atlanta: Georgia Historical Records Advisory Board, 1999), which presents a concise statement of each program element, indicates why it is important, and offers study questions; and a companion loose-leaf manual with many models and examples; and Anne Smith, *Preferred Practices for Historical Repositories: A Resource Manual* (Atlanta: Georgia Historical Records Advisory Board, 1999).

ARCHIVAL THEORY AND PRACTICE

Still worth reading because of their clarity of presentation and influence are Theodore R. Schellenberg, *Modern Archives: Principles and Techniques* (Chicago: University of Chicago Press, 1956) and *The Management of Archives* (New York: Columbia University Press, 1965), both available as reprints from the Society of American Archivists. Frank Burke, *Research and the Manuscript Tradition* (Lanham, Md.: Scarecrow Press and the Society of American Archivists, 1997) describes issues and approaches in the arena of nongovernment, noninstitutional archival records. Richard Berner, *Archival Theory and Practice in the United States: A Historical Analysis* (Seattle: University of Washington, 1983), though dated, is interesting for its views on arrangement and description. James O'Toole, ed., *The Records of American Business* (Chicago: Society of American Archivists, 1997) is a rich series of essays on that topic. The operation of specialty archives is discussed in William J. Maher, *The Management of College and University Archives* (Lanham, Md.: Scarecrow Press and Society of American Archivists, 1992); William Deiss, *Museum Archives: An Introduction* (Chicago: Society of American Archivists, 1983); and Arnita A. Jones and Philip I. Cantelon, eds., *Corporate Archives and History: Making the Past Work* (New York: Krieger Publishing, 1993).

ARCHIVAL TECHNIQUES

Helen Samuels, *Varsity Letters: Documenting Modern Colleges and Universities* (Lanham, Md.: Scarecrow Press and Society of American Archivists, 1992), Richard J. Cox, *Documenting Localities: A Practical Model for American Archivists and Manuscript Curators* (Lanham, Md.: Scarecrow Press and Society of American Archivists, 1996); and Joan K. Haas, Helen W. Samuels, and Barbara Trippel Simmons, *Appraising the Records of Modern Science and Technology: A Guide* (Boston: Massachusetts Institute of Technology, 1985) provide varying perspectives on the concept of documentation strategies. Frank Boles and Julia Marks Young, *Archival Appraisal* (New York: Neal-Schuman, 1991) delves into the practical aspects of appraisal, including impact of appraisal decisions on the repository itself. Steven Hensen, *Archives, Personal Papers, and Manuscripts: A Cataloging Manual for Archival Repositories, Historical Societies, and Manuscript Libraries*, 2d ed. (Chicago: Society of American Archivists, 1989) is the standard manual of rules for archival description. Jackie Dooley, ed., *Encoded Archival Description: Context, Theory, and Case Studies* (Chicago: Society of American Archivists, 1998) and the EAD Working Group of the Society of American Archivists, *EAD Application Guidelines* (Chicago: Society of American Archivists, 1999) introduce this new approach to descriptive practices. Laura B. Cohen, ed., *Reference Services for Archives and Manuscripts* (Binghamton, New York: Haworth Press, 1997) illustrates modern approaches, including reference over the Internet.

Gregory Trinkaus-Randall, *Protecting Your Collections: A Manual of Archival Security* (Chicago: Society of American Archivists, 1995) is a good starting point. Robert Cogswell, *Copyright Law for Unpublished Manuscripts and Archival Collections* (New York: Glanville Publications, 1992) is a good starting point on that topic, but it is advisable to check with the Library of Congress copyright office, the American Library Association, the Society of American Archivists, or other sources to ensure that policies reflect correct statutes and case law. Elsie Freeman Finch, ed., *Advocating Archives: An Introduction to Public Relations for Archivists* (Lanham, Md.: Scarecrow Press and the Society of American Archivists, 1994), covers advocacy, outreach, and fund-raising. Gail A. Farr, *Archives and Manuscripts: Exhibits* (Chicago: Society of American Archivists, 1980) is still the best publication on that topic.

Susan Schwartzberg, *Preserving Library Materials: A Manual*, 2d ed. (Lanham, Md.: Scarecrow Press, 1995) focuses on assessment and planning. Sherlyn Ogden, ed., *Preservation of Library and Archival Materials* (North Andover, Mass.: American Association of Museums and Northeast Document Conservation Center, 1994) is a comprehensive guide to planning. Judith Fortson, *Disaster Planning and Recovery* (New York: Neal-Schuman, 1992) provides practical advice on how to guard against, and how to respond to, just about any conceivable disaster. Lisa Fox, ed., *Preservation Microfilming: A Guide for Librarians and Archivists* (Chicago: American Library Association, 1995) covers selection, technical issues, and project administration. Nancy Elkington, ed., *RLG Archives Microfilming Manual* (Palo Alto: Research Libraries Group, 1994) also covers management as well as technical standards.

ELECTRONIC ARCHIVES

David Bearman, *Electronic Evidence: Strategies for Managing Records in Contemporary Organizations* (Pittsburgh: Archival and Museum Informatics, 1994) has been very influential in asserting that traditional archival approaches won't fit electronic records and in setting forth new approaches. The International Council on Archives' *Guide for the Management of Electronic Records from an Archival Perspective* (Paris: ICA, 1997) is the best guide for the new roles that archivists need to play. William Saffady's *Managing Electronic Records*, 2d ed. (Prairie Village, Kans.: ARMA International, 1998) is the best guide to the physical management of electronic records; his *Computer Storage Technologies: A Guide for Electronic Recordkeeping* (Prairie Village, Kans.: ARMA International, 1996) explains the technical aspects and standards for electronic media. David O. Stephens and Roderick C. Wallace, *Electronic Records Retention: An Introduction* (Prairie Village, Kans.: ARMA International, 1997) covers appraisal, analysis, retention, and disposition of electronic records and includes some material on electronic records. Charles Dollar, *Authentic Electronic Records: Strategies for Long-Term Access* (Chicago: Cohasset Associates, 1999) is a systematic and sensible approach to the management of electronic records. Anne R. Kenney and Stephen Chapman, *Digital Imaging for Libraries and Archives*, Binder (Ithaca: Cornell University, 1996) is a good overview of that topic.

NOTES

INTRODUCTION

1. Copies of these reports are available from the State Historical Records Coordinator's office at the state archives or state historical society in each state. More information on the reports is available from the federal agency that funded them, the National Historical Publications and Records Commission (NHPRC), National Archives, Washington, D.C. 20408 or *www.nara.gov/nhprc*.

2. Victoria Irons Walch, comp., *Where History Begins: A Report on Historical Records Repositories in the United States* (Washington: Council of State Historical Records Coordinators, 1998), 1–29.

3. Michael Kammen, *In the Past Lane: Historical Perspectives on American Culture* (New York: Oxford University Press, 1997), 223.

4. Massachusetts Historical Records Advisory Board, *A Community Treasure: Massachusetts Historical Records—The Summary Strategic Plan* (Boston: Massachusetts Historical Records Advisory Board, 1998), 6.

CHAPTER I: HISTORICAL RECORDS

1. Lewis Bellardo and Lynn Lady Bellardo, comps., *A Glossary for Archivists, Manuscript Curators, and Records Managers* (Chicago: Society of American Archivists, 1992).

2. This discussion of terminology is based on Bruce W. Dearstyne, *The Archival Enterprise: Modern Archival Principles, Practices, and Management Techniques* (Chicago: American Library Association, 1993), 1–4.

3. Bruce W. Dearstyne, *Management of Government Records and Information* (Prairie Village, Kans.: ARMA International, 1999), 234.

4. Bellardo and Bellardo, *Glossary for Archivists*, 32.

5. Philip Brooks, *Research in Archives* (Chicago: University of Chicago Press, 1969), 38.

6. David McCullough, "Introduction" to Herman J. Viola, *The National Archives of the United States* (New York: Harry N. Abrams, 1984), 12–13.

7. James O'Toole, *Understanding Archives and Manuscripts* (Chicago: Society of American Archivists, 1990), 23.

8. The following examples are from O'Toole, *Understanding Archives and Manuscript*, 23–25; Dearstyne, *The Archival Enterprise*, 17–21; New York State Historical Records Advisory Board, *Toward a Usable Past: Historical Records in the Empire State* (Albany: New York State Education Department, 1984), 71–72; and Society of American Archivists, "Who Is the 'I' in Archives?" (Chicago: Society of American Archivists, n.d.); and the author's experience.

9. Barbara Franco, "The History Museum Curator of the 21st Century," *History News* 52 (Summer 1996), 6–9.

10. New York State Historical Records Advisory Board, *Ensuring a Future for Our Past* (Albany: State Historical Records Advisory Board, 1998), 1.

11. Society of American Archivists, "Introduction," in *The Society of American Archivists: Description and Brief History*, undated, from SAA Web site, *www.archivists.org/history/html*, 1/4/2000.

12. Terry Cook, "Archival Appraisal and Collection: Issues, Challenges, New Approaches," Lecture at the National Archives and Records Administration, College Park, Md., April 21, 1999.

13. Society of American Archivists, "Development of a Curriculum for a Master of Archival Studies Degree," adopted June 5, 1994. A directory of educational programs is updated and reissued approximately every two years. Both are available at *www.archivists.org* or by contacting the SAA at 527 S. Wells Street, 5th Floor, Chicago, IL 60607.

14. Academy of Certified Archivists, *Handbook for Archival Certification* (Albany: Academy of Certified Archivists, 1998). The *Handbook* and more information about ACA are available from the ACA office, 48 Howard Street, Albany, NY 12207 or *www.certifiedarchivists.org*.

15. John A. Fleckner, "'Dear Mary Jane': Some Reflections on Being an Archivist," *American Archivist* 54 (Winter 1991), 8–13.

CHAPTER 2: PREREQUISITES FOR PROGRAM SUCCESS

1. Robert R. Archibald, "The Places of Stories, the Stories of Places," *History News* 53 (Winter 1997), 5–6.

2. Albert T. Klyberg, "The Director as Fund Raiser, Marketing Agent, and Cultivator of Institutional Support," in *Leadership for the Future: Changing Directorial Roles in American History Museums and Historical Societies*, ed. Bryant F. Tolles Jr. (Nashville, Tenn.: American Association for State and Local History, 1991), 129–130, 132.

3. Carol Kammen, "On Doing Local History," *History News* 52 (Autumn 1997), 3.

4. Anne W. Ackerson, "New Director! New Directions?" AASLH "Technical Leaflet" in *History News* 53 (Fall 1998), 2, 5.

5. Robert R. Archibald, "No Magic Map," *History News* 53 (Autumn 1998), 10.

CHAPTER 4: LEADERSHIP AND MANAGEMENT

1. The best insights into leadership come from case studies, but there are few of these in the archival field. Bruce W. Dearstyne, ed., special issue of *American Archivist*, "State Archival Programs: Issues, Plans, and Prospects," (60, Spring 1997), illustrates the dynamics of successful programs. Insightful books on leadership include John P. Kotter, *Leading Change* (Boston: Harvard Business School Press, 1996); James Kouzes and Barry Z. Posner, *The Leadership Challenge* (San Francisco: Jossey-Bass, 1996); and Douglas Smith, *Taking Charge of Change* (Reading, Mass.: Addison-Wesley, 1996).

2. This discussion draws extensively on Jeffrey Pfeffer, *The Human Equation: Building Profits by Putting People First* (Boston: Harvard Business School Press, 1998), particularly chapter 3, and Martin W. Sandler and Deborah A. Hudson, *Beyond the Bottom Line: How to Do More with Less in Nonprofit and Public Organizations* (New York: Oxford University Press, 1998).

3. An excellent introduction to team building is *The Wisdom of Teams* by Jon R. Katzenbach and Douglas Smith, (Boston: Harvard Business School Press, 1993).

4. James M. Kouzes and Barry Z. Posner, *Encouraging the Heart: A Leader's Guide to Rewarding and Recognizing Others* (San Francisco: Jossey-Bass, 1999).

5. James M. Fisher and Kathleen M. Cole, *Leadership and Management of Volunteer Programs: A Guide for Volunteer Administrators* (San Francisco: Jossey-Bass, 1993). This is a very helpful introduction to volunteer program administration and the source for many of the ideas presented here. See also David Carmicheal, *Involving Volunteers in Archives* (n.p.: Mid Atlantic Regional Archives Conference, 1990).

CHAPTER 5: SELECTION OF HISTORICAL RECORDS

1. From New York State Documentary Heritage Program, "An Introduction to Appraisal and Selection of Historical Records," curriculum developed for workshops (Albany: New York State Archives and Records Administration, 1994), "Appraisal: Defining the Process."

2. Larry J. Hackman and Joan Warnow-Blewett, "The Documentation Strategy Process: A Model and a Case Study," *American Archivist* 50 (Winter 1987), 12–47.

3. From Richard J. Cox, *Documenting Localities: A Practical Model for American Archivists and Manuscript Curators* (Lanham, Md.: Society of American Archivists and Scarecrow Press, 1996), 133–46.

4. F. Gerald Ham, *Selecting and Appraising Archives and Manuscripts* (Chicago: Society of American Archivists, 1993), 14.

5. Faye Phillips, "Developing Collecting Policies for Manuscript Collections," *American Archivist* 47 (Winter 1984), 40–41.

6. Ham, *Archives and Manuscripts*, 18.

7. Frank Boles and Julia Marks Young, *Archival Appraisal* (New York: Neal-Schuman, 1991) discusses the role that a given selection decision may have on the policies of the repository.

8. Lewis Bellardo and Lynn Lady Bellardo, eds., *A Glossary for Archivists, Manuscript Curators, and Records Managers* (Chicago: Society of American Archivists, 1992), 2.

9. The archival literature includes many versions of "appraisal checklists" besides the one provided here. One of the most extensive is found in Barbara Reed, "Appraisal and Disposal," in *Keeping Archives*, 2d ed., ed. Judith Ellis (Port Melbourne, Victoria, Australia: Australian Society of Archivists, 1993), 172–74.

10. Helen Willa Samuels, *Varsity Letters: Documenting Modern Colleges and Universities* (Metuchen, N.J.: Scarecrow Press, 1992).

11. Terry Cook, "Archival Appraisal and Collection: Issues, Challenges, New Approaches," Lecture at the University of Maryland, April 21, 1999.

12. Ham, *Archives and Manuscripts*, 82–83; Gary M. Peterson and Trudy Huskamp Peterson, *Archives and Manuscripts: Law* (Chicago: Society of American Archivists, 1985), 20–38.

13. Gregory S. Hunter, *Developing and Maintaining Practical Archives* (New York: Neal-Schuman, 1997), 91.

CHAPTER 6: ARRANGEMENT AND DESCRIPTION

1. Paul Brunton and Tim Robinson, "Arrangement and Description," in *Keeping Archives*, 2d ed., ed. Judith Ellis (Port Melbourne, Victoria, Australia: Australian Society of Archivists, 1993), 223.

2. Lewis Bellardo and Lynn Lady Bellardo, *A Glossary for Archivists, Manuscript Curators, and Records Managers* (Chicago: Society of American Archivists, 1992), 4.

3. Oliver W. Holmes, "Archival Arrangement: Five Different Operations at Five Different Levels," *American Archivist* 27 (January 1964), 21–41.

4. Frederic Miller, *Arranging and Describing Archives and Manuscripts* (Chicago: Society of American Archivists, 1990), 25–26.

5. Brunton and Robinson, "Arrangement and Description," in *Keeping Archives*, 226.

6. See Gregory S. Hunter, *Developing and Maintaining Practical Archives* (New York: Neal-Schuman, 1997), 104–07; and Miller, *Archives and Manuscripts*, 48–56.

7. Bellardo and Bellardo, *Glossary*, 10.

8. New York State Archives and Records Administration, *Guidelines for Arrangement and Description of Archives and Manuscripts* (Albany: State Archives and Records Administration, 1995), 4–5.

9. Hunter, *Practical Archives*, 117–20.

10. Miller, *Archives and Manuscripts*, 109–23.

11. Steven Henson, *Archives, Personal Papers, and Manuscripts: A Cataloging Manual for Archival Repositories, Historical Societies, and Manuscript Libraries*, 2d ed. (Chicago: Society of American Archivists, 1990); Vicki Walch, comp., *Standards for Archival Description: A Handbook* (Chicago: Society of American Archivists, 1990). The Walch publication is now online at *www.archivists.org/publications/stds99/index.html*, with links to various sites for standards and organizations mentioned in this text.

12. The best introduction to EAD is in two special issues of the *American Archivist*, "Encoded Archival Description, Part I: Context and Theory," and "Encoded Archival Description, Part II: Case Studies," 60/3 and 60/4, Summer and Fall, 1997 respectively. The two volumes have been drawn together in a book, Jackie Dooley, ed., *Encoded Archival Description: Context, Theory and Case Studies* (Chicago: Society of American Archivists, 1998). The EAD Working Group of the SAA has published *EAD Application Guidelines* (Chicago: SAA, 1999). The Library of Congress, National Development & MARC Standards Office, maintains the Encoded Archival Description Official Web Site, *www.loc.gov/ead.*

CHAPTER 7: SERVICES TO USERS

1. Sigrid McCausland, "Access and Reference Services," in *Keeping Archives*, 2d ed., ed. Judith Ellis (Port Melbourne, Victoria, Australia: Australian Society of Archivists, 1993), 289–90.

2. Mary Jo Pugh, *Providing Reference Services for Archives and Manuscripts* (Chicago: Society of American Archivists. 1992), 44–45.

3. Pugh, *Providing Reference Services for Archives and Manuscripts*, 56.

4. Pugh, *Providing Reference Services for Archives and Manuscripts*, 81–83.

5. Frank G. Burke, *Research and the Manuscript Tradition* (Lanham, Md.: Scarecrow Press, 1997), 244–55. Perhaps the best way to keep track of changes in the Copyright Law and court cases is via the official Library of Congress Copyright Office Web site, *www.loc.gov/copyright.*

6. Thomas J. Ruller, "Open All Night: Using the Internet to Improve Access to Archives," *The Reference Librarian* 56 (1997), 161–70. Lisa Champelli and Howard Rosenbaum, *Web Master* (New York: Neal-Schumann, 1997) is a good introduction to developing Web sites and is intended for the library community and therefore has some applicability to archives.

7. Paul Conway's work over the years has provided considerable insight into how to measure use. His most extensive study is *Partners in Research: Improving Access to the Nation's Archives* (Pittsburgh: Archives and Museum Informatics, 1994), based primarily on user studies conducted at the National Archives.

8. Bruce W. Dearstyne, *The Archival Enterprise: Modern Archival Principles, Practices, and Management Techniques* (Chicago: American Library Association, 1993), 189–91, presents an earlier version of this list of monitoring/reporting areas.

9. The best work on public programs, now somewhat outdated, is Ann E. Pederson and Gail Farr, *Archives and Manuscripts: Public Programs* (Chicago: Society of American Archivists, 1982). On public relations and advocacy, the best work is Elsie Freeman Finch, ed., *Advocating Archives: An Introduction to Public Relations for Archives* (Chicago: Society of American Archivists and Scarecrow Press, 1994).

10. One of the best examples is New York State Archives and Records Administration, *Consider the Source: Teaching with Historical Records* (Albany: New York State Education Department, 1997). Sample documents and lesson plans from this manual are available from the State Archives and Records Administration's Web site, *unix6.nysed.gov/services/teacher.*

CHAPTER 8: PRESERVATION OF HISTORICAL RECORDS

1. Lewis J. Bellardo and Lynn Lady Bellardo, eds., *A Glossary for Archivists, Manuscript Curators, and Records Managers* (Chicago: Society of American Archivists, 1992), 26–27.

2. Mary Lynn Ritzenthaller, *Preserving Archives and Manuscripts* (Chicago: Society of American Archivists, 1993), 9–10.

3. Gregory Hunter, *Developing and Maintaining Practical Archives* (New York: Neal-Schuman, 1997), 142.

4. Ritzenthaller, *Preserving Archives and Manuscripts*, 82–84.

5. Ritzenthaller, *Preserving Archives and Manuscripts*, 110.

6. Bellardo and Bellardo, *Glossary*, 26.

7. Summarized from Hunter, *Practical Archives*, 147–52.

8. Lisa Fox, ed., *Preservation Microfilming: A Guide for Librarians and Archivists* (Chicago: American Library Association, 1995) is an excellent starting point. There are extensive standards, canons of good practice, and advice on selection and technical questions in the publications of the Association for Information and Image Management (AIIM), 1100 Wayne Avenue, Suite 1100, Silver Spring, MD 20910-5603, *www.aiim.org*. AIIM jointly publishes standards issued in this area by the American National Standards Institute (ANSI).

9. Gail A. Farr, *Archives and Manuscripts: Exhibits* (Chicago: Society of American Archivists, 1980).

10. An excellent starting point: Judith Fortson, *Disaster Planning and Recovery* (New York: Neal-Schuman, 1992).

11. Fortson, *Disaster Planning and Recovery*, 88–95.

CHAPTER 9: ELECTRONIC ARCHIVES

1. Society of American Archivists, "Position Paper: Archival Roles for the New Millennium," adopted August 26, 1997. *www.archivists.org/governance/resolutions/millennium*

2. International Council on Archives, *Guide for the Management of Electronic Records from an Archival Perspective* (Paris: International Council on Archives, 1997), 22.

3. Sandra Feldman, "What's Ahead for 2000?" *Information Today* 17 (January 2000), 62.

4. Australian Archives, "Metadata and Contextual Information," in *Keeping Electronic Records: Policy for Recordkeeping in the Commonwealth Government* (Canberra: Australian Archives, 1995), 1.

5. Discussions of record-keeping systems are found in David Bearman, *Electronic Evidence: Strategies for Managing Records in Contemporary Organizations* (Pittsburgh: Archives and Museum Informatics, 1994), 34–116, and in Standards Australia, *Australian Standard: Records Management* (Standard AS 4390.2) (Sydney: Standards Australia, 1996), especially parts 2 and 3.

6. Terry Cook, "Model Approaches to Electronic Records: Effective Strategies and Approaches," Lecture at the University of Maryland, April 20, 1999.

7. Great Britain, Public Records Office, National Archives, *Management, Appraisal, and Preservation of Electronic Records* (London: Public Records Office, 1999), 39.

8. This list appears in Bruce W. Dearstyne, *Managing Government Records and Information* (Prairie Village, Kans.: ARMA International, 1999), 125. It is adopted from State of Florida, Department of State, Division of Library and Information Services, Bureau of Archives and Records Management, *Electronic Records and Records Management Practices* (Tallahassee, Fla.: Department of State, 1996), 19.

9. International Council on Archives, *Electronic Records*, 52–54.

10. Charles Dollar, "Authentic Electronic Records," presentation at annual meeting of National Association of Government Archives and Records Administrators, Columbus, Ohio, July 16, 1999. For an elaboration of Dollar's views, see his book, *Authentic Electronic Records: Strategies for Long-Term Access* (Chicago: Cohasset Associates, 1999).

11. An excellent starting point on this topic is: William Saffady, *Electronic Document Imaging: A State-of-the-Art Report* (Prairie Village, Kans.: ARMA International, 1996).

12. William Saffady, "Managing Electronic Records," Workshop presentation at annual meeting of National Association of Government Archives and Records Administrators, Columbus, Ohio, July 14, 1999. For an overview of the physical management of electronic records, see Saffady's book, *Managing Electronic Records*, 2d ed. (Prairie Village, Kans.: ARMA International, 1998).

INDEX

Bernhardt, Debra, 70
Bernstein, Rachael, 70
budgets, 50–52

cataloging. *See* arrangement and
    description
certification, 12
climate control. *See* preservation
"Code of Ethics," 165–74
collection: defined, 4; development,
    63–83, 210–14; policy, 71–73
collection policy checklist, 82–83
consultants, 40–41
Cook, Terry, 77
cooperative collecting, 23–25, 67–71,
    210–14
coordination in collection, 25–26
copyright law, 113–15
Cox, Richard, 210–14

deed of gift, 80–81, 226–29
description. *See* arrangement and
    description
disaster preparedness, 135–38, 246–48
document, defined, 3
documentation strategy, 25, 66

educational programs, 36–37
electronic document imaging, 153–54
electronic mail (e-mail), 7, 141–42, 153
electronic records, 139–55; appraisal,
    142; checklist, 155; defined, 142;
    functional specifications for electronic
    record-keeping, 151; issues, 142–45;
    physical preservation, 154–55;
    research and development, 144; roll of
    historical records professionals,
    145–48; tools, 148–53; trends, 156–57
elements of historical records programs,
    175–78
educational programs, 36–37

Encoded Archival Description (EAD),
    101, 157
ethics. *See* "Code of Ethics"
exhibits. *See* promotion

finding aids, 95–101, 230–41
Fleckner, John, 13
focus group questions, 28–29
future trends, 156–64

Gates, Bill, 7
Georgia Historical Records Advisory
    Board, 179–209, 249–52
government archives, 7–8, 32–33, 163
grant funding, 41–46
guide, to deeds of gift, 226–29
guidelines, for donating personal family
    papers, 220–25
guides. *See* finding aids

Ham, F. Gerald, 71–72
historical records programs: access and
    reference services checklist, 242–45;
    administration, 47–62; basic elements,
    21–30, 175–78; building a program,
    sources of assistance, 31–46; checklist,
    15; concepts, 1–15; condition and
    need, 29; cooperative approaches to,
    210–14; defined, 3; elements, 175–78;
    future, 158; mission, 16–19; model
    program 37–38; planning and
    evaluation, 215–19; role, 23–27; self-
    assessment guide, 179–209
holdings, defined, 4
Holmes, Oliver Wendell, 85

identification and selection of records.
    See appraisal
Internet, 100–101, 115–18, 157, 163

Kammen, Carol, 17
Kammen, Michael, xii

ABOUT THE AUTHOR

Dr. Bruce W. Dearstyne is a professor at the College of Information Studies, University of Maryland, where he teaches archival and records management courses and coordinates the Archives, Records, and Information Management specialty in the M.L.S. program. Prior to assuming that position in 1997, he was for many years a program director at the New York State Archives and Records Administration. He is the author of many articles and several books, including *The Archival Enterprise* (1993) and *Managing Government Records and Information* (1999).